BLACKSTONE'S GUIDE TO

The Asylum and Immigration (Treatment of Claimants, etc) Act 2004

Peter Morris
Simon Cox
Mark Henderson
Laura Dubinsky
Phil Haywood
Tublu Krishnendu Mukherjee
Shahram Taghavi

barristers of Doughty Street Chambers

OXFORD
UNIVERSITY PRESS

501339997

OXFORD
UNIVERSITY PRESS

342.41082
CHAM.

Great Clarendon Street, Oxford OX2 6DP

Oxford University Press is a department of the University of Oxford.
It furthers the University's objective of excellence in research, scholarship,
and education by publishing worldwide in

Oxford New York

Auckland Bangkok Buenos Aires Cape Town Chennai
Dar es Salaam Delhi Hong Kong Istanbul Karachi Kolkata
Kuala Lumpur Madrid Melbourne Mexico City Mumbai Nairobi
São Paulo Shanghai Taipei Tokyo Toronto

Oxford is a registered trade mark of Oxford University Press
in the UK and in certain other countries

Published in the United States
by Oxford University Press Inc., New York

© Peter Morris, Simon Cox, Mark Henderson, Laura Dubinsky, Phil Haywood,
Tublu Krishnendu Mukherjee, and Shahram Taghavi 2004

The moral rights of the authors have been asserted

Crown copyright material is reproduced under
Class Licence Number C01P0000148 with the permission
of HMSO and the Queen's Printer for Scotland

Database right Oxford University Press (maker)

First published 2004

British Library Cataloguing in Publication Data

Data available

Library of Congress Cataloging-in-Publication Data

Data available

ISBN 0–19–927774–5

1 3 5 7 9 10 8 6 4 2

Typeset in Times New Roman by
Cambrian Typesetters, Frimley, Surrey
Printed in Great Britain
on acid-free paper by
Biddles Ltd.,
King's Lynn

Foreword

The passage of the Asylum and Immigration (Treatment of Claimants, etc) Act 2004, particularly through the House of Lords, provoked an impassioned debate about the rule of law. The rule of law, a concept which the United Kingdom gifted to the world, was being profoundly undermined by the Government's populist desire to be seen to be tough on asylum seekers and illegal immigrants. It was a source of serious concern to peers that the decisions of immigration tribunals were to be excluded from scrutiny by the higher courts. Where did it leave fundamental legal values like natural justice and the need for justice to be seen to be done?

Every eminent lawyer and former judge expressed alarm at the implications of this retreat from principle. Making special rules for asylum seekers meant the creation of differential rights and Lord Mackay, a former Lord Chancellor, echoing Lord Mansfield two centuries before, reminded the House of the old common law principle of equal protection for those within the jurisdiction. The Lord Chief Justice, Lord Woolf, raised the question of whether such a clause was not inconsistent with the spirit of mutual respect between the different arms of government, requiring the courts to act in a manner which would be without precedent. The matters in issue were very practical. Immigration is a complex jurisdiction: there is evidence of poor quality decision-making; claimants are often extremely vulnerable; resources are scarce; instructions often confused and corroboration hard to come by. The record of the tribunal is equivocal. Matters of life and liberty are engaged.

In the end, the Government retreated, replacing the 'ouster' clause with a fairly complicated framework of statutory review. But the devil is in the detail and the retreat was partial. It is important that practitioners, if they are to do justice, understand both the detail and the principles that lie behind it. For this reason I welcome the clear and careful approach of the authors of the Guide in setting out, first, the law as it stands and the principles that underlie it, before then dealing with the clauses in the new Act.

Context is important if we are to do justice. From its origins in the Aliens Act 1905 and the Commonwealth Immigrants Acts of the 1960s, immigration law was born out of a climate of racial hostility. It has been modified by the activity of those who have come here, worked, created new families or brought over existing ones and created or re-created communities. But hostility, particularly towards asylum seekers, reinforced unfortunately by Government ministers and ill informed prejudice in the tabloids, remains a potent influence. It has encouraged a culture of disbelief among officials. For this reason, it is important that the Guide covers such issues as credibility, welfare benefits and accommodation, marriage, detention, enhanced powers for immigration officers, new crimes and procedures for unfounded asylum and human rights claims with rigour and accuracy.

The authors are my colleagues in Doughty Street Chambers. Their writing is informed by a liberal tradition of defending an individual's rights irrespective of the popularity of the cause or the client. I hope, nevertheless, the Guide will be used not only by those representing applicants but by those involved in judicial decisions and representing the Home Office as well. All of us ought to share the aim that no genuine refugee is denied a safe haven. All of us gain from being governed by the rule of law.

Baroness Helena Kennedy QC
Doughty Street Chambers
10 August 2004

Contents—Summary

TABLE OF CASES   xv

TABLE OF STATUTES   xix

TABLE OF SECONDARY LEGISLATION   xxv

TABLE OF INTERNATIONAL LEGISLATION   xxvii

TABLE OF ABBREVIATIONS   xxix

1. INTRODUCTION   1

2. IMMIGRATION OFFENCES (SECTIONS 1–7)   5

3. CREDIBILITY OF ASYLUM AND HUMAN RIGHTS
   CLAIMANTS (SECTION 8)   9

4. WELFARE SUPPORT FOR IMMIGRANTS (SECTIONS 9–13)   25

5. ENFORCEMENT (SECTIONS 14–18)   49

6. MARRIAGE (SECTIONS 19–25)   51

7. APPEALS (SECTIONS 26 AND 28–31; SCHEDULES 1 AND 2)   63

8. UNFOUNDED CLAIMS (SECTION 27)   83

9. THIRD COUNTRY REMOVALS (SECTION 33 AND
   SCHEDULE 3)   95

10. DETENTION (SECTIONS 32 AND 34–36)   111

11. IMMIGRATION SERVICES (SECTIONS 37–41)   127

12. EUROPEAN ASYLUM PROCEDURES DIRECTIVE   137

APPENDIX 1. The Asylum and Immigration (Treatment of Claimants, etc) Act 2004   151

APPENDIX 2. Useful Resources on the Internet   207

INDEX   215

Contents

TABLE OF CASES	XV
TABLE OF STATUTES	xix
TABLE OF SECONDARY LEGISLATION	XXV
TABLE OF INTERNATIONAL LEGISLATION	xxvii
TABLE OF ABBREVIATIONS	xxix

1. INTRODUCTION — 1.01

2. IMMIGRATION OFFENCES (SECTIONS 1–7)
   - A. Assisting unlawful immigration — 2.01
   - B. Entering the United Kingdom without a passport — 2.03
   - C. Forgery of immigration documents — 2.07
   - D. Trafficking people for exploitation — 2.08
   - E. Employment — 2.09

3. CREDIBILITY OF ASYLUM AND HUMAN RIGHTS CLAIMANTS (SECTION 8)
   - A. Introduction — 3.01
   - B. Background — 3.02
   - C. Significance and scope of s 8 — 3.07
     - 1. The significance of s 8 — 3.07
     - 2. Statements to which s 8 applies — 3.15
     - 3. Decision-makers to whom s 8 applies — 3.21
   - D. Behaviour to which s 8 applies — 3.23
     - 1. Behaviour to conceal information or mislead — 3.23
     - 2. Behaviour relating to passports — 3.26
     - 3. Passport not produced — 3.30
     - 4. Passport destroyed, altered or disposed of — 3.35
     - 5. Invalid 'passport' produced — 3.39
     - 6. Ticket or other travel document destroyed, altered or disposed of — 3.49
   - E. Failure to answer question asked by decision-maker — 3.52
     - 1. Explanation for failure to answer question — 3.57
   - F. Timing of the asylum or human rights claim — 3.63
     - 1. Claim after notification of immigration decision — 3.64
     - 2. Claim after arrest under immigration provision — 3.67
   - G. Failure to make asylum or human rights claim in a safe third country — 3.71
   - H. Behaviour obstructing or delaying the handling of claim — 3.76

4. WELFARE SUPPORT FOR IMMIGRANTS (SECTIONS 9–13)

A. Introduction   4.01

B. Section 9—failed asylum-seeker families   4.02
1. Background   4.03
2. Persons affected by s 9(1)   4.10
3. Failure to take reasonable steps to leave the United Kingdom   4.14
4. Support to a child or British citizen—effect of para 2(1)   4.27
5. Breach of ECHR rights   4.34
6. Breach of EC rights   4.45
7. Home Office decision-making   4.54
8. Local authority decision-making under para 7A   4.59
9. Appealing a decision to withdraw asylum support under para 7A   4.64
10. Section 9(3)—removal of right of appeal to asylum support adjudicator   4.80

C. Section 10—failed asylum-seekers: accommodation   4.83
1. Background   4.84
2. The new regulatory scheme   4.89
3. ECHR compatibility   4.94
4. Right of appeal   4.100

D. Section 11—former asylum-seekers: homelessness   4.102
1. Background   4.103
2. NASS accommodation creates local connection   4.108
3. Section 95 accommodation in Scotland   4.113

E. Section 12—end to back-dated benefits   4.116
1. Background   4.117
2. The new provision   4.124

F. Section 13—integration loan for refugees   4.128

5. ENFORCEMENT (SECTIONS 14–18)

A. Immigration officer: power of arrest   5.01

B. Fingerprinting   5.04

C. Information about passengers   5.05

D. Retention of documents   5.06

E. Control of entry   5.07

6. MARRIAGE (SECTIONS 19–25)

A. The new provisions in outline   6.03

B. The present position   6.14

C. Human rights implications   6.23
1. Issues under ECHR Art 12   6.24
2. The existing Strasbourg case law   6.26

D. ECHR compatibility   6.34
    1. The justification   6.34
    2. Potential target groups   6.41
    3. The new measures and existing immigration control   6.43
E. ECHR Art 14: different treatment on the grounds of religion or
    nationality   6.46

7. APPEALS (SECTIONS 26 AND 28–31; SCHEDULES 1 AND 2)
A. Introduction   7.01
B. Background   7.04
C. The new Asylum and Immigration Tribunal   7.15
    1. Membership of the AIT   7.16
    2. Structure of the AIT   7.20
    3. Three-member panels   7.22
    4. Powers of the AIT   7.23
D. Review by the High Court (in Scotland, Court of Session)   7.24
    1. Application for review: time-limit and late applications   7.30
    2. The application for review   7.36
    3. Decision on the review application   7.43
    4. Reference to the appellate court   7.44
    5. Reconsideration by the AIT   7.47
    6. Transitional provision: filter by AIT   7.49
E. Appeal to the Court of Appeal (in Scotland, Court of Session)   7.54
F. Judicial review   7.61
    1. Preliminary, procedural and ancillary decisions   7.62
    2. Power to quash on judicial review   7.68
    3. Judicial review where review has been refused   7.69
G. Public funding of representation for review of AIT and
    reconsideration   7.71
H. Removal of right of appeal before removal in some entry cases   7.77
    1. Work permit holders   7.79
    2. Leave to enter granted before arrival   7.80
    3. Entry clearance holders   7.82
I. Other changes to appeal system   7.83
    1. Entry clearance: power to remove right of appeal   7.83
    2. Right of appeal of certain crew-members of ships and aircraft   7.91
    3. Certification of repeat appeals   7.94

8. UNFOUNDED CLAIMS (SECTION 27)
A. The present law   8.02
B. The new law: removal of the accession states   8.20
C. The new law: extension of the power to designate   8.21
D. Quality of Home Office assessments of countries of origin   8.39
E. Other provisions   8.45

9. THIRD COUNTRY REMOVALS (SECTION 33 AND SCHEDULE 3)

A.	The present law	9.02
B.	The new provisions: the structure of Sch 3	9.12
C.	The deeming provisions	9.14
D.	Scope of human rights deeming provision	9.24
E.	ECHR compatibility of human rights deeming provision	9.29
F.	Amendment of lists of safe third countries	9.40
G.	Introduction of duty to certify clearly unfounded claims	9.52

10. DETENTION (SECTIONS 32 AND 34–36)

A.	Overview	10.01
B.	The power to detain under present legislation	10.04
C.	Limits on power to detain	10.07
	1. Common law	10.08
	2. Art 5 ECHR	10.09
	3. Home Office policy	10.10
D.	Bail under present legislation	10.15
E.	Bail from the Special Immigration Appeals Commission	10.20
F.	Changes introduced by the 2004 Act	10.22
G.	Appeal against a bail decision by the Special Immigration Appeals Commission	10.23
	1. Present legislation and case law	10.23
	2. The new provisions	10.25
	3. Commentary	10.29
H.	Detention pending deportation	10.32
	1. Present legislation	10.32
	2. The new provisions	10.34
	3. Commentary	10.36
I.	Failing to co-operate with the obtaining of a travel document	10.39
	1. Present legislation	10.39
	2. The new provisions	10.41
	3. Powers of arrest, search and entry	10.45
	4. Commentary	10.51
J.	Electronic monitoring	10.53
	1. The new legislation	10.53
	2. Commentary	10.58

11. IMMIGRATION SERVICES (SECTIONS 37–41)

   A. Introduction   11.01

   B. New power to search and seize evidence   11.08
      1. Background   11.08
      2. The new power   11.11
      3. Limits on material that can be seized   11.15
      4. ECHR compatibility   11.27
      5. Extension of power to enter premises   11.35

   C. Power to require information from legal professional bodies   11.36

   D. New offence of offering prohibited immigration services   11.38

   E. Other changes to regulation of immigration services   11.40

12. EUROPEAN ASYLUM PROCEDURES DIRECTIVE

   A. Unfounded claims (safe countries of origin)   12.03

   B. Third country removals   12.15
      1. The European third country scheme   12.15
      2. Correlation between Sch 3 to the 2004 Act and the Asylum Procedures
         Directive   12.31

   C. Rights of appeal   12.34
      1. Article 38: the right to an effective remedy   12.34

APPENDIX 1. The Asylum and Immigration (Treatment of Claimants, etc) Act 2004   151

APPENDIX 2. Useful Resources on the Internet   207

INDEX   215

Table of Cases

A v Secretary of State for the Home Department [2003] EWCA Civ 175, [2003]
  INLR 249 . . . . .8.29
Al-Ameri v Kensington and Chelsea RLBC [2004] UKHL 4, [2004] 2 AC
  159 . . . . .4.107, 4.108
Amuur v France (1996) 22 EHRR 533 . . . . .10.09
Atkinson v Secretary of State for the Home Department [2004] EWCA Civ
  846 . . . . .8.13, 8.30–35

Bagdanavicius v Secretary of State for the Home Department [2003] EWCA Civ
  1605, [2004] 1 WLR 1207 . . . . .8.07, 8.08, 8.13, 9.55
BD (Application of SK and DK) (Croatia) [2004] UKIAT 32 . . . . .7.27
Benes v Austria (1992) 72 DR 118 . . . . .6.26

CA v Secretary of State for the Home Department [2004] EWCA Civ 1165 . . . . .7.27
Campbell v United Kingdom (1992) 15 EHRR 137 . . . . .11.28

Draper v United Kingdom (1981) 24 DR 72 . . . . .6.32, 6.43

F v Switzerland (1987) 10 EHRR 411 . . . . .6.26
Foxley v United Kingdom (2000) 31 EHRR 637 . . . . .11.28

G v Secretary of State for the Home Department [2004] EWCA Civ 265, [2004] 1
  WLR 1349 . . . . .10.24, 10.31
Garcia Avello v Belgium, Case C-148/02 [2004] 1 CMLR 1 . . . . .4.51
Golder v UK (1979–80) 1 EHRR 524 . . . . .6.30

Hamer v United Kingdom (1979) 24 DR 5, 14 Eur Comm HR 6.27, 6.43, 6.44, 6.45
Hilal v UK (2001) 33 EHRR 2 . . . . .12.37

Jabari v Turkey [2001] INLR 136 . . . . .12.37

Karanakaran v Secretary of State for the Home Department [2000] INLR 122,
  [2002] Imm AR 271 . . . . .1.06
Kemal Selim v Cyprus, Application 00047293/99 (2001) 6.33

Litwa v Poland (2000) 33 EHRR 53 . . . . .10.09

M v Islington LBC [2004] EWCA Civ 235, [2004] 2 FCR 363 . . . . .4.29, 4.31
Mahmood (Wasfi), Re [1995] Imm AR 311 . . . . .10.08
MM (Burundi) [2004] UKIAT 182 . . . . .7.64

Nadarajah v Secretary of State for the Home Department [2003] EWCA 1768,
  [2004] INLR 139 . . . . .10.10, 10.12

Naguleswaran v Secretary of State for the Home Department (Elias J,
  3 December 1999) 3.34

Perez de Rada Cavanilles v Spain (1998) 29 EHRR 109 . . . . .7.34

R v Chief Constable of the Metropolitan Police, ex p Gross (DC, 24 July 1998) 11.24
R v Governor of Durham Prison, ex p Singh (Hardial) [1984] 1 WLR 704 . . . . .10.08
R v Governor of Holloway Prison, ex p Giambi [1982] 1 WLR 535 . . . . .10.33
R v Guildhall Magistrates' Court, ex p Primlaks Holdings Co (Panama) Inc [1990]
  1 QB 261 . . . . .11.22
R v Inner London Crown Court, ex p Baines and Baines (a firm) [1988] QB 579 . . . . . . .11.20
R v Maidstone Crown Court, ex p Waitt [1988] Crim LR 384 . . . . .11.33
R v Manchester Crown Court, ex p Rogers [1999] 1 WLR 832 . . . . .11.22
R v Secretary of State for the Home Department, ex p Brezinski and Glowacka
  (QBD, 19 July 1996) 10.16
R v Secretary of State for the Home Department, ex p Bugdaycay [1987] AC 514 . . . . . . .3.09
R v Secretary of State for the Home Department, ex p Kandasamy [1994] Imm AR
  333 . . . . .3.74
R v Secretary of State for the Home Department, ex p Mehari [1994] QB 474 . . . . .3.73
R v Secretary of State for the Home Department, ex p Saadi [2002] UKHL 41,
  [2002] 1 WLR 3131 . . . . .10.14
R v Secretary of State for the Home Department, ex p Sedrati, Butraigo-Lopez and
  Anaghatu (Moses J, 17 May 2001) 10.38
R v Secretary of State for the Home Department, ex p Simms [2000] 2 AC 115 . . . . .3.09
R v Secretary of State for the Home Department, ex p Turkoglu [1988] QB 398 . . . . .10.17
R v Secretary of State for the Home Department, ex p Z [1998] Imm AR 516 . . . . .10.39
R v Secretary of State for Social Security, ex p B and JCWI [1997] 1 WLR 275 . . . . .4.117
R v Special Adjudicator, ex p B [1998] INLR 315 . . . . .10.08
R v Special Adjudicator, ex p Islam (Turner J, 16 October 2000) 3.34
R v Van Binh Lee and Stark [1999] 1 Cr App R (S) 422 . . . . .2.01
R (Abbasi) v Secretary of State for Foreign and Commonwealth Affairs [2002]
  EWCA Civ 1598, [2003] UKHRR 76 . . . . .10.08
R (Ahmadi) v Secretary of State for the Home Department [2002] EWHC 1897
  (Admin), [2003] ACD 14 . . . . .9.27
R (Asif Javed) v Secretary of State for the Home Department [2001] EWCA Civ
  789, [2002] QB 129 . . . . .8.26
R (Bardiqi) v Secretary of State for the Home Department [2003] EWHC 1788
  (Admin) 9.27
R (Erdogan) v Secretary of State for the Home Department [2004] EWCA Civ
  1087 . . . . .7.65
R (G) v Immigration Appeal Tribunal [2004] EWHC 588 (Admin), [2004] 3 All
  ER 286 . . . . .7.70
R (Gibson) v Secretary of State for the Home Department [2003] EWHC 1919
  Admin 8.29
R (Ibrahim) v Secretary of State for the Home Department [2001] EWCA 519,
  [2001] Imm AR 430 . . . . .9.18
R (Kadem D) v Special Adjudicator [2001] EWHC Admin 522 . . . . .3.34
R (Kurtolli) v Secretary of State for the Home Department [2003] EWHC 2744
  (Admin), [2004] INLR 198 . . . . .8.08, 9.27

R (L) v Secretary of State for the Home Department [2003] EWCA Civ 25, [2003]
   1 WLR 1230 . . . . .8.02, 8.06, 8.12, 8.14, 8.15, 8.16, 8.17, 8.18, 8.36, 9.55
R (Mohammed) v Secretary of State for the Home Department [2002] EWHC 57
   (Admin) 9.15, 9.16, 9.20
R (Morgan Grenfell and Co Ltd) v Special Commissioner for Income Tax [2002]
   UKHL 21, [2003] 1 AC 563 . . . . .11.27
R (Q) v Secretary of State for the Home Department [2003] EWCA Civ 364, [2004]
   QB 36 . . . . .3.34, 3.75, 4.35, 4.82, 7.32
R (Secretary of State for the Home Department) v Chief Asylum Support Adjudicator
   and Dogan [2002] EWHC 2218 (Admin) 4.111
R (Subaththeran) v Special Adjudicator [2001] EWHC Admin 12, [2001] Imm AR
   345 . . . . .3.31
R (Tataw) v Immigration Appeal Tribunal [2003] EWCA Civ 925, [2003] INLR 585 . . . .7.29
R (Ullah) v Special Adjudicator [2004] UKHL 26, [2004] 2 AC 323 . . . . . . .9.31, 12.07, 12.30
R (Yogathas) v Secretary of State for the Home Department; R (Thangarasa) v
   Secretary of State for the Home Department [2002] UKHL 36, [2003]
   1 AC 920 . . . . .8.09, 8.10, 9.32
Ravichandran v Secretary of State for the Home Department [1996] Imm AR 97 . . . . .7.27
Rees v UK (1986) 9 EHRR 56 . . . . .6.29

Secretary of State for the Home Department v Razgar [2004] UKHL 27, [2004] 3
   WLR 58, [2003] EWCA Civ 840, [2003] Imm AR 529 . . . . .8.09, 8.10, 8.11, 8.13, 9.27

Tan Te Lam v Superintendent of Tai A Chau Detention Centre [1997] AC 97 . . . . .10.08
TI v United Kingdom [2000] INLR 211 . . . . .9.29, 9.30

Van Der Mussele v Belgium (1984) 6 EHRR 163 . . . . .4.95

Waite and Kennedy v Germany, judgment of 18 February 1999, Reports 1999 . . . . .9.30
Wall's Meat Co Ltd v Khan [1979] ICR 52, CA 7.31

Ziar v Secretary of State for the Home Department [1997] INLR 221 . . . . .3.25

Table of Statutes

Access to Justice Act 1999
  s 6(6) 4.73
  Sch 2, para 2 . . . . .4.73
Anti-Terrorism, Crime and Security Act
  2001
  s 21 . . . . .10.25
  s 23 . . . . .10.21
  s 24 . . . . .10.21
    (5) 10.26, 10.27
  s 27(5), (6) 10.28
Asylum and Immigration Act 1996 . . . .8.26,
                     8.27, 9.28
  s 1 . . . . .3.29
  s 3 . . . . .3.73
  s 8 . . . . .2.09, 2.10
  s 11(2) 4.117
Asylum and Immigration Appeals Act
  1993 .7.02, 7.06
  s 8 . . . . .3.73
  s 9A 10.17
    (1)–(3) 10.17
  Sch 5
    para 5
      (4)(a) 3.33, 3.34
      (10) .3.29
Asylum and Immigration (Treatment of
  Claimants, etc) Act 2004 . . . . . . .4.06,
                7.01–3, 10.22
  see Appendix 1 for full text
  s 1 . . . . .1.04, 2.01
  s 2 . . . . .1.04, 2.03
    (1)–(3) 2.03
    (5) 2.04
    (6) 2.03
    (7) 2.04
    (10) 2.03
  s 3 . . . . .1.04, 2.07
    (2), (3) 2.07
  s 4 . . . . .1.04, 2.08
    (1)–(4) 2.08
    (5) 2.08

Asylum and Immigration (Treatment of
  Claimants, etc) Act 2004—*continued*
  s 4
    (5)
      (a) 2.03
      (b) 2.03
  s 5 . . . . .2.07
  s 6 . . . . .1.04, 2.08, 2.09, 2.10
  s 8 . . . . .1.05, 1.07,
     3.01, 3.06, 3.07, 3.15, 3.22, 3.25
    (1) 3.15, 3.17, 3.19, 3.21
    (2) 3.18, 3.24, 3.26, 3.30,
              3.35–40, 3.49, 3.52, 3.79
    (a), (b) 3.23
    (c) 3.76
    (3) .3.18, 3.23
    (a) 3.26, 3.30, 3.33
    (b) 3.26, 3.39
    (c) 3.26, 3.35
    (d) 3.49
    (4) .3.18, 3.75
    (5) 3.18, 3.63, 3.66
    (6) 3.18, 3.63
    (7) 3.15, 3.21, 3.27, 3.64,
                  3.67–70, 3.72
    (8) 3.41
    (a) 3.40
    (9) 3.72
    (12) 3.13
    (13) 3.21
  s 9 . . . . .1.08, 4.01
    (1) 4.02, 4.10
    (3) . .1.08, 4.01, 4.09, 4.64, 4.80, 4.82
    (4) 4.75
  s 10 . . . . .1.08, 4.01, 4.83
    (1) 4.91
    (2) 4.90
    (3), (4) .4.100
    (5) 4.89
    (6) 4.91
  s 11 . . . . .1.08, 4.01, 4.102
    (1) 4.108

Asylum and Immigration (Treatment of
    Claimants, etc) Act 2004—*continued*
s 11
    (2), (3) 4.115
s 12 . . . . .1.08, 4.01, 4.116, 4.123,
                        4.125, 4.126
    (1) 4.124, 4.126
    (2) 4.118, 4.124
s 13 . . . . .1.08, 4.01, 4.128
    (2) 4.129
    (3) 4.130
        (c) 4.129
        (d)(i) .4.131
s 14 . . . . .1.09, 3.67, 5.02
    (1) 5.02
    (2) 5.03
s 15 . . . . .1.09, 5.04
s 16 . . . . .1.09, 5.05
s 17 . . . . .5.06
s 18 . . . . .5.07
s 19 . . . . .1.10, 6.01
    (1) 6.04
    (2)(a), (b) 6.05
    (3) 6.06
    (4)(a)(ii) 6.07
s 20 . . . . .1.10, 6.01,
    (3) 6.09
ss 21–24 . . . . .1.10, 6.01, 6.08
s 25 . . . . .1.10, 6.01, 6.12
s 26 . . . . .1.11, 7.12, 7.15
    (6) .7.11, 7.71
    (8)
        (a) 7.35
        (b) 7.51
s 27 . . . . .1.12, 8.01
    (4) 8.20
s 28 . . . . .1.11
s 29 . . . . .1.11, 7.88
s 30 . . . . .1.11
    (2) 7.95
s 31 . . . . .1.11, 7.92
s 32 . . . . .1.14, 10.25, 10.29–31
    (1) 10.25–28
    (2) 10.28
s 33 . . . . .1.13, 9.01
s 34 . . . . .1.14, 10.32
s 35 . . . . .1.14, 10.42, 10.45–52
    (1) 10.42

Asylum and Immigration (Treatment of
    Claimants, etc) Act 2004—*continued*
s 35
    (2) 10.43
    (3) 4.41, 10.44
    (4) 10.45
        (a), (b) 10.44
    (5) 10.45
    (6)
        (a) 10.46, 10.47
        (b) 10.48–50
    (9)–(11) 10.44
s 36 . . . . .1.14
    (1)–(3) .10.54
    (6) 10.55
    (7) 10.56
    (8)(a), (b) 10.57
    (10)(b) .10.57
    (11) 10.57
s 37 . . . . .1.15, 11.01
    (1)–(5) .11.42
    (6)
        (a) 11.43
        (b) 11.42
s 38 . . . . .1.15, 11.01
    (1) 11.11
    (2) 11.35
s 39 . . . . .11.38
s 40 . . . . .11.41
s 41 . . . . .11.37
    (5) 11.44
Sch 1 . . . . .7.15
Sch 2
    paras 27, 28 . . . . .7.18
    para 29 . . . . .7.19
        (5)(b) 7.51
    para 30 . . . . .7.51
        (1) 7.49
        (2) 7.51
        (4), (5) 7.51
        (7) 7.53
        (8) 7.49
Sch 3 . . . . .1.13, 9.01, 9.12, 9.13,
                        12.15, 12.31, 12.33
    para 2 . . . . .3.72
        (1) 4.27–33
    para 3 . . . . .9.22
    para 5(4) 9.35

Asylum and Immigration (Treatment of
    Claimants, etc) Act 2004—*continued*
  Sch 3
      para 10(4) .9.35
      para 15(4) .9.35
      para 19(c) .9.35

Children Act 1989
  s 17 . . . . .4.06, 4.29
  s 20 . . . . .4.30
  s 23C 4.06
  s 24A 4.06
  s 24B 4.06
Criminal Justice Act 1982 . . . . .10.36
  s 154 . . . . .10.44

Data Protection Act 1998
  Sch 1, eighth principle 10.39
  Sch 4, para 4(1) 10.39

Forgery and Counterfeiting Act 1981
  s 5 . . . . .2.07

Health Services and Public Health Act
  1968
  s 45 . . . . .4.06
Homelessness etc (Scotland) Act 2003
  asp 10, s 7 . . . . .4.113
Housing Act 1996
  s 188(3) 4.06
  s 189 . . . . .4.106
  s 193 . . . . .4.103
  s 198 . . . . .4.104
  s 199 . . . . .4.104, 4.108
    (6) 4.108–110
    (7) 4.110
  s 204(4) 4.06
  s 217(3) 4.110
Housing (Scotland) Act 1987
  s 27(2)(a)(iii) 4.113
  s 31(2) 4.114
Human Rights Act 1998 . . . . .3.09
  s 3 . . . . .9.33
  s 6 . . . . .9.24

Immigration Act 1971 . . . . . . .2.07, 5.07, 7.05
  s 11 . . . . .4.07
  s 24 . . . . .5.01
  · (1) 3.67
  s 24A 5.01

Immigration Act 1971—*continued*
  s 24A
    (1) 3.67
  s 25 . . . . .2.01, 2.02, 3.67, 5.01
    (7), (8) 2.01
  s 25A 3.67
  s 25B 5.01
  s 25C 5.01
  s 26 . . . . .3.67
  s 26A 3.67
  s 26B 3.67
  s 28(4) 10.50
  s 28AA(1)(b) 3.67
  s 28D 10.47
  s 28E 10.48
  s 28G 10.48
  s 28H 10.49
  Sch 2 .10.04, 10.21
    para 2 . . . . .10.21
      (1) 10.38
    para 2A
      (2) 7.80
      (9) 7.80
    para 8 . . . . .10.05
      (1) 10.40
    para 9 . . . . .10.05
    para 10(1) 10.40
    para 12 . . . . .10.05
      (1), (2) 7.91
    para 13 . . . . .10.05
      (2) 7.93
    para 14 . . . . .7.93, 10.05
    para 16 . . . . .10.05
    para 17 . . . . .3.67
    para 18 . . . . .10.39
    para 21 . . . . .10.06, 10.54
    para 22 . . . . .10.06
      (1) 10.15
      (1A) 7.23, 10.16
      (1B) .10.15
      (2) 10.16
    para 23 . . . . .10.19
    para 24(1) 10.19
    para 25A .10.19
    para 25B .10.19
    para 29
      (1), (2) 10.17, 10.18
      (3) 7.23

Immigration Act 1971—*continued*
  Sch 2
    para 29
      (4) 10.17, 10.18
      (5), (6) 10.18
    para 30(1) 10.19
    para 31 .10.19
    para 33(1) 10.19
    para 34 .10.15
  Sch 3 . . . . .10.04, 10.32, 10.33
    para 1 . . . . .10.40
    para 2
      (1) 10.05, 10.32–10.34, 10.38
      (1A) .10.36
      (2) 10.05, 10.32, 10.33, 10.35
      (3) 10.05, 10.32
      (4A) 7.23, 10.15
      (5) .10.54
Immigration Appeals Act 1969 . . . . .7.04
Immigration and Asylum Act 1999 . . . .1.01,
                        4.06, 7.07
  s 4 . . . . .4.83, 4.85, 4.87, 4.89, 4.100
    (7)(a) 4.91
  s 10 . . . . .3.64
    (1) 10.05
    (7) 10.05
  s 11 . . . .9.03, 9.07, 9.09, 9.10, 9.14–9.21
    (2) 9.06
  s 12 . . . . .9.04, 9.07, 9.10, 9.12
    (2) 9.06, 9.07, 9.09, 9.10
    (5) 9.07
  s 13 . . . . .10.39
    (3), (4) 10.39
  s 18(1)(c) .3.70
  s 24 . . . . .6.02, 6.22
    (2), (3) .6.22
    (5) 6.22
  s 44 . . . . .10.02
  Part IV 4.85, 11.02, 11.03
  s 54 . . . . .10.15
    (3) 10.32
  s 72(2) 8.08
  Part V 11.02, 11.03
  s 83 . . . . .11.05
    (5) 11.30
  ss 84, 85 . . . . .11.03, 11.42
  s 86 . . . . .11.36, 11.37
    (2)(b) .11.37
    (9) 11.03

Immigration and Asylum Act
    1999—*continued*
  s 86
    (9)
      (b)(ii) 11.37
    (9A) 11.37
  s 89 . . . . .11.42
  s 90 . . . . .11.42
    (1) 11.44
  s 91 . . . . .11.05, 11.12, 11.29
  s 92A 11.11, 11.29, 11.34
    (2), (3) 11.12
    (5) 11.14
      (c)(i) 11.15
    (6) 11.14
    (7)
      (a) 11.31
      (b) .11.11
      (c) 11.27
        (ii) 11.16
        (iii) 11.13
    (8)(b) 11.15, 11.27
    (9) 11.16
  s 92B 11.38
    (2) 11.39
  s 93 . . . . .11.29
    (3)(b) 11.30
  s 94 . . . . .4.03
    (3) 4.04, 4.05
    (5) 4.05
  s 95 . . . . .4.03, 4.105, 4.108–114
    (13) 4.13, 4.109
  s 98(2) 4.111
  s 103 . . . . .4.09
  s 111 . . . . .4.84
  s 122 . . . . .4.42
  s 123 . . . . .4.116–118
  s 141 . . . . .5.04
  s 166
    (2) 11.44
    (5)(za) 4.90
  Sch 4, para 6 . . . . .3.47
  Sch 5 . . . . .11.03
    para 1 .11.03
    para 3 .11.03
    para 7 .11.09
    para 21(2)(b) 11.38
  Sch 6 . . . . .11.42
    para 1(1) 11.43

Immigration and Asylum Act
    1999—*continued*
    Sch 9 . . . . .4.13, 4.85, 4.109
Interpretation Act 1978
    s 7 . . . . .4.58

Local Government Act 2000
    s 2 . . . . .4.06

Marriage Act 1949 . . . . .6.05

National Assistance Act 1948
    s 21 . . . . .4.06, 4.33
    s 29 . . . . .4.06
National Health Service Act 1977
    s 21 . . . . .4.06
    Sch 8 . . . . .4.06
Nationality, Immigration and Asylum Act
    2002 . . . . .1.01, 7.02, 7.08
    s 11 . . . . .4.07
    s 18(1)(c) 3.70
    s 44 . . . . .3.70
    s 62 . . . . .10.05, 10.21
      (3), (4) .10.06
    s 65 . . . . .9.04
    s 68 . . . . .10.02
      (2)(b) 10.16
    s 72(2)(a) 9.04
    s 77 . . . . .9.03, 9.04
      (4) 10.18
    s 80 . . . . .9.03
    Part 5 . . . . .10.17
    s 81 . . . . .7.15
      (1)–(5) 7.12
    s 82
      (1) 9.03–06
      (2) 7.92
        (b) 7.09, 7.84
        (g), (h), (i), (j), (k) 5.04
      (3) 7.09
    s 83 . . . . .7.09
    s 88 . . . . .7.85
      (4) 7.86
    s 88A 7.88
      (2)(a) 7.89
    s 90 . . . . .7.84
      (4) 7.86

Nationality, Immigration and Asylum Act
    2002—*continued*
    s 91 . . . . .7.84
      (2) 7.86
    s 92
      (2)(b) 9.04
      (3B) 7.81
      (3C) 7.82
      (3D) 7.79
    s 93 . . . . . . .8.08, 9.06, 9.07, 9.09–11, 9.35
      (2) 9.10, 9.11
        (b) 9.03
      (3) 8.03
    s 94 . . . . .8.01, 8.02, 8.08, 8.20, 8.21,
             8.29, 8.39, 8.41, 9.08, 9.11, 9.55,
                        12.07, 12.12
      (4) 8.04, 8.30
      (5) 8.04, 8.24
      (6)(b) 8.38
      (7) 9.09, 9.10
      (8) 9.09
    s 96 . . . . .7.95, 7.96
      (1) 7.95
      (2) 7.95
    s 101 . . . . .7.27
      (1) 7.27
      (2) 7.65
      (3)(c) 7.70
    s 103A 7.61
      (1) 7.24, 7.27
      (2) 7.28
      (3) 7.30
      (4)(b) 7.31
      (5) 7.36
      (6) 7.69
      (7)(a) 7.26, 7.62
      (8) 7.22, 7.24
      (9) 7.24
      (10) 7.24
    s 103B
      (1) 7.44, 7.54, 7.55
      (2) 7.54
        (b) 7.59
      (3) 7.56
      (4) 7.57
    s 103C
      (1) .7.54, 7.55
      (2) 7.57

Nationality, Immigration and Asylum Act
   2002—*continued*
s 103C
  (2)
     (g) 7.58
s 103D
  (1)–(3) 7.71
  (4)–(6) 7.72
  (8) 7.72
s 103E 7.54
  (2) 7.55
  (3) 7.56
  (4) 7.57
  (7)(a) 7.62
s 104 .... 9.04
  (2) 4.04
s 106(2)(x) 7.47
s 108 .... 3.47
s 113 .... 3.15, 9.03, 9.04
s 115(7) 10.13
s 142 .... 8.42
Sch 3 .... 4.02, 4.29, 4.30, 4.80–82
  para 1 .... 4.06
    (1)(l) 4.13
    (3) 4.13
  para 2 .... 4.08
    (1) 4.27, 4.28
     (a) 4.33
     (b) 4.30–32
    (5), (6) 10.06
  para 3 .... 4.08, 4.34, 4.42
  para 4 .... 4.07, 4.81
  para 5 .... 4.07, 4.50, 4.51, 4.81
  para 6 .... 4.07, 4.81
  para 7 .... 4.07, 4.81
  para 7A ... 4.10–15, 4.28, 4.34–4.82
    (1)
     (a) 4.54

Nationality, Immigration and Asylum Act
   2002—*continued*
Sch 3
  para 7A
    (b) 4.54
    (c) 4.54
    (d) 4.54, 4.66
    (3) 4.54, 4.58, 4.66
    (4) 4.54
Sch 4 .... 7.15
  para 1 .... 7.16
  para 2 .... 7.17
  para 3 .... 7.16
  para 4 .... 7.21
  para 5 .... 7.20
  paras 7, 8 .... 7.21
Sch 7 .... 10.17

Police and Criminal Evidence Act 1984
  s 8(4) 11.13, 11.26
  s 10 .... 11.20
  ss11, 12 .... 11.17
  s 13 .... 11.19, 11.23
  s 14 .... 11.19
  Sch 1 .... 11.26
  para 2 (a)
    (iii) 11.13
    (iv) 11.13, 11.26
  paras 14(a), (b) 11.13
Special Immigration Appeals Commission
   Act 1997
  s 3(2) 10.20
  s 5 .... 10.28
  s 7 .... 10.23
  (2) 10.26
  (3) 10.27

Theft Acts 1968 & 1978 .... 5.03

Table of Secondary Legislation

Asylum (Designated States) Order 2003 (SI 2003/970) 8.05
Asylum (Designated States) (No 2) Order 2003 (SI 2003/1919) 8.05
Asylum Support Appeals (Procedure) Rules 2000 (SI 2000/541)
    r 3 ....4.69
       (3), (4) 4.70
    r 4(1)–(4) 4.70
    r 6(1), (2) 4.70
    r 13(1) 4.70
    r 18(4) 4.70
    Sch 4.69
Asylum Support (Interim Provisions) Regulations 1999 (SI 1999/3056) 4.13, 4.109

Civil Procedure Rules
    PD52.15.4 ....7.42

Human Rights Act 1998 (Designated Derogation) Order 2001 (SI 2001/3644) 10.21

Immigration and Asylum Act 1999 (Part V Exemption: Educational Institutions
    and Health Sector Bodies) Order 2001 (SI 2001/1403) 11.04
Immigration and Asylum Act 1999 (Part V Exemption: Relevant Employers) Order
    2003 (SI 2003/3214) 11.04
Immigration (European Economic Area) Regulations 2000 (SI 2000/2326)
    reg 2(1) 6.18
    reg 5 ....4.51
    reg 14(2) 4.51
Immigration (Leave to Enter) Order 2001 (SI 2001/2590) 5.07
Immigration (Notices) Regulations 2003 (SI 2003/658) 7.86
Immigration (Removal Directions) Regulations 2000 (SI 2000/2243)
    reg 4(2) 10.40
Immigration Rules (HC 395) 6.14
    para 180K 3.73
    paras 277–289 ....6.14
    para 277 ....6.16
    para 278(i) 6.16
    para 284
       (i) 6.17
       (iv) 6.17
       (v) 6.17
    para 341 ....3.05

Nationality, Immigration and Asylum Act 2002 (Consequential and Incidental
    Provisions) Order 2003 (SI 2003/1016) 9.04

Police and Criminal Evidence Act 1984 Code B 'Code of Practice for searches of
    premises by police officers and the seizure of property found by police officers
    on persons or premises
    para 3.4 . . . . .11.31
    para 3.6 . . . . .11.31
    para 3.8 . . . . .11.31
    paras 6.7–6.8, 6.9–6.13 . . . . .11.31
Police and Criminal Evidence (Northern Ireland) Order 1989 (SI 1989/1341)
    Arts 13–14 . . . . .11.17

SIAC (Procedure) Rules 2003 (SI 2003/1034)
    r 2(1)(i) 10.28
    r 29(g) 10.30

Withholding and Withdrawal of Support (Travel Assistance and Temporary Accommodation)
    Regulations 2002 (SI 2002/3078)
    reg 2(2) 4.11

Table of International Legislation

Council Directive (EC) 2002/90 defining the facilitation of unauthorized entry,
   transit and residence [2002] OJ L328/17 . . . . .2.02
Council Directive (EC) 2003/9 laying down minimum standards for the reception
   of asylum seekers [2003] OJ L31/18
   Art 2(c) 4.47
   Art 3 . . . . .4.47
   Art 13 . . . . .4.47
   Art 16(1)(a) 4.48
   Art 18(1). 4.49
   Art 26(1). 4.46
Council Directive (EC) 2004/83 on minimum standards for the qualification and
   status of third country nationals or stateless persons as refugees or as persons
   who otherwise need international protection and the content of the protection
   granted [2004] OJ L304/12 . . . . .12.38
Council Directive on minimum standards on procedures in Member States for
   granting and withdrawing refugee status (draft) 9.01, 12.01–03, 12.15–18
   Art 3A(2)(a) 12.30
   Art 27 . . . . .12.28, 12.29, 12.33
   Art 30 . . . . .12.04, 12.09, 12.13
      (1) 12.05
      (2) 12.05
      (3)–(6) 12.05
   Art 30A 12.06, 12.09
      (1) 12.13
      (5) 12.08
   Art 30B 12.08, 12.09
      (1) 12.10
      (2) 12.11
   Art 35A 12.20
      (1) 12.27, 12.29
      (4) 12.27
   Art 38 . . . . .12.34
      (1) 12.35
      (2) 12.36
      (3) 12.37
      (4) 12.36
      (5) 12.38
   Art 39(6) 12.39
   Annex II 12.06
Council Regulation (EC) 343/2003 establishing the criteria and mechanisms for
   determining the Member State responsible for examining an asylum
   application lodged in one of the Member States by a third-country national
   [2003] OJ L50/1 ("Dublin II") 9.40, 9.41, 12.15–12.17

Dublin II, *see* Council Regulation (EC) 343/2003

EU Council Framework Decision 2002/946, 28 November 2002 on the strengthening
    of the penal framework to prevent the facilitation of unauthorized entry,
    transit and residence [2002] OJ L328/1 .... .2.02
European Convention on Human Rights (1950) 3.66, 9.23
    Art 3 .... .1.08, 3.09, 4.03, 4.10, 4.35, 4.99, 9.26, 9.29–33, 10.21, 12.07, 12.22, 12.30
    Art 4 .... .2.08
        (2) 4.94
        (3) 4.95
    Art 5 .... .10.09, 10.10, 10.14, 10.37
        (1) 10.09, 10.21
          (f) 10.09
        (2) 10.09
        (4) 10.09
    Art 6(1) 7.34, 7.90
    Art 8 .... .4.38, 4.40–44, 4.49, 9.26, 11.34
    Art 12 .... .1.10, 6.23, 6.45
    Art 13 .... .7.90
    Art 14 .... .1.10, 4.99, 6.23, 7.90

Geneva Convention relating to the status of refugees (Refugee Convention) 3.66, 9.14–23
    Arts 23, 24 .... .4.127
    Art 28 .... .3.28
    Art 33(1) 3.08

International Labour Convention No 29, Forced Labour Convention (1930)
    Art 2(1) 4.95

New York Convention on the status of stateless persons (1954) 3.28

Table of Abbreviations

AIT	Asylum and Immigration Tribunal
APCI	Advisory Panel on Country Information
CIPU	Home Office Country Information and Policy Unit
EC	European Community
ECHR	European Convention on Human Rights and Fundamental Freedoms
ECRE	European Council on Refugees and Exiles
EEA	European Economic Area
EU	European Union
IAS	Immigration Advisory Service
IDI	Immigration Directorate Instructions
JCHR	Joint Committee on Human Rights
NASS	National Asylum Support Service
RLC	Refugee Legal Centre
SIAC	Special Immigration Appeals Commission
UN	United Nations

1

INTRODUCTION

The Asylum and Immigration (Treatment of Claimants, etc) Act 2004, the third **1.01** major piece of legislation in this area in five years,[1] radically reshapes the system for immigration and asylum appeals and introduces important changes, particularly in the welfare rights of immigrants, the designation of countries to which removal of claimants is deemed safe on human rights grounds, and the powers of the Secretary of State to detain.

The passage of the Bill through the House of Lords provoked huge controversy. **1.02** The interventions of the Lord Chief Justice, a former Lord Chancellor and senior Law Lords were unprecedented in modern times. If the decisions of immigration tribunals were to be excluded from scrutiny by the higher courts, where did it leave the careful (unwritten) constitutional balance between the powers of the executive and the powers of the courts? The Bill was amended.

This Guide follows the structure of the Act. It sets out the background to the law, **1.03** describes the changes introduced by the Act and provides commentary on the implication of the changes:

New offences: Sections 1–6 of the 2004 Act create a series of new offences (or, by **1.04** amendment to existing legislation, clarify existing offences). They include assisting unlawful immigration (s 1); entering the United Kingdom without a passport (s 2); forgery of immigration documents (s 3); trafficking people for exploitation (s 4); and changes in employer's liability for illegal working, allowing for conviction on indictment rather than, as before, a fine on summary conviction (s 6). They are described in Chapter 2.

Credibility: Section 8 of the 2004 Act requires decision-makers to presume that a **1.05** claimant's credibility is damaged by certain specified behaviour. Such behaviour includes concealing information, failure to produce a passport, destroying or altering a passport, producing an invalid passport, destroying or altering a ticket or other travel document, failing to answer questions asked by a decision-maker, making a claim after notification of an immigration decision, or arrest under an immigration provision and delaying or obstructing the resolution of the claim.

Unlike most other jurisdictions, the evidence in asylum and human rights claims **1.06**

---

[1] Immigration and Asylum Act 1999; Nationality, Immigration and Asylum Act 2002.

is derived almost entirely from the claimant. Assessment has frequently to be made on the basis of fragmented, incomplete and confused information; from people who are bewildered, frightened and perhaps desperate.[2] In this context, Home Office officials have, for a number of years, sought to argue that certain behaviour is inconsistent with being a genuine refugee.

1.07   Chapter 3 examines these presumptions. Against the backdrop of the United Kingdom's obligations under the Refugee and Human Rights Conventions, it suggests that if, looking at all the evidence in the round, a decision-maker considers a claimant is telling the truth about a certain event, it would be unlawful to disbelieve him or her simply on the basis of the factors set out in s 8. The decision-maker's duty is to determine whether a claimant's actions have so damaged his or her credibility that there is not even a real risk that their account is true.

1.08   *Welfare support for immigrants:* A person who makes an asylum claim or a claim under Art 3 of the European Convention on Human Rights (ECHR) is entitled to receive asylum support if he or she is destitute. Sections 9–13 of the 2004 Act make important changes in the scheme of support: s 9 disqualifies failed asylum-seeker families who have failed to leave the United Kingdom voluntarily from receiving asylum or social services support; s 9(3) removes rights of appeal to an asylum support adjudicator; s 10 gives powers to the Home Office to require failed asylum-seekers who cannot leave the United Kingdom to work unpaid as a condition of receiving support; s 11 amends the scheme on homelessness for former asylum-seekers; s 12 ends back-dated benefits; s 13 introduces integration loans for refugees. Chapter 4 carefully analyzes the impact of these changes and provides an up-to-date commentary on the new scheme.

1.09   *New enforcement powers:* Sections 14–18 of the 2004 Act extend immigration officers' powers of arrest (s 14); widen the scope under which fingerprints can be taken (s 15); widen the scope by which an immigration officer can obtain information about a passenger from a carrier (s 16); give new powers to retain documents that come into an immigration officer's (or Secretary of State's) possession (s 17); and allow an immigration officer to examine a person granted entry clearance (s 18). The powers are described in Chapter 5.

1.10   *Marriage:* Sections 19–25 of the 2004 Act, which provide a special procedure for the registration of marriages, were introduced at a very late stage of the Bill. The Government amendment provoked sharp criticism that the failure to allow adequate time for proper scrutiny amounted to an abuse of Parliament. The Act only provides a general framework for the new procedure: its full effect will not become clear until detailed regulations and guidance have been published. Chapter 6 examines, in particular, the compatibility of the new procedure with Arts 12 and 14 ECHR.

1.11   *Appeals:* Section 26 of the 2004 Act radically changes the system for immigration and asylum appeals:

---

[2] *Karanakaran v Secretary of State for the Home Department* [2000] INLR 122, [2002] Imm AR 271.

- Section 26 replaces the existing two levels of appeal, to an adjudicator and the Immigration Appeal Tribunal, with a new single tier body, the Asylum and Immigration Tribunal (AIT). The most important distinction in the new AIT is that an appeal determined by a panel of three or more members cannot be challenged on statutory review, but only on appeal to the Court of Appeal.

- A complex scheme of statutory review by the High Court is restricted by a five-day time-limit, severely criticized by the UN High Commissioner for Refugees for falling short of international standards of fairness by seriously compromising the ability of claimants to access their rights of appeal; and the introduction, in effect, of a conditional fee approach, criticized in the House of Lords as inappropriate to human rights cases which require, as the courts have repeatedly stated, the most anxious scrutiny.

- There is a new (and complex) scheme by which an appeal can be considered by the Court of Appeal.

Other changes to the appeals system are set out in ss 28–31. Chapter 7 describes the background to the changes, sets out the requirements under the new scheme, and provides practical guidance in making an application for review.

Unfounded claims: Section 27 extends the Secretary of State's powers to certify   **1.12** claims as 'clearly unfounded' and so deny in-country rights of appeal. Chapter 8 carefully reviews recent case law, particularly in the Court of Appeal, on the designation of countries that are generally free from persecution and the relevant human rights abuses; sets out the basis for challenging designation; and analyses the quality of Home Office country assessments.

Third country removals: Section 33 of and Sch. 3 to the 2004 Act now contain all   **1.13** the 'safe third country' provisions which were previously dispersed between the 1999 and 2002 Acts. Chapter 9 analyzes the four categories of third countries to which removals may be effected and assesses the compatibility of the deeming provisions with the ECHR.

Detention: Sections 32 and 34–36 of the 2004 Act introduce four changes in the   **1.14** area of detention, bail and temporary admission: there is a new right of appeal on a point of law against a decision by the Special Immigration Appeals Commission on bail; where a person is liable to be deported, he can be detained by the Secretary of State even though he has been bailed by a court with the power to grant them bail; a new offence is created of failing to co-operate in the obtaining of a travel document; and electronic monitoring can now be imposed as a condition of temporary admission or bail. Chapter 10 provides a comprehensive commentary on the law, as amended, on detention and bail.

Immigration services: Sections 37–40 of the 2004 Act give the Immigration   **1.15** Services Commissioner new powers to search and seize evidence (including legally privileged material); powers to require legal professional bodies to provide information to him and the Secretary of State (and powers to remove a body from the approved list if it fails to comply); and create an offence of offering immigration services when not qualified to do so. Chapter 11 describes these changes in the regulation of immigration services. The power to seize evidence can be used to seize material from solicitors' offices and barristers' chambers.

1.16   *European Asylum Directive:* Chapter 12 examines the implications of the Directive for unfounded claims, third country removals, and the right to an effective remedy.

1.17   Access to a great deal of information is available through the internet. Appendix 2 provides a list of useful resources.

1.18   *Commencement.* **References in this book to the 'present' or 'current' law are to the law as it stood before amendment by the 2004 Act.** The 2004 Act received Royal Assent on 22 July 2004. At the time of writing, the following provisions are in force:

Section(s)	Date in force	Commencement provision
1	1 October 2004	SI 2004/2523
2	22 September 2004	2004 Act, s 48(1)
3	1 October 2004	SI 2004/2523
6	1 October 2004	SI 2004/2523
8(7), (10), (11)	1 October 2004*	SI 2004/2523
15	1 October 2004	SI 2004/2523
18	1 October 2004	SI 2004/2523
27–31	1 October 2004	SI 2004/2523
32(1)	22 September 2004**	2004 Act, s 48(2)
32(2)	22 September 2004	2004 Act, s 48(1)
33	1 October 2004	SI 2004/2523
34	1 October 2004	SI 2004/2523
35	22 September 2004	2004 Act, s 48(1)
36–46	1 October 2004	SI 2004/2523

*only for the purposes of enabling subordinate legislation to be made
**SIAC determinations made on or after this date

1.19   Our thanks are due to our colleagues at Doughty Street, particularly other members of the immigration team from whom we have gained through discussion at every stage of the book; to our clerks, Paul Friend, Richard Bayliss, Melanie Stephenson and Jason Savage and other members of the Doughty Street staff; and to Helena Kennedy who not only wrote the foreword but is a great fighter for a decent and humane approach to the law. Migration has shaped British society for centuries. The measure with which we treat strangers is a measure of our own values of decency, humanity and justice.

Doughty Street
18 August 2004

2

IMMIGRATION OFFENCES
(SECTIONS 1–7)

A. Assisting unlawful immigration	2.01
B. Entering the United Kingdom without a passport	2.03
C. Forgery of immigration documents	2.07
D. Trafficking people for exploitation	2.08
E. Employment	2.09

A. ASSISTING UNLAWFUL IMMIGRATION

Section 1 of the Asylum and Immigration (Treatment of Claimants, etc) Act 2004 **2.01** amends s 25 of the Immigration Act 1971 (assisting unlawful immigration to a member state).[1] The offence is assisting a person who is not a national of a member state to enter and reside in a member state contrary to the laws of the member state.[2] The amendment corrects an omission in that section by which 'member state' was

---

[1] Immigration Act 1971, s 25, substituted by Nationality, Immigration and Asylum Act 2002, s 143 from 10 February 2003.

[2] For sentencing guidelines for this offence see *R v Van Binh Lee and Stark* [1999] 1 Cr App R (S) 422, 425 *per* Lord Bingham: 'In the ordinary way the appropriate penalty for all but the most minor offences against section 25(1) is one of immediate custody. The offence is one which calls very often for deterrent sentences and, as the statistics make plain, the problem of illegal entry is on the increase. Plainly the seven year maximum sentence must accommodate offences with the most aggravating features. There are indeed a number of features which may aggravate the commission of this offence ... where the offence has been repeated and the defendant comes to court with a record of violations against this provision ... where the offence has been committed for financial gain ... where the illegal entry has been facilitated for strangers as opposed to a spouse or a close member of the family. In cases of conspiracy the offence is aggravated by a high degree of planning, and sophistication. Plainly the more prominent the role of the defendant the greater the aggravation of the offence. It is further aggravated if it is committed in relation to a large number of illegal entrants as opposed to a small number ... [T]he maximum must cater for the case in which the defendant has contested the charge and so failed to earn the discount which a plea of guilty would have earned. The more of those aggravating features that are present, the higher the sentence will be, and conversely the absence of those features will militate in favour of a defendant, and he will ordinarily be entitled as in any other case to some discount for a plea of guilty.'

restricted only to members of the European Union. It allows the Secretary of State to make an order prescribing additional states which are to be regarded as 'member states' for the purposes of the section[3] if he considers it necessary for the purposes of complying with the United Kingdom's EU obligations.[4] The nationals of these states are also to be deemed to be citizens of the European Union for the purposes of s 25 of the 1971 Act.[5]

2.02 The purpose of the amendment is to ensure that the United Kingdom is compliant with EU law in including Schengen signatories as EU states.[6] An order by the Secretary of State is meant to add any new Schengen signatories,[7] hence the naming of the list as 'Section 25 List of Schengen Acquis States'. If this is its purpose it is not clear why the amendment does not simply state that 'member states' should also include Schengen states rather than giving the Secretary of State the power to add states by list.

B. ENTERING THE UNITED KINGDOM WITHOUT A PASSPORT

2.03 Section 2 creates a new offence of entering the United Kingdom without a valid[8] passport or a document which is designed to serve the same as a passport[9] which satisfactorily establishes his/her identity and nationality or citizenship.[10] The commission of the offence takes place when the person is first interviewed by an immigration officer after arrival in the United Kingdom.[11] There is a statutory presumption that the person will not have such a document if he fails to produce one to an immigration officer on request.[12] The section also criminalizes travelling with a dependent child without the requisite immigration document.[13] The defence to these offences is that the person or child is an EEA national[14] or the person has a reasonable excuse for not being in possession of the document.[15]

2.04 The fact that the document was deliberately destroyed is not a reasonable excuse

---

[3] Immigration Act 1971, s 25(7)(a) (as amended).

[4] ibid, s 25(8) (as amended).

[5] ibid, s 25(7)(b) (as amended).

[6] Council Directive (EC) 2002/90 of 28 November 2002 defining the facilitation of unauthorized entry, transit and residence [2002] OJ L328/17 and EU Council Framework Decision 2002/946 of 28 November 2002 on the strengthening of the penal framework to prevent the facilitation of unauthorized entry, transit and residence [2002] OJ L328/1. The current non-EU Schengen States are Norway and Iceland.

[7] Statement of Minister for Immigration, Beverley Hughes, HC Standing Committee B, col 11 (8 January 2004).

[8] Asylum and Immigration (Treatment of Claimants, etc) Act 2004, s 2(1)(a).

[9] ibid, s 2(10).

[10] ibid, s 2(1)(b).

[11] ibid, s 2(1).

[12] ibid, s 2(6).

[13] ibid, s 2(2).

[14] ibid, s 2(3)(a) and (4)(a).

[15] ibid, s 2(3)(b) and (4)(b).

for not being in possession of the document unless the destruction was for a reasonable cause or was beyond the control of the person charged with the offence.[16] A reasonable cause does not include delaying the handling or resolution of a claim or application; or taking a decision that increases the chances of success of a claim or application; or complying with instructions or advice given by a person who offers advice about, or facilitates, immigration into the United Kingdom.[17]

A constable or immigration officer who reasonably suspects that a person has 2.05 committed an offence under this section may arrest the person without a warrant.[18] A person who is convicted of the offence if tried summarily will not be imprisoned for more than six months; or if tried in the Crown Court, for more than two years.[19]

Although drafted very widely, the Government's apparent intention is to prose- 2.06 cute people who deliberately destroy or dispose of their documentation between embarkation and claiming asylum; not to try to prosecute people where it believes that they never had documents in the first place or that they have not destroyed documents, whether false or not.[20] Consequently, the number of prosecutions of people who have destroyed their documents ought only to constitute a small percentage of the total number who are guilty and should comprise a number of high-profile cases in order to deter this behaviour.[21]

C. FORGERY OF IMMIGRATION DOCUMENTS

Section 3 amends s 5 of the Forgery and Counterfeiting Act 1981 so that 'immigra- 2.07 tion documents' become instruments to which s 5 of the 1981 Act applies.[22] 'Immigration documents' are cards or stickers designed to be given to a person to show whether that person is subject to control under the Immigration Act 1971 and, if so, what conditions have been attached to any grant of leave to enter or remain in the United Kingdom.[23]

---

[16] ibid, s 2(5)(a).

[17] ibid, s 2(5)(b).

[18] ibid, s 2(8).

[19] ibid, s 2(7).

[20] Statement of Minister for Immigration, Beverley Hughes, HC Standing Committee B, col 44 (8 January 2004): 'I shall make some specific points, but it is important at the outset to go back to the intention of the clause, which we discussed this morning: it is to catch those who deliberately destroy the documents that they used for embarkation to the UK in the first place. It is not to catch the people who may be able to arrive here without the passport or other documentation that enables them to travel but perhaps with some evidence of experiences testifying to their claim to be refugees and in need of asylum. The clause is not to catch those people; it is precisely to catch people who we believe have deliberately destroyed their documents.'

[21] Statement of Minister for Immigration, Beverley Hughes, HC Standing Committee B, col 64 (8 January 2004).

[22] Asylum and Immigration (Treatment of Claimants, etc) Act 2004, s 3(2).

[23] ibid, s 3(3).

D. TRAFFICKING PEOPLE FOR EXPLOITATION

2.08 Section 4 introduces a new criminal offence of trafficking people into, or out of, the United Kingdom for the purposes of exploitation. Trafficking is arranging or facilitating the arrival, travel within or departure from the United Kingdom of an individual.[24] The offence is committed if the person intends to exploit the passenger in the United Kingdom or elsewhere, or believes that another person is likely to exploit the passenger in the United Kingdom or elsewhere.[25] For commission of the offence caused by trafficking within the United Kingdom, the trafficker has to believe that the person was brought into the country for exploitation.[26] An exploited person is defined in s 4(4) which includes behaviour contrary to Art 4 of the European Convention on Human Rights (ECHR).[27] It carries on conviction on indictment a term of imprisonment not exceeding 14 years, or on summary conviction not more than six months.[28]

E. EMPLOYMENT

2.09 Section 6 applies to the criminal offence of employer's liability for illegal working under s 8 of the Asylum and Immigration Act 1996. The section stipulates that the penalty on conviction shall be a fine not exceeding the statutory maximum either on indictment or summary conviction. This allows conviction on indictment, rather than the previous position which only allowed for summary conviction with a maximum level 5 fine.

2.10 Section 6 also abolishes an extension of time for prosecution under s 8 of the 1996 Act. The previous regime allowed for an extension of time from the date that evidence sufficient to justify proceedings came to the notice of a police officer (in England and Wales) with corresponding provisions for the rest of the United Kingdom.

---

[24] Asylum and Immigration (Treatment of Claimants, etc) Act 2004, s 4(1), (2) and (3).
[25] ibid, s 4(1), (2) and (3).
[26] ibid, s 4(2).
[27] ibid, s 4(4).
[28] ibid, s 4(5).

3

CREDIBILITY OF ASYLUM AND HUMAN RIGHTS CLAIMANTS (SECTION 8)

A.	Introduction	3.01
B.	Background	3.02
C.	Significance and scope of s 8	3.07
D.	Behaviour to which s 8 applies	3.23
E.	Failure to answer question asked by decision-maker	3.52
F.	Timing of the asylum or human rights claim	3.63
G.	Failure to make asylum or human rights claim in a safe third country	3.71
H.	Behaviour obstructing or delaying the handling of claim	3.76

A. INTRODUCTION

Section 8 of the Asylum and Immigration (Treatment of Claimants, etc) Act 2004 **3.01** requires immigration decision-makers, including the Asylum and Immigration Tribunal, to presume that a claimant's credibility is damaged by certain specified actions. However, the requirement properly to determine asylum and human rights claims means that the decision-maker is entitled to accept the claimant's statement notwithstanding any presumed damage to credibility.

B. BACKGROUND

Disputes of fact in asylum and human rights claims differ from those in other areas of **3.02** law (such as in a road traffic accident or a robbery), in that evidence is usually only presented by one party: the claimant, often supported by other sources of evidence such as witnesses, experts and/or general material on the country concerned. The Secretary of State rarely presents evidence going to the events which led to the asylum claim. His only regular practice is to present his 'assessment' of the claimant's country of origin, which is a document summarizing (but not analysing) what others have said about that country's systems and practices. Only in very rare cases does the Secretary of State advance any evidence directed to the particular facts of the claimant's case. This reluctance to investigate the claimant's account independently is at odds with the guidance given by the UN High Commissioner for Refugees' *Handbook on Procedures and Criteria for Determining Refugee Status*, para 196.

3.03   The Home Office stance means that, whereas most judicial decision-makers choose between two or more differing accounts of factual events, those who determine asylum and human rights claims are generally only presented with one account of events.

3.04   It is in this context that the behaviour of the claimant can assume far greater significance than it does in other fields. Presented with an account which is consistent with independent reports of the country concerned, which is detailed and internally consistent, some Home Office officials nevertheless seek to argue that the account is not true because the claimant's behaviour shows that it is not. For a number of years, Home Office officials have sought to create an environment in which certain behaviour is regarded as inconsistent with being a genuine refugee. No empirical evidence has been gathered to support the contention that this behaviour is a valuable guide to whether a person is telling the truth.

3.05   Paragraph 341 of the Immigration Rules[1] therefore provides that certain matters may damage the credibility of a person claiming asylum, including:

(a) failure without reasonable explanation to claim asylum forthwith upon arrival in the United Kingdom, unless the claim is based upon events which took place after arrival;

(b) that the claim is made after refusal of leave to enter, recommendation for deportation or notification of decision to make a deportation order;

(c) failure to produce a passport without reasonable explanation;

(d) production of an invalid passport with failure to inform the immigration officer.

3.06   Section 8 can therefore be seen as the newest Home Office mechanism for focusing attention on the behaviour of asylum claimants. It is hoped that conscientious decision-makers, at all levels, will nevertheless continue to concentrate on determining the truth of the claimant's account.

C. SIGNIFICANCE AND SCOPE OF S 8

1. The significance of s 8

3.07   The significance of s 8 must be considered in the light of the overriding obligations imposed upon decision-makers to determine asylum and human rights claims correctly.

---

[1] HC 395.

The United Kingdom has accepted the obligations imposed by the Geneva and **3.08** Human Rights Conventions. In particular, the United Kingdom is prohibited from expelling a person who is a Convention refugee to the frontiers of a territory where her or his life or freedom would be threatened.[2] The United Kingdom is also prohibited from expelling a person where to do so would expose him or her to a real risk of inhuman or degrading treatment or punishment.[3]

The obligation imposed by Art 3 ECHR is incorporated into domestic law by **3.09** Human Rights Act 1998, s 6. The obligation imposed by Geneva Convention, Art 33(1) has not been incorporated in the same way. However, only a clear, unambiguous statute could cut down the Geneva Convention obligation, given that it concerns fundamental human rights.[4]

Where a decision-maker is considering whether expulsion would breach those **3.10** obligations, she is obliged to consider all the material presented and reach a conclusion that is true to the assessment of that material. If that decision-maker considers that a claimed historical event is true, then the decision-maker would be acting contrary to the Refugee and Human Rights Conventions if she determined the claim on the basis that it was not true. That course is also prohibited by domestic law (see para 3.09 above).

During the passage of the Act, the Government accepted that: 'The deciding **3.11** authority will have discretion to decide the weight to give to [failures], taking into account all factors relevant to the claim. The requirement to take that behaviour into account is not determinative of credibility and does not displace the obligation to consider all the circumstances of the case.'[5]

If, on all the evidence presented, the decision-maker considers that the claimant is **3.12** telling the truth about a certain event, it would be unlawful to disbelieve him or her on the basis that s 8 requires additional damage to credibility. Thus, even in cases where there is good reason to believe that the account is untrue, it would be unlawful to allow s 8 damage to tip the balance against the claimant.

Section 8 does not prevent the decision-maker from deciding that other kinds of **3.13** behaviour damage credibility.[6]

It is therefore submitted that s 8 has only very limited effect. The effect of s 8 is **3.14** no more than to stipulate matters which damage credibility. It does not require the decision-maker to disbelieve the claimant. Nor does it relieve the decision-maker of the duty to determine whether a claimant's actions have so damaged his credibility that there is not even a real risk that the account is correct. The determination of the

---

[2] Geneva Convention, Art 33(1).

[3] Art 3 ECHR.

[4] See *R v Secretary of State for the Home Department, ex p Simms* [2000] 2 AC 115, 131, *per* Lord Hoffmann; *R v Secretary of State for the Home Department, ex p Bugdaycay* [1987] AC 514, 531, *per* Lord Bridge.

[5] Letter from Beverley Hughes MP, to the Parliamentary Joint Committee on Human Rights, 27 January 2004, published as Appendix to the Committee's Fifth Report of Session 2003–04 (HL Paper 35, HC Paper 304) 37.

[6] Asylum and Immigration (Treatment of Claimants, etc) Act 2004, s 8(12).

extent of any damage arising from actions or failures remains entirely with the decision-maker. The decision-maker is entitled to say that, having taken account of any s 8 damage, the claimant's account is accepted.

2. Statements to which s 8 applies

3.15 Section 8 only applies to a decision whether to believe a statement made by or on behalf of a person who makes an asylum or human rights claim.[7] 'Asylum claim' and 'human rights claim' have the meanings given by Nationality, Immigration and Asylum Act 2002, s 113.[8]

3.16 Section 8 has no application to a person who has not made such a claim, but is making some other immigration application, for example, to remain as a student or work permit holder. It is unclear from the wording of s 8 whether it is to apply to every immigration aspect of the case of a person who has made an asylum or human rights claim. It is submitted that it does not, and that it is intended to apply solely to the consideration of statements in the context of a pending asylum/human rights claim or appeal.

3.17 Section 8 applies to statements made 'on behalf' of an asylum or human rights claimant.[9] It therefore applies to statements made by a representative on behalf of a client. It is important to note that the behaviour of representatives does not damage credibility under s 8: it is only the claimant's behaviour which counts.

3.18 Section 8 does not apply to statements made by witnesses and family members. Those statements are made in support of, but not 'on behalf of' the claimant, and the credibility of their own statements is not damaged by the actions of the claimant. Section 8 does not require a decision-maker to treat a witness's credibility as damaged by that witness's own actions: it is concerned only with the actions of the claimant.[10]

3.19 Section 8 applies when considering whether to believe a statement.[11] Clearly, that relates only to statements of fact. This includes statements by the claimant about the factual circumstances surrounding physical evidence presented to a decision-maker, such as photographs and official documents.

3.20 Once the facts are established, s 8 does not affect the exercise of a judgment or discretion. For example, once the decision-maker has found the relevant facts and is then concerned with whether it would be proportionate to remove the claimant from the United Kingdom, that judgment is not affected by s 8.

---

[7] Asylum and Immigration (Treatment of Claimants, etc) Act 2004, s 8(1).
[8] ibid, s 8(7).
[9] ibid, s 8(1).
[10] ibid, s 8(2)–(6).
[11] ibid, s 8(1).

3. Decision-makers to whom s 8 applies

Section 8 applies to each 'deciding authority', ie immigration officers, the Secretary **3.21** of State, the Asylum and Immigration Tribunal and the Special Immigration Appeals Commission.[12] Section 8 also applies to immigration adjudicators and the Immigration Appeal Tribunal, if it is brought into force before they are abolished.[13]

Section 8 does not apply to the High Court or Court of Appeal (or, in Scotland, **3.22** Court of Session). In cases where those courts are considering the legality of a decision of the Secretary of State or the Asylum and Immigration Tribunal, that will not normally matter. However, in those unusual cases where the court considers a factual issue for itself, s 8 has no application.

D. BEHAVIOUR TO WHICH S 8 APPLIES

1. Behaviour to conceal information or mislead

Section 8 applies to behaviour by the claimant which the deciding authority thinks is **3.23** designed or likely to conceal information or to mislead.[14] Under s 8(3), certain behaviours are treated as designed or likely to conceal information or mislead. These are largely concerned with passports and the route of travel to the United Kingdom and are dealt with specifically below.

Section 8(2) speaks of behaviour which is designed or likely to 'conceal informa- **3.24** tion' or to 'mislead'. It is suggested that the information to which s 8 refers must be information which the decision-maker does not have which, it is considered, would be relevant to the determination of the asylum or human rights claim.

Section 8 only applies where the decision-maker is satisfied that certain facts **3.25** adverse to the claimant are made out, for example, that a document was produced as if it were a passport, or that a claimant had a reasonable opportunity to make an asylum claim in a third country. In some appeal cases there will be a dispute about such facts. It is suggested that the burden of proving those facts rests upon the Secretary of State to the balance of probabilities.[15]

2. Behaviour relating to passports

Section 8(2) applies where the claimant (s 8(3)(a)–(c)): **3.26**

(a) fails without reasonable explanation to produce a passport on request to an immigration officer or to the Secretary of State;

---

[12] ibid, s 8(1), (7).
[13] ibid, s 8(13). For abolition of adjudicators and Tribunal, see para 7.15 below.
[14] ibid, s 8(2)(a)–(b).
[15] See, by analogy, *Ziar v Secretary of State for the Home Department* [1997] INLR 221, 233–234, IAT.

(b) destroys, alters or disposes of a passport without reasonable explanation; or

(c) produces a document which is not a valid passport as if it were.

3.27 'Passport' includes any document relating to a non-UK national 'which is designed to serve the same purpose as a passport'.[16] A passport is a document authorizing travel abroad and requesting the governments of other countries to offer protection.[17]

3.28 'Passport' therefore includes documents designed to facilitate international travel. That would include travel documents such as those issued under Geneva Convention, Art 28 or under Art 28 of the 1954 New York Convention relating to the status of stateless persons, as well as those issued by national bodies on an ad hoc basis, such as the UK Government's 'Certificate of Identity'.

3.29 A national identity card is designed for internal use in the state concerned and not for international travel and protection. It follows that, even where permitted to be used for international travel, for example, within the European Union, a national identity card is not a passport under s 8. Parliament chose not to define passport as including 'some other document satisfactorily establishing his identity and nationality or citizenship' as it did in the old provisions for certification preventing a right of appeal to the Immigration Appeal Tribunal.[18]

3. Passport not produced

3.30 Section 8(2) applies where the claimant fails without reasonable explanation to produce a passport on request to an immigration officer or to the Secretary of State.[19]

3.31 The claimant may accept that a request for a passport was made. In a case where the claimant does not deny that such a request was made, the evidence may entitle the adjudicator to infer that one was made.[20] However, where there is a denial, it is suggested that the Secretary of State must produce evidence establishing that a request was made for a passport in a language which the claimant understood at the time.

3.32 Once that has been proved, the claimant must then provide a reasonable excuse for his failure to produce a passport.

3.33 Section 8(3)(a) is very similar to the provision for certification in Asylum and Immigration Appeals Act 1993, Sch 5, para 5(4)(a). However, there is one important difference. Old para 5(4)(a) applied if the claimant 'failed to produce a passport without giving a reasonable explanation for his failure to do so'. It was held that this

---

[16] Asylum and Immigration (Treatment of Claimants, etc) Act 2004, s 8(7).

[17] *Oxford English Dictionary*.

[18] Asylum and Immigration Appeals Act 1993, Sch 5, para 5(10), inserted by Asylum and Immigration Act 1996, s 1.

[19] Asylum and Immigration (Treatment of Claimants, etc) Act 2004, s 8(3)(a).

[20] *R (Subaththeran) v Special Adjudicator* [2001] EWHC Admin 12, [2001] Imm AR 345 at [15].

required an explanation to be volunteered to the immigration officer at the time.[21] Section 8(3)(a) is worded differently and it is suggested that the explanation need not be volunteered at the time the passport is requested.

Apart from that, the case law on old para 5(4)(a) is relevant to the interpretation **3.34** of the new provision:

(a) '[I]t is the explanation that must be reasonable not the conduct of the applicant. That may not be reasonable even if the explanation was. For example, if I have an accident that prevents me from attending work, there is a reasonable excuse for my non-attendance notwithstanding that the accident was entirely my fault.'[22]

(b) 'If the traveller is unsophisticated, bemused, or otherwise very much in the hands of his agent or travelling companion, it may be perfectly understandable that he will hand his documents to such a person. Often that person will be someone who has assumed some responsibility for the asylum [seeker and] in whom the asylum seeker may have reposed considerable confidence. They may, at least to some extent, be in a position of trust towards the asylum seeker.'[23] That view was affirmed in a different context by the Court of Appeal: '[There is] the possibility of duress by threats against the families of asylum seekers, and this phenomenon is recorded in the Home Office research. It is also clear that some asylum seekers are so much under the influence of the agents who are shepherding them into the country that they cannot be criticised for accepting implicitly what they are told by them ... To disregard the effect that they may have on their charges would be both unrealistic and unjust.'[24]

(c) Where the explanation was that no passport had been applied for because it would not have been issued, and the decision-maker decides that a passport would have been issued, the explanation may not be a reasonable one.[25] (It is suggested that the result in that case would have been different if the adjudicator had accepted that the claimant had genuinely, but mistakenly, believed that no passport would have been issued on application.)

(d) Where an explanation is given which is not fanciful, the decision-maker must explain why it is not a reasonable one.[26]

4. Passport destroyed, altered or disposed of

Section 8(2) applies where the claimant destroys, alters or disposes of a passport **3.35** without a reasonable explanation.[27]

---

[21] ibid at [17].

[22] *Naguleswaran v Secretary of State for the Home Department* (Elias J, 3 December 1999) at [28] followed in *R (Kadem D) v Special Adjudicator* [2001] EWHC Admin 522 at [12].

[23] *Naguleswaran*, ibid at [33]: text in square brackets corrects apparent error in transcript.

[24] *R (Q) v Secretary of State for the Home Department* [2003] EWCA Civ 364, [2004] QB 36 at [40].

[25] *Kadem D*, n 22 above, at [6]–[8].

[26] *R v Special Adjudicator, ex p Islam* (Turner J, 16 October 2000) at [13]–[14].

[27] Asylum and Immigration (Treatment of Claimants, etc) Act 2004, s 8(3)(c).

3.36   Where a claimant arrives in the United Kingdom without a passport, he may accept that he had a passport but destroyed it or disposed of it en route. He may present a damaged passport.

3.37   Where the claimant denies that he has engaged in this behaviour, it is suggested that on appeal the Secretary of State must show that he has so engaged. This may be done by, for example, producing the passport which the claimant disposed of en route (such passports are sometimes retained by the aeroplane's toilet mechanism), or demonstrating that he boarded the plane with a passport (carriers often keep photocopies of records of documents used when boarding).

3.38   When considering whether the explanation for the behaviour is reasonable, it is suggested that the case law on the old certification provisions is relevant: see para 3.34 above.

5. Invalid 'passport' produced

3.39   Section 8(2) applies where the claimant produces a document which is not a valid passport as if it were.[28] The context indicates that this applies only where the document is produced to an immigration officer or the Secretary of State, and not where another person, such as a local authority official, is presented with such a document. The equivalent Immigration Rule refers expressly to production to the immigration officer.[29]

3.40   Section 8(2) applies where the claimant produced the document on behalf of another person.[30] However, it does not apply where another person produced such a document on behalf of the claimant. That is because s 8(2) only applies to behaviour by the claimant, and not behaviour on his behalf.

3.41   The effect of s 8(8) is that a document is not a valid passport if it:

(a) does not relate to the person by whom or on whose behalf it is produced;

(b) has been altered otherwise than by or with permission of the authority who issued it; or

(c) was obtained by deception.

3.42   Bribery of the issuing authority is not a ground upon which a passport is to be regarded as invalid. (In several refugee-producing countries, bribery is necessary to persuade the authorities to issue a valid passport.)

3.43   In many cases the claimant will accept that the passport does not relate to him or her. In others the decision-maker will decide that the person shown in the passport photograph is not the claimant. However, where it cannot be shown that the passport does not relate to the claimant, the other provisions may give rise to difficulty.

3.44   As for the alteration limb, the Secretary of State must show that an alteration was

---

[28] Asylum and Immigration (Treatment of Claimants, etc) Act 2004, s 8(3)(b).

[29] HC 395, para 341(iv)(b).

[30] Asylum and Immigration (Treatment of Claimants, etc) Act 2004, s 8(8)(a).

made and that this was without the permission of the authority who issued the document. Unless the photograph has been covertly substituted, that may be difficult. The Secretary of State can hardly refer the document itself to the authority who issued the passport while the asylum claim or appeal is still pending. He may however be able to produce general information from the issuing authority about passport alteration procedures.

As for the deception limb, the personal details in the passport may differ from **3.45** those said by the claimant to be correct: a name may be spelt differently, or a date of birth differs. That may be because the issuing authority was deceived, or because of a mistake made when entering the details on the passport, or in the documents produced to obtain it. Given the difficulty of obtaining the issuing authority's passport application file without compromising the confidentiality of the asylum claim, it may be hard to show that such a passport was obtained by deception.

Where it is disputed on appeal that an invalid document was presented, it is **3.46** suggested that the Secretary of State must produce evidence establishing that:

(a) the document was produced by the claimant, and not by another person on his behalf;

(b) the claimant produced the document as if it were a valid passport. (A claimant may have presented the document and been unable, for example, through lack of English, to communicate its invalidity. In such cases, it is suggested that the Secretary of State will need to show that the claimant had the facilities to communicate the nature of the document, but did not do so.)

(c) the document is invalid (see paras 3.41–3.45 above).

If the Secretary of State alleges that the document produced is a forgery and that **3.47** disclosure to the claimant of a matter relating to the detection of the forgery would be contrary to the public interest, then the Tribunal must investigate that allegation in private.[31] Having done so, the Tribunal has power to proceed in private in so far as necessary to prevent the disclosure of the matter relating to the detection of the forgery. It is believed that the Secretary of State has rarely invoked this provision or its predecessors.[32] It is a fundamental principle of English law that litigants are equal before the court, and are entitled to know all of the evidence presented against them. This provision permits a serious departure from that principle and must be construed narrowly and applied with caution.

In cases where this provision is invoked, it is suggested that the Tribunal should **3.48** consider the following:

(a) Whether the Secretary of State has demonstrated that disclosure of the matter relating to the detection would be contrary to the public interest. Many methods

---

[31] Nationality, Immigration and Asylum Act 2002, s 108.
[32] The predecessors are Immigration and Asylum Act 1999, Sch 4, para 6; Asylum Appeals (Procedure) Rules 1996, SI 1996/2070, r 30.

of detection are well-known, or information on them is available from public sources such as the internet. Disclosure that such a method has been deployed cannot be said to be contrary to the public interest. If the Secretary of State's concern is disclosure of the method, has he produced reliable evidence that this method is one which remains secret from the public?

(b) Which parts of the case against the claimant can be made known to him without disclosing the matter which must be kept secret. The Tribunal must ensure that the fundamental rights are only derogated from to the minimum extent required. For example, if substitution of the photograph has been detected, is there a compelling reason why the claimant cannot be told this, albeit without being told how it was detected?

(c) Whether the forgery allegation is proved, given that the claimant might have been able to present rebuttal evidence if he knew of the matter kept secret. The fact that the evidence cannot be tested and challenged reduces the weight that can be attached to it.

6. Ticket or other travel document destroyed, altered or disposed of

3.49   Section 8(2) applies where the claimant destroys, alters or disposes of a ticket or other document connected with travel without a reasonable explanation.[33] 'Other document connected with travel' may include boarding cards and baggage labels.

3.50   As for passports, it is suggested that where the claimant denies that he destroyed, disposed of or altered such a document, it is for the Secretary of State so to prove: see para 3.25 above.

3.51   Where the claimant accepts that the document has been disposed of, the explanation offered may be that it was no longer important. In many cases that may be a reasonable explanation. It may not be unreasonable for a person to regard a ticket or boarding card as unimportant once he has taken up his seat.

E. FAILURE TO ANSWER QUESTION ASKED BY DECISION-MAKER

3.52   Section 8(2) applies where the claimant fails to answer a decision-maker's question without reasonable explanation, see s 8(3)(e). It is suggested that a question is only asked if it is asked in a way in which the claimant can understand.

3.53   In some cases, the claimant denies having been asked the question in the way alleged and/or denies having given the answer claimed. Where the Secretary of State alleges on appeal that the claimant failed to answer a question asked by him in interview, it is suggested that he must show that the question was asked of the claimant.

3.54   It is suggested that the Tribunal should be careful to weigh up the evidence presented to it in such cases. It is rare for the Secretary of State to present oral

---

[33] Asylum and Immigration (Treatment of Claimants, etc) Act 2004, s 8(3)(d).

evidence about what occurred at interview. The evidence relied upon to that end is normally the interviewer's note of the questions asked and answers given, usually through an interpreter. Such evidence must be treated with caution. The interviewer's note is exactly that: a note. It is not in practice a verbatim transcript of exactly what was said in the interview. Interviewers, interpreters and interviewees often make side comments, interrupt, rephrase or clarify without full notation of the exchanges. Since many words permit of different meanings, misunderstanding is an ever-present risk in interpretation. The note of interview is no longer read back to the interviewee to check for errors in understanding, translation and notation. Public funding is now only available for a solicitor's representative to attend interview in special cases. Indeed, even where a representative does attend, unless she is fluent in the language of the interview it is unlikely that she would detect errors. Unless such a representative takes a note, there is never a note of the questions and answers as spoken in the claimant's own language. It is inevitable that notes of interview will not always be an accurate record of the questions as put through an interpreter and of the claimant's replies in his own language. It is significant that the police have long been required to tape-record interviews of suspects even for minor crimes, though such interviews are almost always in English.

3.55 The claimant's evidence is capable of bearing much more weight. Typically, it is oral evidence from the claimant about what was said at interview. The claimant was there and heard the question actually posed and the answer given.

3.56 Where the claimant's evidence is that the note is inaccurate, it is suggested that it will be hard for the Secretary of State to show that his officer's note of interview is to be preferred. Absent tape-recording or professional transcription in the language of the questions and answers, the likelihood of error in translation or notation is simply too great.

1. Explanation for failure to answer question

3.57 In many cases, there will be no dispute about the question asked and the failure to answer it. The most likely explanation for a failure to answer a question is that the claimant did not understand the question or did not know the answer.

3.58 Home Office interviewers sometimes ask questions which, even in translation, may not be capable of being understood by the interviewee. For example, a claimant ignorant of political parties may be asked whether a relative 'held office' in a party or what the 'policies' of the party were. It may be that by careful questioning using terms the claimant does understand, an answer can be provided. In such cases, the claimant's explanation will be a reasonable one: 'I did not understand what the Home Office was getting at'.

3.59 More often, questions are asked to which the claimant does not know the answer. If that is accepted, it will be a reasonable explanation. In considering whether a claimant would know a particular answer, it is important that decision-makers should not assume that British cultural traditions are universal. For example, in many parts of the world (such as Iraq), most people do not celebrate birthdays and dates of birth are often unknown to close relatives or even the person concerned. It is therefore not surprising that some claimants do not know the dates of birth, or exact ages, of their spouse, siblings or children. Similarly, in many towns and cities (such as Khartoum, Sudan) there are no systems of house address in use. Before concluding that the explanation 'I do not know' is not to be accepted even to the lower standard, the adjudicator must be satisfied that the answer is one that the claimant is very likely to know and that he is therefore lying.

3.60   Often individuals cannot recall information they probably knew or observed at some time: names of those involved in events; periods of time; location of events; details of journeys. Many Home Office officials and some appellate decision-makers appear to consider that it is unusual for individuals to be unable to recall such matters. Yet consideration of the faculties of memory of oneself and one's family and friends strongly indicates that it is normal for people to forget details in their life: even those details important in English culture, such as anniversaries. Political commitment does not mean that one will necessarily have a good recall of the dates on which one was arrested or the names of fellow activists, or be observant during the journey to the United Kingdom.

3.61   Sometimes, after the Home Office interview, a claimant may recall information which he did not give at the interview. The subject of Home Office questions can be events occurring over many years, in many different places, involving many different people and often traumatic events. Interviewees often want to present their history in the way in which they remember it. However, interviewers rarely assist them to do so, instead interrupting the flow of the history (and thus of the recollection) with questions about matters occurring at other times or in other contexts. Many Home Office officials do not seem to heed the advice of the UN High Commissioner for Refugees that they should aim to 'gain the confidence of the applicant in order to assist the latter in putting forward his case'.[34] In such cases, it is hardly surprising that interviewees can find it difficult to recollect the information sought at the moment when the question is asked.

3.62   There may be other reasonable explanations for a failure to answer: the claimant may have been ashamed of referring to the events or fearful that his answer will reach the authorities of his country or be used against him in some other way. In such cases, the reasonableness of the claimant's explanation must be assessed in the light of his state of knowledge and belief.

F. TIMING OF THE ASYLUM OR HUMAN RIGHTS CLAIM

3.63   Credibility is treated as damaged (see s 8(5)–(6)) if the asylum or human rights claim is made after:

---

[34] *Handbook on Procedures and Criteria for Determining Refugee Status*, para 200.

(a) notification of an immigration decision to the claimant; or

(b) the arrest of the claimant under an immigration provision.

1. Claim after notification of immigration decision

An immigration decision means (s 8(7)): **3.64**

(a) refusal of leave to enter the United Kingdom;

(b) refusal to vary leave to enter or remain in the United Kingdom;

(c) grant of leave to enter or remain in the United Kingdom;

(d) a decision that a person is to be removed from the United Kingdom as a person refused leave to enter, as an illegal entrant or by way of directions under Immigration and Asylum Act 1999, s 10;

(e) a decision to make a deportation order;

(f) a decision to take action in connection with extradition from the United Kingdom.

This provision applies to claims made after the notification of the decision. The form **3.65** of notification is to be defined by regulations.[35]

The provision does not apply if 'the claim relies wholly on matters arising after **3.66** the notification'.[36] On the face of it, s 8(5) may apply where any event of relevance to current risk occurred before the immigration decision was made. It is suggested that such an interpretation would be mistaken. The claim is that removal would breach the Geneva or Human Rights Convention. The matters on which that claim relies are those which show that the risk is now a real risk (and no longer a fanciful one). It follows that s 8(5) only applies if the claimant argues that matters of which he was already aware show that his claim is well-founded. For example, if the government of a country began persecuting members of a particular faith, it would be absurd if s 8(5) applied on the basis that the claimant was already a member of that faith when the immigration decision was made.

2. Claim after arrest under immigration provision

Arrest under the following immigration provisions counts for this purpose (s 8(7)): **3.67**

(a) illegal entry and obtaining leave to remain by deception;[37]

(b) overstaying or breach of conditions of leave;[38]

(c) failure to report to an immigration medical officer;[39]

---

[35] Asylum and Immigration (Treatment of Claimants, etc) Act 2004, s 8(9) definition of 'notification' and s 8(10)–(11).

[36] ibid, s 8(5).

[37] Immigration Act 1971, ss 24(1)(a) and 24A(1)(a).

[38] ibid, s 24(1)(b) and (c).

[39] ibid, s 24(1)(d).

(d) breach of conditions of temporary admission;[40]

(e) incitement or conspiracy to work without immigration permission to do so;[41]

(f) avoiding enforcement action by deception;[42]

(g) disembarkation while pending removal or while a restriction on embarkation is imposed on nationals of that country;[43]

(h) assisting a breach of UK immigration law or the immigration law of an EU state, or of a deportation order in respect of a national of such a state;[44]

(i) helping an asylum-seeker to enter the United Kingdom;[45]

(j) possession of a false or altered Asylum Registration Card or of a replica immigration stamp (and related offences);[46]

(k) power to arrest a person liable to administrative detention;[47]

(l) immigration officer's power of arrest for marriage or theft offences;[48]

(m) a provision of the Extradition Acts 1989 or 2003.

3.68 This provision only applies to a claimant arrested in the exercise of one of these powers, and not to a person who is merely detained by an immigration officer in the exercise of an administrative immigration law.

3.69 This provision does not apply if:

(a) the claim relies wholly on matters arising after arrest (see para 3.66 above) or;
(b) the claimant had no reasonable opportunity to make the claim before arrest.

3.70 When considering whether or not the claimant had a reasonable opportunity, it may be necessary to consider the procedure for making asylum claims and whether it could reasonably have been invoked by the claimant. The Secretary of State can designate places where asylum claims are to be made.[49] The formal position remains unclear, but it seems that the Secretary of State may have designated the Asylum Screening Units as the only places in which claims may be made by persons who have already entered the United Kingdom. If that is correct, then, save for those arrested before entry, the question will be whether there was a reasonable opportunity to attend an Asylum Screening Unit before the arrest took place.

---

[40] Immigration Act 1971, s 24(1)(e).

[41] ibid, s 28AA(1)(b).

[42] ibid, s 24A(1)(b).

[43] ibid, s 24(1)(f) and (g).

[44] ibid, ss 25 and 25B.

[45] ibid, s 25A.

[46] ibid, ss 26A and 26B.

[47] ibid, Sch 2, para 17.

[48] Asylum and Immigration (Treatment of Claimants, etc) Act 2004, s 14.

[49] See definition of 'asylum-seeker' in Nationality, Immigration and Asylum Act 2002, s 18(1)(c) and Immigration and Asylum Act 1999, s 94(1) (as amended by Nationality, Immigration and Asylum Act 2002, s 44).

G. FAILURE TO MAKE ASYLUM OR HUMAN RIGHTS CLAIM IN A SAFE THIRD COUNTRY

The credibility of a claimant's statement is treated as damaged if he fails to take   3.71
advantage of a reasonable opportunity to make an asylum or human rights claim
while in a safe country.

A safe country means one of the member states of the European Economic Area   3.72
(EEA) listed in Asylum and Immigration (Treatment of Claimants, etc) Act 2004,
Sch 3, para 2.[50] Asylum or human rights claim includes a claim which is analogous
in the country concerned.[51]

The concept of 'opportunity to make an asylum claim in a third country' was the   3.73
subject of litigation in the early 1990s. From 1993 to 1996, decisions to remove an
asylum-seeker to a third country attracted a right of appeal prior to removal.[52] This
right was removed by Asylum and Immigration Act 1996, s 3 and the appeal became
exercisable only after removal. During the period of the in-country right of appeal,
the Immigration Rules provided that the Secretary of State could remove an asylum-
seeker to a third country if he had 'not arrived in the United Kingdom directly from
the country in which he claims to fear persecution and has had an opportunity, at the
border or within the territory of a third country, to make contact with that country's
authorities in order to seek their protection'.[53]

In *R v Secretary of State for the Home Department, ex p Kandasamy*,[54] Hidden J   3.74
accepted that this provision was satisfied in a case where:

(a) the claimant was aware that he was outside the country in which he feared persecution;

(b) the claimant was physically able, directly or indirectly, to contact the authorities
of the state in which he found himself; and

(c) there was no reason to believe that those authorities would not receive an application.

The wording of s 8(4) is significantly different to that of the Immigration Rule   3.75
considered in *Kandasamy*. Section 8(4) only applies if the claimant had a reasonable
opportunity while in the country concerned. It is suggested that the issue of a reasonable opportunity is to be determined having regard to the claimant's state of knowledge and belief. The better analogy for the form of words used is that dealt with in

---

[50] See definition of 'safe country' in Asylum and Immigration (Treatment of Claimants, etc) Act 2004,
s 8(7).

[51] ibid, s 8(9).

[52] Asylum and Immigration Appeals Act 1993, s 8.

[53] HC 725, para 180K; see *R v Secretary of State for the Home Department, ex p Mehari* [1994] QB
474, 484, *per* Laws J.

[54] [1994] Imm AR 333.

R (Q) v Secretary of State for the Home Department.[55] There the Court of Appeal held that the presence of an agent may make it not reasonably practicable for a claimant to make an asylum claim at the port of entry to the United Kingdom: see para 3.34(b) above. It would seem therefore to follow that the presence or actions of an agent may so direct the conduct of a claimant that he has no reasonable opportunity to claim asylum in the third country in question.

H. BEHAVIOUR OBSTRUCTING OR DELAYING THE HANDLING OF CLAIM

3.76 If a claimant's behaviour is designed or likely to obstruct or delay the handling or resolution of the asylum or human rights claim or the taking of a decision in relation to the claimant, then the credibility of his statements is treated as damaged.[56]

3.77 This provision can only apply where the delay is contrary to proper decision-making. Delay is often an important feature in proper decision-making. A decision may be delayed for a report to be received, or for a more senior Home Office colleague to be consulted. The submission of new material is unlikely to cause delay of the kind to which the provision must be directed.

3.78 An obvious example of a case where the provision may apply is an unreasonable failure to attend an interview. It is suggested that not all failures are caught by the provision. Where failure to attend was because of illness it is suggested that the claimant's behaviour did not delay a proper decision, but merely followed from the fact that he was not well enough to be interviewed.

3.79 Section 8(2) refers to the obstruction or delay to the 'resolution of the claim or the taking of a decision in relation to the claimant'. The reference to 'resolution' would seem to encompass the Secretary of State's decision on the asylum or human rights claim. It therefore seems probable that the 'decision' referred to is an 'immigration decision' (see para 3.64 above).

---

[55] [2003] EWCA Civ 364, [2004] QB 36.
[56] Asylum and Immigration (Treatment of Claimants, etc) Act 2004, s 8(2)(c).

4

WELFARE SUPPORT FOR IMMIGRANTS
(SECTIONS 9–13)

A.	Introduction	4.01
B.	Section 9—failed asylum-seeker families	4.02
C.	Section 10—failed asylum-seekers: accommodation	4.83
D.	Section 11—former asylum-seekers: homelessness	4.102
E.	Section 12—end to back-dated benefits	4.116
F.	Section 13—integration loan for refugees	4.128

A. INTRODUCTION

The Asylum and Immigration (Treatment of Claimants, etc) Act 2004 makes **4.01** changes to the scheme of support for immigrants, in particular:

(a) failed asylum-seeker families who have failed to leave the United Kingdom voluntarily are disqualified from receiving asylum support and social services (s 9);

(b) the Act removes the right of appeal to an asylum support adjudicator for asylum-seekers disqualified from asylum support because they have failed to comply with removal directions or are EEA nationals (s 9(3));

(c) the Home Office can require failed asylum-seekers who cannot leave the United Kingdom to work unpaid as a condition of receiving 'hard cases' support (s 10);

(d) asylum-seekers given permission to remain in the United Kingdom who then apply for homelessness assistance are treated as having a 'local connection' with any local authority where they were accommodated by the National Asylum Support Service (NASS) (s 11);

(e) refugees lose entitlement to claim back-dated social security benefits to cover the period waiting for the decision on their asylum claim (s 12);

(f) refugees are to be eligible for a discretionary Home Office 'integration loan' instead of back-dated benefits (s 13).

25

B. SECTION 9—FAILED ASYLUM-SEEKER FAMILIES

4.02 Section 9(1) disqualifies failed asylum-seeker families who have failed to leave the United Kingdom voluntarily from receiving asylum support and social services. It does so by adding a new class of excluded person to Sch 3 to the Nationality, Immigration and Asylum Act 2003.

1. Background

4.03 A person who has made an asylum claim or a claim under Art 3 of the European Convention on Human Rights (ECHR) is entitled to receive asylum support if he is destitute.[1]

4.04 Eligibility to support continues during any appeal against a Home Office decision on the asylum/human rights claim.[2]

4.05 Eligibility to support stops once the appeal is finally disposed of, unless the claimant's household includes a child aged under 18.[3] Support continues for 21 days after the final appeal decision is received by the claimant.[4]

4.06 Schedule 3 to the Nationality, Immigration and Asylum Act 2002 excludes certain classes of immigrants from entitlement to asylum support and social services. The welfare provisions affected are listed in para 1 of Sch 3:

(a) National Assistance Act 1948, ss 21 and 29 (local authority: accommodation and welfare),

(b) Health Services and Public Health Act 1968, s 45 (local authority: welfare of elderly),

(e) National Health Service Act 1977, s 21 and Sch 8 (social services),

(g) Children Act 1989, ss 17, 23C, 24A and 24B (welfare and other powers which can be exercised in relation to adults),

(j) Housing Act 1996, ss 188(3) and 204(4) (accommodation pending review or appeal),

(k) Local Government Act 2000, s 2 (promotion of well-being),

(l) those in the Immigration and Asylum Act 1999, or

(m) those in the Nationality, Immigration and Asylum Act 2002.

4.07 Before the 2004 Act comes into force, Sch 3 applies to the following classes of ineligible persons (paras 4–7):

---

[1] Immigration and Asylum Act 1999, ss 94–95.

[2] ibid, s 94(3). Appeal includes any further appeal, as defined in Nationality, Immigration and Asylum Act 2002, s 104(2).

[3] ibid, s 94(5).

[4] ibid, s 94(3); Asylum Support Regulations 2000, SI 2000/704, reg 2(2).

First class: refugee status abroad (para 4). A person who has been recognized as a Geneva Convention refugee by an EEA state other than the United Kingdom. Also, a dependant of such a person (for definition of dependant, see para 4.11 below);

Second class: citizens of other EEA states (para 5). Those states are Austria, Belgium, Cyprus, Czech Republic, Denmark, Estonia, Finland, France, Germany, Greece, Hungary, Iceland, Ireland, Italy, Latvia, Liechtenstein, Lithuania, Luxembourg, Malta, Netherlands, Norway, Poland, Portugal, Slovakia, Slovenia, Spain, Sweden. Also, a dependant of such a person (see para 4.11 below);

Third class: failed asylum-seeker (para 6). An asylum-seeker who has exhausted rights of appeal and who has failed to co-operate with removal directions issued in respect of him;

Fourth class: person unlawfully in the United Kingdom who is not an asylum-seeker (para 7). A person is unlawfully in the United Kingdom if he entered illegally, has breached the terms of his leave or has stayed beyond the period of limited leave.[5] A person granted temporary admission on arrival is not unlawfully in the United Kingdom.[6] It is unclear whether this provision overlaps with the third class, or whether it is intended only to apply to those who have never claimed asylum.

Schedule 3 as expressed does not affect provision of support to a child or a British **4.08** citizen, or where to deny support would breach EC or ECHR rights (paras 2 and 3).

Until s 9(3) comes into force, a person refused asylum support because of Sch 3 **4.09** has a right of appeal to an asylum support adjudicator from that decision.[7]

2. Persons affected by s 9(1)

Section 9(1) inserts a new para 7A in Nationality, Immigration and Asylum Act **4.10** 2002, Sch 3. This adds a fifth class of excluded persons to Sch 3. The principal persons affected by para 7A are those who:

(a) have exhausted any rights of appeal from a Home Office decision refusing an asylum claim or claim under Art 3 ECHR; and

(b) would only be eligible for asylum support because there is a dependent child aged under 18 in the household; and

(c) have failed to take reasonable steps to leave the United Kingdom or be able to leave the United Kingdom.

Dependants of the principal are also caught by para 7A, whether or not they have **4.11** failed to take reasonable steps. A dependant of the principal is a person who:[8]

---

[5] Nationality, Immigration and Asylum Act 2002, s 11.
[6] Immigration Act 1971, s 11.
[7] Immigration and Asylum Act 1999, s 103(1)–(2).
[8] Withholding and Withdrawal of Support (Travel Assistance and Temporary Accommodation) Regulations 2002, SI 2002/3078, reg 2(2).

(a) is his spouse;

(b) is a child of his or of his spouse;

(c) is a member of his or his spouse's close family and is under 18;

(d) is under 18 and has been living as part of his household—
- (i) for at least six of the last twelve months, or
- (ii) since birth;

(e) is in need of care and attention from him or a member of his household by reason of a disability and would fall under (c) or (d) but for the fact that he is not under 18;

(f) has been living with him as an unmarried couple for at least two of the last three years.

4.12 Thus, a dependant is not limited to persons dependent on the principal. In the case of a failed asylum-seeker living in the same household as her sister (a recognised refugee) and the sister's minor son, the Chief Asylum Support Adjudicator held that the sister's son is a 'dependant' of her failed asylum-seeker aunt.[9] A more restricted construction of 'dependant' may be necessary in the context of this provision. Otherwise, the failure of one part of the family to leave the United Kingdom may affect the rights of those with leave to remain.

4.13 Paragraph 7A is not limited to persons receiving or seeking asylum support from NASS. It will apply equally to those receiving support from a local authority under any of the provisions listed in para 1 of Sch 3 (see para 4.06 above). It is suggested that para 1 does not catch support provided by a local authority under the Asylum Support (Interim Provisions) Regulations 1999.[10] These regulations are made under Immigration and Asylum Act 1999, s 95(13) and Sch 9, and are neither a provision of that Act (which would be caught by para 1(1)(l)) nor approval or directions given under that Act (which would be caught by para 1(3)).

3. Failure to take reasonable steps to leave the United Kingdom

(a) *Who must take the steps?*

4.14 Paragraph 7A is not applied automatically. It only applies to a failed asylum-seeker whom the Home Office certifies has failed to take reasonable steps to leave the United Kingdom or be able to leave the United Kingdom.

4.15 It is the failed asylum-seeker's failures that allow the Home Office to certify. Paragraph 7A does not allow the Home Office to certify on the grounds that the failed asylum-seeker has failed to take steps to enable a dependant to leave the United Kingdom, or that a dependant has failed to take steps. However, where the

---

[9] ASA Ref ASA/04/05/8109.
[10] SI 1999/3056.

28

inability of the failed asylum-seeker to leave the United Kingdom is caused by someone else (for example, a failure to provide documentation), reasonable steps are likely to include trying to persuade that person to assist.

(b) *What kind of steps?*

Paragraph 7A can apply to two cases: **4.16**

(a) those who are able to leave the United Kingdom voluntarily, but fail to take reasonable steps to do so; and

(b) those who are presently unable to leave the United Kingdom, but fail to take steps to become able to leave voluntarily.

The steps required must be those which would lead to the claimant leaving the **4.17** United Kingdom, or being able to leave the United Kingdom and not, for example, steps to provide the Home Office with information about an unrelated or purely historical matter.

An example of a person able to leave is someone from a country to which sched- **4.18** uled flights are made and who has a valid national passport. He can leave by arranging a voluntary departure with an immigration officer. If an immigration officer asks him to do so and he refuses without a reasonable excuse, then a certificate could be issued.

An example of a person unable to leave is a person lacking a valid national pass- **4.19** port from a country which will not accept returnees without a passport. It may be reasonable for him to attend his national embassy and complete an application form for a passport.

(c) *Reasonable steps and reasonable excuses*

Paragraph 7A applies only to claimants who have failed to make good an asylum or **4.20** human rights claim in respect of a country identified in the decision refusing that claim. It follows that, when considering what is reasonable, it must be assumed that the claimant's arrival in that country would not breach his human rights. If the claimant considers that a change in circumstance means his arrival there would breach his human rights, he can seek to make a fresh claim to the Home Office.

Steps which are impossible for the claimant to take are clearly not reasonable. **4.21** These would include obtaining a birth certificate to prove identity when no certificate exists or producing witnesses to affirm one's nationality when there are none known. A claimant may not know his true date of birth, his parentage or his past, especially if he arrived in the United Kingdom as a minor. It would be impossible for him to provide such details as one of the steps to be able to leave the United Kingdom.

If the claimant would not be able to leave the United Kingdom regardless of **4.22** steps, for example because the country he is supposed to go to has made it clear that it will not admit him, then there are no reasonable steps he can take.

Not all possible steps are reasonable. It may not be reasonable for the claimant to **4.23** depart at a particular moment, or by a particular route or to take particular steps to facilitate departure. Parliament has not expressed the test as 'possible' nor even limited it to those steps which would not breach human rights.

4.24 Examples of steps to leave the United Kingdom which may not be reasonable include: travelling when the claimant or dependant is ill or pregnant; travelling by a route which the claimant reasonably considers is unsafe; arriving at a destination in the country concerned from which the claimant reasonably considers onward travel to his home area would be unsafe. Examples of a reasonable excuse might include: awaiting a visa from a country which will accept him as a refugee, and which he could not apply for from his own country; completing a series of medical treatments; wishing to stay for a temporary period with a seriously ill relative in the United Kingdom.

4.25 Examples of steps to be able to leave the United Kingdom which may be unreasonable include those which certain countries might require to issue a passport: paying a bribe; making a declaration of political allegiance or religious observance; undertaking not to engage in political activities; informing on the activities of other exiles.

4.26 In some cases, the Home Office may have decided that the claimant is not of his claimed nationality and/or identity. Clearly, it is a reasonable step to tell the Home Office the truth about those matters. Where that Home Office decision has been upheld on appeal, then it may be unreasonable for the claimant to deny that conclusion. However, in some cases there is no right of appeal and, in others, the appeal will have been dismissed on the ground that, even if of the claimed nationality, he can safely be returned. In those cases, it may not be reasonable to require the claimant to accept a nationality other than the one he claims to have.

4. Support to a child or British citizen—effect of para 2(1)

4.27 Paragraph 2(1) of Sch 3 provides that: 'Paragraph (1) does not prevent the provision of support or assistance (a) to a British citizen, or (b) to a child . . .'.

4.28 At first sight, it would seem that para 2(1) lifts the Sch 3 exclusion to enable a power or a duty in respect of a child or a British citizen to be discharged. If that is correct then para 7A does not prevent the provision of support to the children of the family.

4.29 However, in *M v Islington LBC*[11] the Court of Appeal held that Sch 3 removes the power to provide support to a British citizen child under Children Act 1989, s 17, where the mother to whom support is also provided was caught by Sch 3. Buxton LJ (with whom Maurice Kay and Waller LJJ agreed) reached that conclusion with considerable reluctance, the contrary argument not having been seriously pursued by the claimant.[12] The claimant succeeded on other grounds.

---

[11] [2004] EWCA Civ 235, [2004] 2 FCR 363.
[12] ibid at [15]–[19].

The correctness of the Court's conclusion must be open to doubt. Schedule 3 is **4.30** directed essentially at services provided to adults living alone or with children. Schedule 3 does not apply to Children Act 1989, s 20, the most important power to provide for children living alone. Paragraph 2(1)(b) must therefore have been intended to prevent the withdrawal of support under para 1 where it is being provided in part to a child. In a case where the support cannot be provided to the child alone, it must follow that Parliament intended para 2(1)(b) to disapply para 1. If it were the other way around, para 2(1)(b) would have no real effect.

The Court in *M v Islington* was concerned with a power to provide support.[13] **4.31** Section 122 of Immigration and Asylum Act 1999 imposes a duty to provide asylum support to a child, as part of the eligible person's household. It is suggested that para 2(1)(b) saves this duty. It may be that support can be withdrawn from some adult members of the household without depriving the child of its accommodation and essential living needs.

However, it is suggested that para 1 cannot be construed as removing the s 122 **4.32** duty to the child unless para 2(1)(b) is to be robbed of all real effect.

It is therefore also suggested that, where a dependant of the failed asylum-seeker **4.33** is a British citizen, the effect of para 2(1)(a) is that para 1 cannot lead to the withdrawal of support (for example, under National Assistance Act 1948, s 21) from that person where there is a statutory duty to provide it.

5. Breach of ECHR rights

Paragraph 7A only removes eligibility to support if the denial of that support does **4.34** not breach the rights of the claimant or his dependants under the ECHR.[14]

(a) *Art 3*
The denial of asylum support to an asylum-seeker who has no permission to work and **4.35** who will be unable to fend for himself is capable of being 'inhuman or degrading treatment' contrary to Art 3 ECHR.[15] In *Q*, the withdrawal was based upon a past failure by the asylum-seeker to claim asylum as soon as reasonably practicable.

However, para 7A will often concern cases where a claimant maintains a deliber- **4.36** ate unreasonable refusal to take steps to go to another country where he would be supported or be able to support himself. It is submitted that withdrawal of support in such a case would not of itself breach Art 3. The cause of the lack of support would be the continuing refusal to take steps, not the withdrawal of support. There may be unusual cases, such as mental illness, where that is not the case. During the passage of the Bill the Government accepted that the absolute duty under Art 3 might be engaged by a decision under para 7A.[16]

---

[13] ibid at [19].
[14] Nationality, Immigration and Asylum Act 2002, Sch 3, para 3.
[15] *R (Q) v Secretary of State for the Home Department* [2003] EWCA Civ 364, [2004] QB 36, CA.
[16] *Hansard*, HL col 702 (18 May 2004).

(b) *Art 8*

4.37 A consequence of a withdrawal of support by para 7A is that the local authority concerned may bring care proceedings under Children Act 1989, s 31. The effect of this may be to separate the children from their parents, a serious interference with the right to respect for family life of all concerned.

4.38   Where withdrawal of support may lead to the separation of the children from the parents, the obligation of 'proportionality' imposed by Art 8 requires the Home Office to consider whether an alternative approach would be a lesser interference with the family life concerned. The Government has accepted that withdrawal of support leading to separation must be a last resort. Beverley Hughes MP told the House of Commons Home Affairs Committee that 'it is not our intention that any child should come into care as a result of this measure and we will implement the policy in such a way as to prevent this happening as a consequence, as far as we possibly can'.[17]

4.39   One alternative to denial of support is to enforce removal of the family from the United Kingdom. Indeed, the Government has said that it intends to avoid separating children from their parents by 'ensuring that families who are refusing to co-operate with voluntary departure processes will be targeted for compulsory removal so that we can ensure that all its members leave the country together'.[18]

4.40   It is suggested that where removal of the family is possible despite their non-co-operation, a decision denying support will breach Art 8 ECHR, if there is a real risk that it would lead to the children being taken into local authority care. It is incumbent upon the Home Office to have thoroughly explored the possibility of removal before withdrawing support. This may include requesting the Government of the receiving state (or a transit country) to waive their documentary requirements for the family, or removing the family by an alternative route to that normally used.

4.41   In some cases, removal will be impossible without co-operation. In such cases, the Home Office can prosecute the claimant for refusing to co-operate.[19] The relevant provisions mirror para 7A. Where prosecution of the claimant is possible, it is submitted that, where there is a risk that the children would be taken into care, it would breach Art 8 to withdraw support without serious consideration of such a course. The proportionate course may be to seek to punish the claimant as a means of securing co-operation, rather than to separate the children from their parents.

4.42   It may be suggested that the Home Office does not need to concern itself with the possibility that the children will be taken into care, since the local authority and the family court hearing any care order application would also have the duty to act proportionately. It is suggested that such an approach would be wrong. If Art 8 requires that the children be accommodated with their parents pending further attempts to remove them or to secure co-operation, then the performance of the

---

[17] Supplementary Memorandum submitted by the Home Office, 8 December 2003, published in House of Commons Home Affairs Committee, 1st Report of 2003–04 (HC 109) Ev45.

[18] ibid.

[19] Asylum and Immigration (Treatment of Claimants, etc) Act 2004, s 35(3), see para 10.39, below.

duty imposed on the Home Office by Immigration and Asylum Act 1999, s 122 is not affected by Sch 3 para 7A.[20]

(c) *Compliance after issue of the certificate*

In some cases the claimant will take steps after the certificate is issued. The Home **4.43** Office undoubtedly has power to withdraw the certificate at any time, but para 7A does not require that to be done. Cases may therefore arise where the claimant is now trying to leave the United Kingdom but is to be denied support while he does so.

It is suggested that in such cases Art 8 ECHR would prohibit denial of support as **4.44** a disproportionate response to a breach which occurred in the past.

6. Breach of EC rights

Paragraph 7A only removes eligibility to support if the denial of that support does **4.45** not breach the EC rights of the claimant or his dependants.[21]

(a) *Council Directive (EC) 2003/9*

Council Directive (EC) 2003/9 of 27 January 2003 laying down minimum standards **4.46** for the reception of asylum seekers[22] is not yet in force. However, it must be implemented in the United Kingdom by 6 February 2005.[23]

The Directive requires member states to provide support to asylum-seekers.[24] It is **4.47** unclear to what extent the Directive will be held to apply to asylum-seekers who have been refused asylum and exhausted their appeal rights, but in respect of whom a final removal decision has yet to be taken. The Directive is expressed to apply to all those allowed to remain as 'asylum-seekers',[25] a phrase defined as those who have made an application 'in respect of which no final decision has been taken'.[26] It may be that the Directive will be held to have no effect where appeal rights are exhausted, although no actual removal directions have been made.

Even if the Directive does apply to persons caught by para 7A, it permits member **4.48** states to withdraw support from a person who 'does not comply with reporting duties or with requests to provide information or to appear for personal interviews concerning the asylum procedure during a reasonable period laid down in national law . . .'.[27]

However, where the Directive does apply, 'the best interests of the child shall be **4.49** a primary consideration for member states when implementing the provisions of this Directive that involve minors'.[28] It is suggested that this provision underlines the

---

[20] Nationality, Immigration and Asylum Act 2002, Sch 3, para 3(a).
[21] ibid, Sch 3, para 3(b).
[22] [2003] OJ L31/18.
[23] ibid, Art 26(1).
[24] ibid, Art 13.
[25] ibid, Art 3.
[26] ibid, Art 2(c).
[27] ibid, Art 16(1)(a), second indent.
[28] ibid, Art 18(1).

requirement imposed by Art 8 ECHR, that the Home Office pursue all possible alternatives to a withdrawal of support which would affect children.

(b) *Other EC law rights*

4.50   Where the claimant or his partner is a national of an EC or other EEA state (for example, one of the states which joined the EC and EEA on 1 May 2004), para 7A will not need to be invoked since para 5 of Sch 3 will already apply.

4.51   The only circumstances in which the Home Office might invoke para 7A rather than para 5 is where the claimant's partner has dual citizenship, ie British citizenship and that of another EC country. Such a dual national can invoke EC law against their own member state.[29] In such a case, it may be contrary to EC law to expel the non-EU spouse, even if the EC national spouse is not presently working.[30]

4.52   There may also be cases where a non-EC national has rights under EC law to reside in the United Kingdom which have been hitherto overlooked. For example, a 19-year-old failed asylum-seeker has a right to reside under EC law if her mother marries an economically active EC national who lives in the UK.[31]

4.53   In cases where the claimant or family member has an EC law right to reside, it is submitted that it would be contrary to that right to withdraw support on the ground that the person is seeking to enjoy the right by refusing to take steps to leave the United Kingdom.

7. Home Office decision-making

4.54   For the para 7A disqualification to take effect, the Home Office must:

(a) determine that the claimant is only treated as an asylum-seeker because there is a dependent child in the household;[32]

(b) exercise its discretion to certify that the claimant has failed without reasonable excuse to take reasonable steps voluntarily to leave the United Kingdom or to be able to do so;[33]

(c) ensure that the claimant has received a copy of that certificate.[34] Where the certificate is sent by first class post, receipt is deemed to occur on the second day after posting;[35] and

(d) allow 14 days to elapse.[36] This period may be varied by statutory instrument.[37]

---

[29] Case C-148/02 *Garcia Avello v Belgium* [2004] 1 CMLR 1, para 10.
[30] See Immigration (European Economic Area) Regulations 2000, SI 2000/2326, regs 5 and 14(2).
[31] ibid, reg 6(4)(a).
[32] Nationality, Immigration and Asylum Act 2002, Sch 3, para 7A(1)(a).
[33] ibid, para 7A(1)(b).
[34] ibid, para 7A(1)(c).
[35] ibid, para 7A(3).
[36] ibid, para 7A(1)(d).
[37] ibid, para 7A(4).

There is no statutory procedure for Home Office consideration of whether to certify. **4.55** During the passage of the Bill, the House of Commons Home Affairs Committee asked Ministers to explain the proposed procedure. Beverley Hughes MP replied that the decision to certify would be made by the Immigration Service, who would be issued with detailed guidance. She continued:

... the Immigration Service would be looking for clear evidence that the family has refused or intends to refuse an opportunity to leave the country and has no reasonable excuse (such as the serious illness of a family member); or that it is failing to co-operate with steps to obtain travel documents which will enable it to leave (for instance, by missing appointments or refusing to supply necessary information).

Again, we envisage that when the Immigration Service had reached that view it would seek to interview the family. At the interview it would explain the consequences of its non-compliance to the family and give it an opportunity to explain what has happened or to undertake to co-operate for the future. Failure by the family to attend for the interview, or to give credible assurances about its future conduct, or subsequent failure to live up to those assurances, would lead to the ending of support.[38]

The Minister appears to have overlooked the fact that para 7A is only concerned **4.56** with the failures of the failed asylum-seeker and not 'the family' (see para 4.15 above). The guidance mentioned has not yet been published.

It is suggested that the minimum procedural steps would include the following: **4.57**

(a) all communication with the claimant to be in a form he understands (it is still the case that the Home Office often communicates in written English);

(b) Home Office to advise the claimant in a form which he understands of the precise steps the Home Office considers it reasonable for him to take;

(c) Home Office to make a written record of any response from the claimant to those proposed steps;

(d) Home Office to consider any explanation offered;

(e) Home Office to consider whether it is necessary to issue a certificate or whether there is some other way of securing the claimant's departure;

(f) any certificate (again, in a form understood by the claimant) to identify precisely when and how the claimant was asked to take a particular step and how he has failed to take it; if any excuse has been advanced, why the Home Office considers it unreasonable.

Under para 7A, a certificate sent to the claimant's last known address is treated as **4.58** having been served on the second day after posting.[39] If the claimant proves that the certificate reached him later than this, or not at all, then this presumption is rebutted.[40]

---

[38] Supplementary Memorandum, n 17 above, Ev44–45.
[39] Nationality, Immigration and Asylum Act 2002, Sch 3, para 7A(3).
[40] Interpretation Act 1978, s 7.

8. Local authority decision-making under para 7A

4.59 A Home Office certificate under para 7A is intended to operate to deny social services listed in para 1 (see para 4.06 above). Such cases will be rare, since virtually all failed asylum-seeker families who require support receive it from NASS. Almost all the old asylum cases receiving support under the Asylum Support (Interim Provisions) Regulations 1999 are likely to be granted indefinite leave to remain under the Government's 'One-Off Exercise', announced by the Home Secretary on 24 October 2003.

4.60 However, local authority support may be affected in some cases. For example, some old asylum cases may have been disqualified under the One-Off Exercise for criminal offences. In such cases, the claimant and dependants will continue to receive local authority asylum support.

4.61 Another possible example is where the local authority is providing social services to a disabled adult who is a dependant of a NASS-supported asylum-seeker family.

4.62 Where support is provided by the local authority, decision-making is split with the Home Office. The Home Office determines whether to issue a certificate. The local authority decides whether the certificate means that support must be denied. Therefore, the local authority must decide whether:

(a) the support requested or provided is caught by para 1 of Sch 3. Paragraph 1 may not apply to support under the Asylum Support (Interim Provisions) Regulations 1999 (see para 4.13 above);

(b) para 2 of Sch 3 (British citizens and children) requires support to be provided notwithstanding the certificate (see paras 4.27–4.33 above);

(c) para 3 of Sch 3 (ECHR and EC rights) requires support to be provided notwithstanding the certificate (see paras 4.34–4.53 above).

4.63 Only a claimant seeking asylum support has a right of appeal to an asylum support adjudicator. In local authority cases the remedy is judicial review, which can be claimed in respect of both the Home Office decision to issue a certificate and the local authority decision to deny support.

9. Appealing a decision to withdraw asylum support under para 7A

4.64 A person denied asylum support under para 7A has a right of appeal from that decision to an asylum support adjudicator.[41] It is important that claimants appeal where possible. Even if it is considered that the local authority may provide social services, if there are grounds for challenging the certificate an appeal should be brought. If it is not, and judicial review of the local authority becomes necessary, the court may refuse to entertain a challenge to the certificate on the ground that the claimant failed to exhaust his appeal remedy.

---

[41] Asylum and Immigration (Treatment of Claimants, etc) Act 2004, s 9(3).

A person denied social services has no right of appeal to an asylum support adju- **4.65**
dicator. Judicial review is the only remedy.

It seems likely that the certificate will be accompanied by a decision letter termi- **4.66**
nating entitlement to support effective on the 16th day after the date of the letter, ie
14 days after the date of deemed receipt.[42] This period will normally be sufficient for
any appeal to be heard: see para 4.70 below.

There is no further appeal from the asylum support adjudicator. Judicial review is **4.67**
the remedy.

(a) *Appeal procedure*

Home Office decisions denying asylum support are, in practice, notified to the **4.68**
claimant in writing with a statement of the right of appeal, though this is not
expressly required. Where an appeal is made from a decision which NASS denies is
appealable, the adjudicator will admit the appeal if she determines that there is a
right of appeal.

Notice must be on the prescribed form, or one to like effect.[43] The notice requires **4.69**
grounds of appeal and points of dispute to be stated: these should be particularized
on the form. In practice they can be amplified later.

The appeal procedure is very quick: **4.70**

(a) Notice of appeal must be received by the asylum support adjudicator by the third
working day after the day the claimant received the decision letter.[44] The adjudicator has power to extend time and the power has been exercised liberally.[45]

(b) NASS must file and serve the appeal bundle within three working days.[46]

(c) Any appeal hearing must take place within six working days of receipt of the
NASS appeal bundle.[47]

(d) The adjudicator must give her decision orally on the day of the hearing, and
issue written reasons within three working days.[48]

(e) If the appellant does not request a hearing and the adjudicator does not direct
one, the appeal is decided within five days of receipt of the NASS bundle.[49]

In practice, the asylum support appeals service has met the statutory time-limits, **4.71**
except where there has been a sudden influx of appeals.

Oral hearings are relatively informal and NASS is almost always represented. **4.72**

---

[42] Nationality, Immigration and Asylum Act 2002, Sch 3, para 7A(1)(d) and (3).
[43] Asylum Support Appeals (Procedure) Rules 2000, SI 2000/541, r 3 & Sch.
[44] ibid, rr 3(3) and 18(4).
[45] ibid, r 3(4).
[46] ibid, r 4(1) and (2).
[47] ibid, rr 4(3), (4) and 6(1).
[48] ibid, r 13(1).
[49] ibid, r 6(2).

4.73 A solicitor may assist the claimant under 'Legal Help', for example by drafting grounds of appeal, witness statements and submissions. Public funding is not available for advocacy before the asylum support adjudicator.[50] In exceptional cases, the Lord Chancellor may authorize funding for advocacy.[51] In practice, any such funding would almost certainly be retrospective.

4.74 At the time of writing, the Asylum Support Appeals Project provides two independent legally qualified 'duty advocates' to represent appellants attending for a hearing without an advocate. They are based in the asylum support adjudicators' building and have access to interpreters by telephone to take instructions. The advocates only attend on Thursdays. The Project can be contacted via the asylum support adjudicators.

(b) *Appeals from para 7A decisions*

4.75 The issue on most appeals under para 7A will be whether the Home Office was correct to certify under para 7A. The adjudicator has power to annul the certificate or require the Home Office to reconsider.[52] It is submitted that the adjudicator should decide for herself on all the evidence and explanations provided whether to uphold the certificate.

4.76 Paragraph 7A operates to disqualify a claimant and dependants from entitlement to asylum support. It is strongly suggested that therefore the Home Office has the burden of establishing unreasonable failure to take steps.

4.77 It is suggested that the starting point is for the Home Office to prove that the claimant was specifically requested to take a step which would lead towards him leaving the United Kingdom and that he has had sufficient time to take that step. The adjudicator would then need to be persuaded that the step or steps required were reasonable for this claimant to take, and that any excuse provided is not a reasonable one. This may involve factual disputes: for example, did the claimant attend at the embassy or immigration office? Was the claimant properly informed of the steps he was expected to take? There will also be questions of judgment about whether the claimant acted reasonably. Even if the conditions for the certificate are made out, the adjudicator will need to consider whether she should exercise her discretion to certify.

4.78 If the certificate is to be upheld, the adjudicator will then need to consider whether denial of support, and its effect on the children, is a necessary step towards ensuring the claimant's departure. At this stage, the Home Office may need to show that it has tried or considered other ways of effecting departure, such as enforced removal, prosecution of the claimant, or a special approach to the government of the country concerned.

4.79 It may be that the adjudicator will be persuaded that the claimant will now take

---

[50] Access to Justice Act 1999, s 6(6) and Sch 2, para 2.

[51] ibid, s 6(8)(b).

[52] Asylum and Immigration (Treatment of Claimants, etc) Act 2004, s 9(4).

reasonable steps. It is suggested that in such a case, Art 8 ECHR would require the adjudicator to direct the Home Office to allow time for those steps to be taken before reconsidering whether to certify.

10. Section 9(3)—removal of right of appeal to asylum support adjudicator

Section 9(3) of the 2004 Act removes the right of appeal to an asylum support adju- **4.80** dicator from a decision denying asylum support made under Sch 3 to the Nationality, Immigration and Asylum Act 2002, other than one made under para 7A of that Schedule (for which, see para 4.10 above).

Each of paras 4–7 of Sch 3 are capable of applying to those eligible for asylum **4.81** support. However, it seems that relatively few asylum support decisions have been based on Sch 3. The only significant group affected is asylum-seekers with children from the countries which joined the European Union and the European Economic Area on 1 May 2004. At the time of writing, NASS expects to end support for hundreds of families of failed asylum-seekers from those countries, mainly Poland, the Czech Republic and Lithuania.

Once s 9(3) comes into force, those denied asylum support under Sch 3 (other **4.82** than para 7A) can only bring a challenge by judicial review. The lack of the right of appeal will impose upon the Home Office the stringent requirements of fairness set out in *R (Q) v Secretary of State for the Home Department.*[53]

C. SECTION 10—FAILED ASYLUM-SEEKERS: ACCOMMODATION

Section 10 of the 2004 Act empowers the Home Secretary to make regulations **4.83** governing access to support under Immigration and Asylum Act 1999, s 4. Controversially, regulations may be made requiring a person to perform unpaid community work as a condition of receiving support. Section 4 support is commonly known as 'hard cases' support, because it is the power used to support certain failed asylum-seekers without dependent children. Section 10 also provides for a right of appeal from a denial of s 4 support.

1. Background

Under the Immigration and Asylum Act 1999, eligibility for asylum support ends **4.84** when any appeal is finally determined. Only families with children remain eligible for support. During the passage of the Bill which became the 1999 Act, there was concern at the lack of any power to provide support for 'hard cases', ie, those of individuals who had lost their appeals but had meritorious reasons for not leaving the United Kingdom immediately. The Government intended to establish a fund for

---

[53] [2003] EWCA Civ 364, [2004] QB 36, CA.

charities to provide such support under s 111 of the 1999 Act. However, no charities could be found to operate the fund. Section 4 of the 1999 Act had been included in the Bill as a power to provide accommodation short of detention. After commencement, the s 4 power was used for the 'hard cases' for which s 111 had been intended.

4.85 The s 4 power is exercised by NASS. There is no regulatory scheme. At the time of writing, support is available to a person:

(a) whose claim for asylum has been determined (within the meaning of Pt VI of the 1999 Act);

(b) who has been supported by NASS or by a local authority under Sch 9 to the 1999 Act;

(c) who is no longer an asylum-seeker within the meaning of Pt VI of the 1999 Act;

(d) who appears to the Secretary of State to be destitute within the meaning of Pt VI of the 1999 Act; and

(e) who has no other avenue of support.

4.86 Each case is considered on its merits, but support will not normally be made available to claimants unless they are:

(a) unable to leave the United Kingdom by reason of a physical impediment to travel, for example, through illness or late pregnancy;

(b) complying with an attempt to obtain a travel document to facilitate return (this includes a person who has elected to return voluntarily under the Voluntary Assisted Returns and Reintegration Programme (VARRP) administered by the International Organisation for Migration (IOM) but who cannot leave immediately because he requires a travel document);

(c) unable to leave because there is no route or safe viable route of return available;

(d) applying for judicial review of the decision to refuse them asylum and have been granted permission to proceed or in Scotland have applied for judicial review (Scotland does not have a formal permission to proceed stage); or

(e) the circumstances of the case are otherwise wholly exceptional or compassionate.

4.87 NASS policy about support provision is:

Support under section 4 of the Act is normally provided as basic full board accommodation mostly outside of London and the south-east. There is no separate financial support and the accommodation will be offered on a no choice basis. While every effort will be made, in exceptional circumstances, to provide accommodation in the area a claimant was previously dispersed to, it may be necessary for claimants to relocate.

If the conduct of a supported person causes an accommodation provider to refuse to continue to provide accommodation, Section 4 support will be withdrawn.

Those supported may be required to subject themselves to regular reviews and, other than in cases where judicial proceedings are outstanding, be able to show that they are taking all reasonable steps to leave the United Kingdom and in any event are complying fully with efforts to remove them.

During the passage of the Bill through Parliament, the Minister responsible stated **4.88** that fewer than 500 people are supported under s 4.[54] The majority of them are failed asylum-seekers from Iraq who cannot presently be removed there.

2. The new regulatory scheme

Section 10(5) amends s 4 of the Immigration and Asylum Act 1999 by empowering **4.89** the Home Secretary to make regulations specifying the criteria to be used to determine whether to provide or continue to provide accommodation. No draft regulations have been published.

Regulations must be made by the affirmative procedure.[55] **4.90**

Section 10(6) permits the regulations to make performance of, or participation in, **4.91** community activities a condition of providing support. 'Community activities' means activities which appear to the Home Office to be beneficial to the public or a section of the public.[56] During the passage of the Bill through Parliament examples of community activities suggested by Ministers were: maintenance of the failed asylum-seekers' own accommodation and providing services to minority groups, perhaps for 15 to 20 hours per week.[57]

The Home Office will have power to pay an allowance, which may include travel **4.92** expenses.[58]

The Government intends that those who breach the conditions should first be **4.93** given a warning and that failure to participate thereafter would lead to support ending.[59]

3. ECHR compatibility

Article 4(2) ECHR provides: 'No one shall be required to perform forced or compul- **4.94** sory labour'.

Article 4(3) states that 'the term "forced or compulsory labour" shall not include **4.95** ... (d) any work or service which forms part of normal civic obligations'. International Labour Convention No 29, Forced Labour Convention, 1930, Art 2(1) defines 'forced or compulsory labour' as 'all work or service which is exacted from any person under the menace of any penalty and for which the said person has not offered himself voluntarily'.[60]

The opinion of the Parliamentary Joint Committee on Human Rights was that **4.96**

---

[54] *Hansard*, HC col 1185 (12 July 2004).

[55] Immigration and Asylum Act 1999, s 166(5)(za), as amended by Asylum and Immigration (Treatment of Claimants, etc) Act 2004, s 10(2).

[56] Immigration and Asylum Act 1999, s 4(7)(a), inserted by Asylum and Immigration (Treatment of Claimants, etc) Act 2004, s 10(1).

[57] *Hansard*, HC col 1190 (12 July 2004); *Hansard*, HL col 649 (15 June 2004), col 29 (28 June 2004).

[58] *Hansard*, HL col 647 (15 June 2004).

[59] *Hansard*, HL cols 29–30 (28 June 2004).

[60] *Van Der Mussele v Belgium* (1984) 6 EHRR 163, para 32.

there is a significant risk that requiring failed asylum-seekers to work as a condition of receiving support would breach Art 4(2).[61] The Committee considered that:

(a) the threat of destitution is the menace of a penalty;[62]

(b) such work is not part of a normal civic duty imposed upon anyone else in the United Kingdom.[63]

4.97   The response of Ministers was that work is not a penalty[64] and that 'it is not incompatible with a person's civic responsibilities to participate in the sort of community activity proposed'.[65]

4.98   It is suggested that the Government's response does not answer the Committee's argument. The work will be required on pain of the penalty of destitution. No one else is required to work unpaid as a condition of receiving state support: social security recipients are required to be available for paid work.

4.99   The Committee also argues that the new regulations may breach other ECHR obligations. Denial of support for a refusal to work may result in destitution breaching Art 3, while the singling out of failed asylum-seekers for an enforced requirement to work may breach Art 14.[66]

4. Right of appeal

4.100   Section 10(3) and (4) provides for a right of appeal to an asylum support adjudicator from a decision refusing or ending support under s 4. This right will be exercisable where s 4 support is denied on any ground.

4.101   Asylum support appeals procedure is described at paras 4.68–4.74 above. Issues raised on such appeals may be under one or more of the criteria translated into regulations.

D. SECTION 11—FORMER ASYLUM-SEEKERS: HOMELESSNESS

4.102   Section 11 of the 2004 Act amends the scheme of homelessness legislation in England and Wales to provide that a former asylum-seeker has a 'local connection' for homelessness purposes with an English or Welsh district in which he was last provided with asylum support accommodation. The section removes the normal homelessness duty in England or Wales in a case where a person was last accommodated in Scotland.

---

[61] Fourteenth Report of Session 2003–04 (HL Paper 130, HC Paper 828) paras 9–16.
[62] ibid, para 12.
[63] ibid, para 15.
[64] *Hansard*, HC col 1191 (12 July 2004); *Hansard*, HL col 648 (15 June 2004).
[65] *Hansard*, HL col 648 (15 June 2004).
[66] Fourteenth Report, n 61 above, paras 17–24.

1. Background

Section 193 of the Housing Act 1996 requires a local authority to provide accommo- **4.103** dation to homeless persons in priority need who are not intentionally homeless. The different scheme which operates in Scotland is explained at paras 4.113–4.115 below.

A local connection with an authority is not necessary for the authority to owe a **4.104** duty to such a person. However, if the applicant or his family has a 'local connec- tion' with another authority, and no such connection with the authority to which the application was made, that authority may refer the application to the authority with the local connection.[67] 'Local connection' means: past residence of choice; employ- ment; family connections; or other special circumstances.[68] If the applicant has no local connection with any authority, then the authority to whom he applies owes him the duty.

Section 95 of the Immigration and Asylum Act 1999 empowers NASS to arrange **4.105** accommodation for destitute asylum-seekers. That accommodation is arranged on a 'no choice' basis, normally by 'dispersal' to an English or Welsh authority outside the South-East, or to Glasgow.

Asylum-seekers granted leave to remain (either as refugees or on some other **4.106** basis) often become homeless when their NASS accommodation is withdrawn. Those in priority need (for example, with dependent children[69]) are eligible for homelessness assistance. They may wish to be accommodated by an authority where they have family or other connections, and not the authority where NASS placed them.

In *Al-Ameri v Kensington and Chelsea RLBC*[70] two families had been accommo- **4.107** dated by NASS in Glasgow. They were granted leave to remain and became home- less. They applied to local authorities in London which sought to refer their cases to Glasgow. The House of Lords held that the 'no choice' nature of their NASS accom- modation meant that their residence in Glasgow did not give rise to a local connec- tion

2. NASS accommodation creates local connection

Section 11(1) reverses the effect of *Al-Ameri v Kensington and Chelsea RLBC*, by **4.108** adding new subss (6) and (7) to Housing Act 1996, s 199. Under s 199(6), a person has a 'local connection' with a district in England or Wales in which he was accom- modated under Immigration and Asylum Act 1999, s 95. This does not prevent the person also having a local connection with another district, for example, because of family connections or previous residence there. Where the person has no local

---

[67] Housing Act 1996, s 198.
[68] ibid, s 199.
[69] ibid, s 189.
[70] [2004] UKHL 4, [2004] 2 AC 159, HL.

connection with another district in the United Kingdom, the duty will be owed by the district in which the s 95 accommodation was provided.

4.109 Section 199(6) only applies if accommodation was provided by NASS. It does not apply where only 'essential living needs' were provided by NASS. Section 199(6) refers to accommodation provided under s 95. It is unclear whether s 199(6) applies to accommodation provided by a local authority under the Asylum Support (Interim Provisions) Regulations 1999, which are made under Immigration and Asylum Act 1999, s 95(13) and Sch 9.

4.110 Section 199(6) only applies to the last accommodation provided under s 95.[71] Thus, where a person is accommodated in two different districts under s 95, only the last accommodation provided creates this local connection. The reference in the English and Welsh scheme to 'districts' includes Scottish districts[72] so, if the last s 95 accommodation was provided in Scotland, previous s 95 accommodation in England or Wales will not create a local connection with that English or Welsh authority.

4.111 In some cases, a person provided with emergency accommodation refuses to take up dispersal accommodation. Emergency accommodation is initially provided under Immigration and Asylum Act 1999, s 98. NASS then decides that the person qualifies for s 95 accommodation and arranges for him to travel some short time later to his 'dispersal' accommodation. However, from the point at which NASS decides the person qualifies, accommodation cannot be provided under s 98 and so must be provided under s 95.[73] It follows that from the date of decision, the emergency accommodation is provided under s 95.[74] If the person does not travel to his new accommodation then this emergency s 95 accommodation will have created a local connection with the district where it is located.

4.112 While there is always a local connection with the district of the last s 95 accommodation, that does not mean that no local connection was established during an earlier stay in another district (whether in NASS accommodation or not), or during a stay.[75]

3. Section 95 accommodation in Scotland

4.113 A person whose last s 95 accommodation was in Scotland will not thereby have a local connection with the district of that accommodation. That is because the Scottish homelessness scheme does not regard s 95 accommodation as creating a local connection.[76]

---

[71] Housing Act 1996, s 199(7).

[72] ibid, s 217(3).

[73] Immigration and Asylum Act 1999, s 98(2).

[74] See *R (Secretary of State for the Home Department) v Chief Asylum Support Adjudicator and Dogan* [2002] EWHC 2218 (Admin) at [6].

[75] Guidance on 'local connection' adopted by the local government associations is reproduced in the Homelessness Code of Guidance for Local Authorities (Office of the Deputy Prime Minister, July 2002) Annex 11, para 4.

[76] Housing (Scotland) Act 1987, s 27(2)(a)(iii), inserted by Homelessness etc (Scotland) Act 2003, asp 10, s 7.

This does not mean that the Scottish authority can refuse to provide accommodation to such a person who applies for it. If the applicant has no local connection with any other authority in the United Kingdom, then the Scottish authority to which the application is made will owe a duty to provide accommodation.[77] Unlike in England, a Scottish authority cannot refer the applicant to a different Scottish district on the ground that s 95 accommodation was provided there.[78] **4.114**

4.115

Section 11(2) and (3) of the 2004 Act allows English and Welsh councils to refuse to provide accommodation to a person who was provided with his last s 95 accommodation in Scotland and who does not have a local connection with the English or Welsh district concerned. There is no equivalent provision to this in Scottish homelessness legislation. The applicant will need to apply to a Scottish authority, which will owe him a duty. If that authority considers that the applicant has a local connection with a different UK authority it may refer the applicant back to that authority.

E. SECTION 12—END TO BACK-DATED BENEFITS

Section 12 of the 2004 Act abolishes provision for awarding recognized refugees back-dated means-tested benefits for the period during which their asylum claim and any appeal was pending. It does so by repealing Immigration and Asylum Act 1999 Act, s 123. Section 12 also expressly repeals the regulations for back-dating income support, housing benefit and council tax benefit. It is the Government's intention to end the existing arrangements under which other benefits are back-dated for recognized refugees, i.e. child benefit, guardian's allowance, child tax credit and working tax credit. This is expected to be done by statutory instrument. **4.116**

1. Background

The power to award back-dated benefits was first contained in Asylum and Immigration Act 1996, s 11(2). It was part of a package of amendments introduced by the Conservative Government to reverse *R v Secretary of State for Social Security, ex p B and JCWI*,[79] which had quashed regulations denying benefits to asylum-seekers.[80] The Government's intention was to 'bring the treatment of refugees into line with that of British citizens who win an appeal'.[81] Section 11(2) was replaced by Immigration and Asylum Act 1999, s 123.[82] **4.117**

---

[77] Housing (Scotland) Act 1987, s 31(2).
[78] See also Code of Guidance on Homelessness (Scottish Executive, 2003) para 236.
[79] [1997] 1 WLR 275, CA.
[80] *Hansard*, HL col 596 (24 June 1996), col 1220 (1 July 1996).
[81] *Hansard*, HL col 1223 (1 July 1996).
[82] See Explanatory Notes to the 1999 Act, para 351.

4.118   Applications for back-dated benefits are administered in the same way as other benefit claims. The effect of the regulations made under s 123[83] are that:

(a) a person recognized as a refugee,

(b) who would have been entitled to a means-tested benefit if his refugee status had been recognized when he originally claimed, and

(c) who claims those benefits within 28 days of receiving notification,

is entitled to receive those benefits back-dated to the date of the asylum claim (or, the date social security stopped, if later), but giving credit for any asylum support already provided. The normal benefit rules mean that periods of other income (for example, from work) lead to lower or nil payments.

4.119   The outcome is that the claimant is in the same position he would have been in if his asylum claim had been decided correctly immediately.

4.120   Virtually all back-dated claims are for income support only. The amount paid is usually the 30 per cent difference between income support and asylum support. Where the period of delay is six months the payment for a single person would be about £500. Because asylum claims are now normally dealt with speedily, few payments exceed this amount. In practice, the back-dated sum enables the refugee to 'catch up' by purchasing capital items (shoes, clothing, household items, children's toys) which NASS payments did not cover.

4.121   Only a small minority of claimants are eligible for back-dated housing benefit, since most were accommodated by NASS or free of charge by relatives. However, some will have been tenants and the back-dated payment means that their rent arrears are cleared. Any amount unspent after 52 weeks counts towards capital for ongoing benefit entitlement. The Government does not have records of the number or amount of back-payments.[84]

4.122   Those granted indefinite leave (for example, under Government concessions), exceptional leave, discretionary leave or humanitarian protection are not eligible for back-dated benefits.

4.123   The Government's proposal of s 12 seems to have been triggered by an article in the *Sun* newspaper,[85] which described s 123 as a 'loophole' and wrongly claimed that half of those who claimed asylum in 2002 were eligible for back-dated benefits.

2. The new provision

4.124   Section 12(1) abolishes the power to make provision for paying newly recognised refugees back-dated income support, housing benefit and/or council tax benefit. Section 12(2) provides that the regulations made under that provision are to lapse.

4.125   The Government intends to delay abolition until the new system of integration

---

[83] listed in Asylum and Immigration (Treatment of Claimants, etc) Act 2004, s 12(2).

[84] *Hansard*, HL col 668 (15 June 2004).

[85] 17 March 2004.

loans (see paras 4.128–4.132 below) is ready.[86] The Government intends that no one recognized as a refugee after commencement of s 12 will be eligible to claim a back-dated payment.[87] Transitional provision is not envisaged.[88]

Section 12 does not directly repeal the regulations for back-payments to recog- **4.126** nized refugees of child tax credit, working tax credit, child benefit and guardian's allowance. However, those provisions can be revoked by statutory instrument.

Articles 23 and 24 of the Geneva Convention relating to the Status of Refugees **4.127** require contracting states (which include the United Kingdom) to 'accord refugees lawfully staying in their territory the same treatment' as their own nationals with respect to public relief and assistance (Art 23) and social security (Art 24). The Government considers that this obligation is discharged because asylum support is 'on average only 4% lower than income support levels'.[89]

F. SECTION 13—INTEGRATION LOAN FOR REFUGEES

Section 13 of the 2004 Act empowers the Home Office to establish a regulatory **4.128** scheme for making 'integration loans' to refugees. The aim of the loan is to enable the refugee to establish himself in his new life in the United Kingdom.[90]

The loans can be made to any refugee who has been granted indefinite leave to **4.129** remain[91] and who is over 18.[92] Only one loan can be made,[93] but regulations may provide for a single loan to be advanced in instalments.[94]

At the time of writing, the detail of the intended regulatory scheme has yet to be **4.130** made public. Regulations will specify the circumstances in which loans will be made, the amount of the loan and the terms of repayment.[95]

The Government has the power to charge interest, but does not intend to exercise **4.131** it.[96]

The loan scheme will be funded by the savings from abolishing back-dated bene- **4.132** fits.[97] The Government intends the loan scheme to begin when back-dated benefits are abolished.[98]

---

[86] *Hansard*, HL col 87 (28 June 2004); *Hansard*, HC col 1210 (12 July 2004).
[87] *Hansard*, HC col 1209 (12 July 2004).
[88] *Hansard*, HL col 669 (15 June 2004).
[89] *Hansard*, HL col 711 (6 July 2004).
[90] *Hansard*, HL col 673 (15 June 2004).
[91] Asylum and Immigration (Treatment of Claimants, etc) Act 2004, s 13(2).
[92] ibid, s 13(3)(c)(i).
[93] ibid, s 13(c)(iii).
[94] *Hansard*, HL col 715 (6 July 2004).
[95] Asylum and Immigration (Treatment of Claimants, etc) Act 2004, s 13(3).
[96] ibid, s 13(3)(d)(i); *Hansard*, HL col 678 (15 June 2004), col 46 (28 June 2004).
[97] *Hansard*, HL col 715 (6 July 2004).
[98] *Hansard*, HL col 87 (28 June 2004); *Hansard*, HC col 1210 (12 July 2004).

5

ENFORCEMENT
(SECTIONS 14–18)

A. Immigration officer: power of arrest	5.01
B. Fingerprinting	5.04
C. Information about passengers	5.05
D. Retention of documents	5.06
E. Control of entry	5.07

A. IMMIGRATION OFFICER: POWER OF ARREST

Immigration officers already have the power of arrest in relation to a number of **5.01** immigration offences, for example under ss 24, 24A, 25, 25B and 25C of the Immigration Act 1971, which include illegal entry, overstaying and related offences such as breach of conditions.

Section 14 of the Asylum and Immigration (Treatment of Claimants, etc) Act **5.02** 2004 allows an immigration officer to arrest for a specified offence only when it comes to their notice in 'the course of exercising a function under the Immigration Acts',[1] in other words in pursuit of their ordinary duties under immigration law. It does not allow any immigration officer to initiate any investigations into theft or any other of the specified offences. So, in an example given by the Immigration Minister, an immigration officer who, while mowing her lawn, sees her neighbour acting suspiciously cannot bound over the hedge and arrest that person. She has to call a police officer in the same way as a member of the public.[2]

The arrests can only be made where the immigration officer has a reasonable **5.03** suspicion that a person has committed or attempted to commit an offence in subs (2) and in conformity with the Immigration (PACE Codes of Practice) Direction 2000. The range of specified offences is an attempt to combat stolen identity documents

---

[1] s 14(1).

[2] Statement of Minister for Immigration, Beverley Hughes, HC Standing Committee B, col 214 (15 January 2004).

(offences under the Theft Acts 1968 and 1978); obtaining support through deception; and bigamy to facilitate immigration abuse. The section is excluded from the Race Relations Act 1976.

B. FINGERPRINTING

5.04 Section 15 widens the scope of s 141 of the Immigration and Asylum Act 1999 as to when an authorized person may take fingerprints from someone subject to immigration control. It allows fingerprints to be taken from any person (except a minor in certain circumstances) subject to an immigration decision under s 82(2)(g), (h), (i), (j) or (k) of the Nationality, Immigration and Asylum Act 2002 until such decision or deportation order ceases to have effect.

C. INFORMATION ABOUT PASSENGERS

5.05 Section 16 widens the scope by which an immigration officer can obtain information about a passenger from a carrier. A carrier must provide in addition a copy of a document or part of a document that relates to a passenger and provides passenger information.

D. RETENTION OF DOCUMENTS

5.06 Section 17 provides the Secretary of State or an immigration officer with a new power to retain a document which has come into his possession in the course of the exercise of an immigration function if he believes that the person to whom the document may relate may be liable to removal under the Immigration Acts or that retention of the document may facilitate the removal.

E. CONTROL OF ENTRY

5.07 Section 18 amends the Immigration Act 1971 to allow an immigration officer to examine a person who has been granted leave to enter as entry clearance by virtue of an order of the Secretary of State such as the Immigration (Leave to Enter) Order 2001.[3] This is to establish whether leave to enter should be cancelled on the grounds that the person's purpose in arriving in the United Kingdom is different to that specified in the entry clearance. This completes an immigration officer's power to examine on entry the intention of arriving passengers in the United Kingdom.

---

[3] SI 2001/2590.

6

MARRIAGE
(SECTIONS 19–25)

A.	The new provisions in outline	6.03
B.	The present position	6.14
C.	Human Rights implications	6.23
D.	ECHR compatibility	6.34
E.	ECHR Art 14: different treatment on the grounds of religion or nationality	6.46

Sections 19–25 of the Asylum and Immigration (Treatment of Claimants, etc) Act **6.01** 2004 introduce a special procedure for the registration of marriages. These provisions were introduced at a late stage[1] in the passage of the Bill, leading members of the House of Lords to complain that the tranche of new measures, of which the provisions relating to marriage were part, had not received proper parliamentary scrutiny—a sentiment shared by the Joint Committee on Human Rights (JCHR) in their report.[2]

The Government stated that its purpose in introducing the new measures was to **6.02** respond to the increasing prevalence of 'sham marriages', ie marriages deliberately entered into for the purpose of circumventing immigration control.[3] According to the Minister of State, 'it has become clear through intelligence and other channels that abuse by those seeking to enter into sham marriages as a means of circumventing immigration control is on the increase'.[4] It was admitted in debate, however, that it was difficult to collate evidence to establish the extent of the abuses being committed.[5]

---

[1] Amendments to the Bill tabled at the recommittal stage of the Bill in the House of Lords on 15 June 2004; indication of intention to consider the introduction of such measures originally indicated in a statement to the House on 30 March 2004.

[2] Fourteenth Report of Session 2003–04 (HL Paper 130, HC Paper 828).

[3] Immigration and Asylum Act 1999, s 24.

[4] Letter from Baroness Scotland QC to Lord McNally, 7 June 2004.

[5] Lord Rooker; *Hansard*, HL col 681 (15 June 2004).

A. THE NEW PROVISIONS IN OUTLINE

6.03   The Government's intention in tabling the new measures was to attempt to deal with 'marriage abuse' at the earliest stage possible—that is, before the marriage has actually taken place. Lord Rooker observed, however, during the course of debate that:

> In many ways we are dealing with a highly targeted commercial operation ... We are not dealing with whether people love each other, whether they are going to get on with each other or whether the marriage is genuine. That is not our purpose; it is not the function of Government to be involved with that. We are dealing with a narrow aspect of the matter.[6]

6.04   The new provisions relate to all marriages before a Registrar of Marriages, where a party to the proposed marriage is subject to immigration control.[7] In England, therefore, a marriage solemnized in a Church of England religious ceremony would not be within the ambit of the new provisions.

6.05   There is provision for the designation of particular districts in which applicants covered by the new provisions must give notice of their intention to marry in accordance with the terms of the Marriage Act 1949.[8] An application may be made only to a registrar in one of the districts specified in regulations made by the Secretary of State.[9] The parties to the marriage also need to have resided in a registration district for seven days prior to the giving of the notice, although this need not be the district in which the notice is given.

6.06   A proposed marriage cannot take place (because the registrar will not enter notice of the marriage into the marriage notice book) unless an applicant, who is covered by the terms of the new provisions because they are subject to immigration control, satisfies the requirements identified in s 19(3).

6.07   Section 19(4) defines the meaning of 'subject to immigration control'. The provisions will apply where a party to the marriage is not an EEA national and requires leave to enter or remain in the United Kingdom under the terms of the Immigration Act 1971 (the provision applies even where this has already been granted, 'whether or not leave has been given'[10]).

6.08   Similar provisions are also enacted in relation to an intention to marry in Scotland[11] and Northern Ireland.[12]

6.09   The superintendent registrar shall not enter the proposed marriage into the marriage notice book[13] unless satisfied 'by the provision of specified evidence' (to

---

[6] *Hansard*, HL col 696 (15 June 2004).

[7] Asylum and Immigration (Treatment of Claimants, etc) Act 2004, s 19(1).

[8] ibid, s 19(2).

[9] ibid, s 19(2)(a) and (b).

[10] ibid, s 19(4)(a)(ii).

[11] ibid, ss 21 and 22.

[12] ibid, ss 23 and 24.

[13] ibid, s 19(3).

be defined in regulations to be published by the Registrar General of Marriages) that the party to the marriage who is subject to immigration control:

(a) has entry clearance for the purpose of enabling him to marry in the United Kingdom; or

(b) has written permission from the Secretary of State to marry (termed a 'certificate of approval' in the debates); or

(c) is within a class of applicants identified in regulations made by the Secretary of State (s 20(3) provides for the making of regulations).

In relation to the criteria by which the Secretary of State might grant permission to marry (a certificate of approval) Lord Rooker indicated during the course of the debate on the amendment: 6.10

> The exact details will be set out at a later date, but we envisage that those who are legally resident in the UK and who have been granted six months or more leave would normally be granted approval to marry, in what would be known as a certificate of approval. Where they do not hold the appropriate leave to remain—that is, they have something less than six months—they will be expected to leave the United Kingdom and apply for entry clearance from abroad, like hundreds of thousands of others do, unless on the facts of a particular case it is unreasonable to expect them to do so. In the example I gave, such a consideration would be given where a lady is heavily pregnant and therefore unable to travel.
>
> I must say that the phrase 'unable to travel', as written here, is almost the answer of a wordsmith or jobsmith.[14]

In responding to concerns about the position of children, and the possibility that children might be born illegitimate, as a result of the new provisions, he added: 6.11

> ... it is not our intention deliberately to force children into being born out of wedlock. The ability to travel might be a factor for a heavily pregnant woman, but I cannot see the marriage being refused for that. It would be wholly inequitable because we would be bringing in legislation almost forcing children to be born out of wedlock.[15]

The Secretary of State is given the power to make regulations specifying that an application for permission to marry, where required, must be made in writing, and a power to designate what information must be provided within the application.[16]   6.12

There is also provision permitting the Secretary of State to require payment of a fee (with the provision that certain classes of applicants identified in regulations may be able to make an application at reduced or no fee).[17] During the course of debate, it was suggested that this might be in the region of £155–250, on the basis that the fee would be comparable to that currently charged for applications for leave to remain.[18]   6.13

---

[14] Lord Rooker; *Hansard*, HL col 69–70 (28 June 2004).
[15] ibid.
[16] Asylum and Immigration (Treatment of Claimants, etc) Act 2004, s 25.
[17] ibid, s 25.
[18] Lord Rooker; *Hansard*, HL col 685 (15 June 2004).

B. THE PRESENT POSITION

6.14 The position of those seeking entry clearance or leave to enter or remain on the basis of marriage is regulated by Immigration Rules,[19] paras 277–289. Guidance on the interpretation and application of the rules is published in the Immigration Directorate Instructions (IDI).[20] Paragraph 281 of the Immigration Rules sets out the general framework. It provides:

> 281. The requirements to be met by a person seeking leave to enter the United Kingdom with a view to settlement as the spouse of a person present and settled in the United Kingdom or who is on the same occasion being admitted for settlement are that:
>
> (i)   (a) the applicant is married to a person present and settled in the United Kingdom or who is on the same occasion being admitted for settlement; or
>
>   (b) the applicant is married to a person who has a right of abode in the United Kingdom or indefinite leave to enter or remain in the United Kingdom and is on the same occasion seeking admission to the United Kingdom for the purposes of settlement and the parties were married at least 4 years ago, since which time they have been living together outside the United Kingdom; and
>
> (ii) the parties to the marriage have met; and . . .
>
> (iii) each of the parties intends to live permanently with the other as his or her spouse and the marriage is subsisting; and
>
> (iv) there will be adequate accommodation for the parties and any dependants without recourse to public funds in accommodation which they own or occupy exclusively; and
>
> (v) the parties will be able to maintain themselves and any dependants adequately without recourse to public funds; and
>
> (vi) the applicant holds a valid United Kingdom entry clearance for entry in this capacity.

6.15 The existing rules accordingly provide for 'orderly' immigration control through a general requirement for entry clearance. Marriage, as a potential basis to remain in the United Kingdom, will only be recognized where the Secretary of State is satisfied that the marriage is genuine and subsisting. The rules provide that the parties to the marriage must have met, and there must be an intention to live together on a permanent basis. In the Internal Instructions, the Secretary of State indicates that he interprets the provision relating to the intention of the couple:

> 'Intention to live permanently with the other' means an intention to live together, evidenced by a clear commitment from both parties that they will live together permanently in the United Kingdom immediately following the outcome of the application in question or as soon as circumstances permit thereafter, and 'intends to live permanently with the other' shall be construed accordingly.[21]

---

[19] HC 395.

[20] IDI, Ch 8, s 1 and Ch 8, annex B.

[21] ibid, Ch 8, s 1, Pt 1, para 2.2.

There are also provisions in the Immigration Rules limiting the recognition of **6.16** marriage for immigration purposes on general public policy grounds. Such considerations include the possibility that the marriage may be polygamous,[22] and that the spouse seeking entry is under the age of 16 (or the sponsor is under 18).[23]

Paragraph 284 of the Immigration Rules sets out provisions against 'switching' **6.17** following entry in another capacity, when initial leave granted had been for less than six months, unless the initial entry had been as a fiancée.[24] An extension of stay on the basis of marriage is not to be granted where the applicant had remained in breach of the Immigration Rules,[25] or where marriage had post-dated the instigation of deportation proceedings.[26] The initial grant of leave will be for a 'probationary' period of two years; thereafter, it is open for an applicant to apply to remain in the United Kingdom indefinitely if the marriage is still subsisting and continues to meet the provisions of the relevant rules.

For EEA nationals, the position is less restrictive but there is no obligation on the **6.18** Secretary of State to take account of the position of a spouse in a marriage that is a marriage of convenience.[27]

The IDIs also indicate that further enquiries should be conducted where there are **6.19** grounds to suspect that the marriage is not genuine or subsisting; this would potentially lead to a home visit or interview with the couple being conducted.[28]

The circumstances under which there might be a departure from a strict applica- **6.20** tion of the rules is also identified in internal guidance: the most important of these internal policies is DP3/96.[29]

Pre-existing provisions therefore limited the circumstances under which the **6.21** Secretary of State was bound to recognize marriage as a basis on which an applicant would be entitled to remain in the United Kingdom. The Secretary of State's own guidance also provides for investigations to be conducted where there are serious doubts about the genuine nature of a particular marriage.

Section 24 of the Immigration and Asylum Act 1999 placed an obligation on a **6.22** registrar to report her suspicions to the Secretary of State where there were reasonable grounds for suspecting that the marriage would be a sham marriage.[30] The Act

---

[22] Immigration Rules, HC 395, para 278(i).

[23] ibid, para 277.

[24] ibid, para 284(i).

[25] ibid, para 284(iv).

[26] ibid, para 284(v).

[27] 'Spouse' in relation to EEA nationals exercising community law rights does not include a party to a marriage of convenience: see Immigration (European Economic Area) Regulations 2000, SI 2326/2000, reg 2(1).

[28] IDI, Ch 8, s 1, Pt 1, para 3.

[29] The policy covers the position of illegal entrants and those facing deportation action. As a general rule, where (a) there is a genuine marriage which has subsisted for two or more years by the time of enforcement action (the meaning of which is defined in the policy) with a person who is settled in the UK, and married life has been conducted in this country; and (b) it is unreasonable to expect the settled spouse to accompany his or her partner on removal, enforcement action will not normally be pursued.

[30] Immigration and Asylum Act 1999, s 24(2) and (3).

defines a 'sham marriage' as a marriage involving a person who was neither a British citizen or EEA national and where the marriage was entered into 'for the purpose of avoiding the effect of one or more provisions of United Kingdom immigration law or the immigration rules'.[31]

C. HUMAN RIGHTS IMPLICATIONS

6.23 The potential human rights implications of the new measures fall to be analyzed within Art 12 (right to marry and found a family) and Art 14 (in relation to discrimination in the exercise of substantive rights under the European Convention on Human Rights (ECHR)).

1. Issues under ECHR Art 12

6.24 Article 12 provides:

Men and women of marriageable age have the right to marry and to found a family, according to the national laws governing the exercise of this right.

6.25 If ss 19–25 and the regulations made under those sections are to comply with Art 12 ECHR, they must satisfy a number of conditions. The new provisions must pursue a legitimate aim. The means employed must be rationally connected to the pursuit of that aim. They must constitute a proportionate response to the abuses with which they attempt to deal. The new provisions cannot act in such a way that the very essence of the rights protected by Art 12 is impaired. Article 14 is relevant potentially because of the difference in treatment on the basis of nationality and religion that the measures create.[32]

2. The existing Strasbourg case law

6.26 The preservation of the integrity of marriage as an institution constitutes a legitimate aim which is in the public interest.[33] In *Benes v Austria*,[34] the Commission declared as inadmissible a complaint in relation to a decision in Austria to declare a marriage null and void, when it subsequently emerged that the marriage had been one of convenience. The evidence indicated that the sole purpose of the marriage had been to obtain Austrian nationality; in those circumstances, in an application decided under Art 8 ECHR, proceedings to nullify a marriage of convenience prevented disorder and protected the interests of others, and were therefore legitimately instigated. Further, the Commission accepted that it was for the national authorities to lay

---

[31] Immigration and Asylum Act 1999, s 24(5).
[32] The JCHR report on the new amendments produced a cogent analysis of the potential conflicts.
[33] See, eg, *F v Switzerland* (1987) 10 EHRR 411, para 36.
[34] (1992) 72 DR 118.

down the rules according to which the validity of a marriage could be determined and to draw the legal consequences of such a decision, including proceedings to have the marriage concerned declared null and void.

An interference with the right to marry cannot be to such an extent that the very **6.27** essence of the right itself is impaired. *Hamer v United Kingdom*[35] concerned an application by a serving prisoner to marry. Policy in force at that time was in effect a blanket prohibition on marriage by prisoners, unless the purpose of the marriage was to legitimize a child. The justification advanced was that it would have been unduly onerous administratively for the prison authorities to decide which marriages should be allowed to proceed on the basis that they were 'desirable'.[36] The Commission found that the protected right was the right to form a legal relationship. The facts of the case presented no countervailing considerations justifying an interference in the exercise of the right on the basis, for example, that prison order or security would be compromised if the marriage were allowed to proceed.

In relation to the interpretation to be afforded to Art 12:   **6.28**

. . . Article 12 guarantees a fundamental 'right to marry'. Whilst this is expressed as a 'right to marry . . . according to the national laws governing the exercise of this right', this does not mean that the scope afforded to national law is unlimited. If it were, Article 12 would be redundant. The role of national law, as the wording of the Article indicates, is to govern the exercise of the right.[37]

National laws could govern the exercise of the right to marry, but in seeking to **6.29** 'regulate' the exercise of the right, they could not injure its substance.[38] In relation to the imposition of rules within national law, the Commission stated in *Hamer*:

Such laws may thus lay down formal rules concerning matters such as notice, publicity and the formalities whereby marriage is solemnised . . . They may also lay down rules of substance based on generally recognised considerations of public interest. Examples are rules concerning capacity, consent, prohibited degrees of consanguinity or the prevention of bigamy . . . However, in the Commission's opinion national law may not otherwise deprive a person or category of persons of full legal capacity of the right to marry. Nor may it substantially interfere with their exercise of the right.[39]

The Commission further noted that there might be a breach even where the interfer- **6.30** ence in the right was an effectively temporary one: 'hindrance in fact can contravene the Convention just like a legal impediment'; 'hindering the effective exercise of a right may amount to a breach of that right, even if the hindrance is of a temporary character'.[40]

---

[35] (1979) 24 DR 5, 14 Eur Comm HR 35 .

[36] ibid, para 17.

[37] ibid, para 60.

[38] ibid, para 61: see also *Rees v UK* (1986) 9 EHRR 56, para 50. Limitations imposed by national law 'must not restrict or reduce the right in such a way or to such an extent that the very essence of the right is impaired'.

[39] ibid, para 62.

[40] Citation by the Commission at para 65 from *Golder v UK* (1979–80) 1 EHRR 524.

6.31 The Commission noted that personal liberty was not a necessary precondition for the exercise of the right to marry; further:

> The essence of the right to marry, in the Commission's opinion, is the formation of a legally binding association between a man and a woman. It is for them to decide whether or not they wish to enter an association in circumstances where they cannot cohabit.[41]

6.32 On the basis of the general circumstances, and also because there was no evidence demonstrating that it was 'harmful to the public interest' to allow the marriage of prisoners, the Commission found that the substantial delay created by the measure created a breach of Art 12. In *Draper v United Kingdom*,[42] the Commission, while not prepared to speculate in the abstract, suggested that there might be cases, particularly because the offence committed by the prisoner had been serious, where considerations of policy might mean that an interference with the Art 12 right would be permitted. It was careful to add, however, that a blanket prohibition on marriage with respect to all life prisoners was unlikely to be justified.[43]

6.33 It is clear, therefore, that it is legitimate for a public authority to interfere in cases where marriages are in fact marriages of convenience. Rights protected by Art 12 must not however be fundamentally impaired. In regulating the procedure for marriage, it is for the state to decide on the national legal framework; again, however, it is clear that the applicable law cannot impair the very essence of the protected right.[44]

D. ECHR COMPATIBILITY

1. The justification

6.34 The 2004 Act only provides a general framework for implementation. The JCHR was clearly unhappy that the provisions had been introduced at such a late stage in the progress of the Bill. Their concern that detailed scrutiny of the measures was limited was evidently shared by a number of speakers in the debate in the House of Lords.

6.35 The full impact of the new provisions will only become clear once the detailed regulations and guidance have been published. It is therefore only possible, at the

---

[41] *Hamer*, para 71.

[42] (1981) 24 DR 72.

[43] ibid, para 62.

[44] In an admissibility decision in *Kemal Selim v Cyprus*, Application 00047293/99 (2001) (subsequently the subject of a friendly settlement), the Court considered the issue of impairment of the right protected by Art 12. The Court declared admissible a complaint by a Cypriot national of Turkish origin who wished to marry his Romanian fiancée. Under Cypriot law, there was no basis for someone of Turkish origin professing the Muslim faith to enter into a civil marriage. The applicant had been forced to marry in Romania without any of his friends or family being present.

time of writing, to make general observations about some of the potential difficulties that the new legislation might create.

The professed intention behind the new provisions is to prevent sham marriages. **6.36** This, however, sits rather uneasily with the observations made during the debate by Lord Rooker that: 'We are not dealing with whether people love each other, whether they are going to get on with each other or whether the marriage is genuine. That is not our purpose; it is not the function of Government to be involved with that.'[45]

During the course of debate on the measures in the Lords, there were strong reser- **6.37** vations about the need for the new amendments, given objections based upon the somewhat equivocal nature of the evidence relied upon by the Government in contending that there was a serious issue of abuse to be tackled. The Government cited, in support of its case that new measures were needed, evidence from reporting of 'suspicious' marriages by registrars, contending that the number of reports had increased significantly. In debate, it was suggested that the increase in the number of reports might, in part, be due to the greater assiduity of registrars in reporting suspicious marriages now that they had become accustomed to the reporting requirement.[46]

The available evidence made it clear that there had been a comparatively small **6.38** number of arrests and criminal charges arising from the reports made. No statistics were presented to demonstrate the impact of reporting on subsequent decisions to grant leave to enter or remain in the target group comprising those who had been reported. Of the more than 2,000 reports, there were only 37 instances in which criminal charges followed, and no statistics were provided to indicate how many of those charged were actually convicted of an offence, although it was suggested that a number of removals from the United Kingdom had followed interventions by the Immigration Service because of concerns about 'suspicious' marriages.[47]

It is suggested that the intentions of the parties to a particular marriage must be **6.39** relevant in assessing whether an interference in the Art 12 protected right is justified. This must logically be the case with the new framework introduced by ss 19–25 because of the professed intention behind the measures and the potentially harsh interference with what is clearly a fundamental right.

While it is difficult to gauge exactly what form the regulations will take, criteria **6.40** such as lawful residence, or the length of extant leave held are not logically germane to this question. In effect, and as noted by the JCHR, the criteria for permission to marry, if they follow the indications provided during the debates,[48] may introduce a bar to genuine marriages because of considerations that have no rational bearing on the good faith of the couple intending marriage. Someone who has leave to remain of short duration may have a perfectly genuine intention in marrying; the limitations created by the proposed framework may not therefore be rationally connected to the intended purpose in the legislation.

---

[45] See n 6 above.
[46] *Hansard*, HL col 686 (15 June 2004).
[47] *Hansard*, HL col 681 (15 June 2004); JCHR report, n 2 above, paras 38 and 57.
[48] See n 14 above.

2. Potential target groups

6.41   All non-EEA nationals are potentially covered by the new requirements. It was said in the course of debate that there were particular concerns about sham marriages being contracted with EEA nationals. Marriage to an EEA national confers advantages over and above those obtained from marrying a British citizen.[49] While there would be no obligation to recognize the validity of a sham marriage involving an EU national exercising treaty rights in this country, the burden of so demonstrating might arguably fall on the Secretary of State. The Secretary of State is bound to exercise care in order to ensure that genuine marriages to EEA nationals by fiancées subject to immigration control do not create interferences in Community law rights.

6.42   While a claim remains under consideration, an asylum applicant cannot reasonably be expected to return to his country of origin to obtain entry clearance. That is for the obvious reason that an applicant may eventually be determined to be at risk and therefore recognized as a refugee. In such circumstances, it will be difficult to refuse to permit a genuine marriage to take place if it is argued that the couple could be expected to return to marry in the asylum-seeker's country of origin.

3. The new measures and existing immigration control

6.43   In the immigration context, there is an important point of comparison with *Hamer*. The Commission held that liberty was not a condition precedent for a serving prisoner to be able to marry; a couple could marry even though they would not be free to cohabit. A general prohibition on marriage by serving prisoners was not justified. The exercise of such rights, as *Hamer* and *Draper* make clear, is not wholly unrestricted and may be subject to public policy considerations. It is difficult to see, in line with the approach in *Hamer*, however, why British or EEA nationality should be necessary per se for the exercise of an unrestricted right to marry.

6.44   It was a point forcefully made during the debate in the Lords that an individual subject to immigration control, and who was seeking to remain on the basis of his conjugal status would, if he did not otherwise satisfy the requirements of the Immigration Rules, have to return to obtain entry clearance. It is striking that the indications provided in the debates were that the new guidance setting out the circumstances in which permission to marry would normally be given would appear simply to mirror the provisions already in place with regard to the requirements to be met in granting leave on the basis of marriage. In this context, it might be said that the new enactments add little to the existing position in terms of the ability to enforce immigration control. The Government, during debate, clearly held a different view, citing the additional difficulties in taking enforcement action once a marriage had actually taken place as a compelling reason behind the introduction of the new measures.[50]

---

[49] *Hansard*, HL col 70 (28 June 2004).
[50] *Hansard*, HL col 682 (15 June 2004).

As *Hamer* makes clear, delays in a couple's ability to marry, because an individ- **6.45** ual applicant will have to return to obtain entry clearance, may also be relevant in determining whether the essence of the Art 12 right is damaged.

E. ECHR ART 14: DIFFERENT TREATMENT ON THE GROUNDS OF RELIGION OR NATIONALITY

The new measures apply to all non-EEA nationals, and to cases where a marriage is **6.46** not solemnized in a ceremony conducted before a recognized Church. As a conse- quence, there is a difference in treatment, according to the nationality or religion of the individuals intending to marry.

Where there is a difference in treatment between particular groups, Art 14 **6.47** requires that the difference in approach must be predicated on a rational and objec- tive justification.

In analyzing the new measures in the context of English law, the JCHR drew **6.48** attention to the potentially discriminatory impact of the provisions.[51] All marriages conducted by a registrar will be within the ambit of the new provisions; marriages solemnized in ceremonies in the Church of England will not be covered. The new provisions potentially apply to all religious marriages outside the Church of England and to all non-religious marriages in a registry office.

As the JCHR pointed out, the measures raise an issue of difference of treatment **6.49** on the basis of religion or nationality, of groups in an essentially analogous position. The only substantial justification for excluding marriages solemnized in the Church of England from the new provisions was that there was 'no evidence' of sham marriages being contracted in such ceremonies. As the JCHR note, that might well be a relatively weak justification for the differences in treatment; particularly where there is a potentially blanket restriction in relation to an important core human right.

---

[51] JCHR report, n 2 above, paras 69–76.

7

APPEALS
(SECTIONS 26 AND 28–31;
SCHEDULES 1 AND 2)

A. Introduction   7.01
B. Background   7.04
C. The new Asylum and Immigration Tribunal   7.15
D. Review by the High Court (in Scotland, Court of Session)   7.24
E. Appeal to the Court of Appeal (in Scotland, Court of Session)   7.54
F. Judicial review   7.61
G. Public funding of representation for review of AIT and
    reconsideration   7.71
H. Removal of right of appeal before removal in some entry cases   7.77
I. Other changes to appeal system   7.83

A. INTRODUCTION

The Asylum and Immigration (Treatment of Claimants, etc) Act 2004 radically **7.01** changes the system for immigration and asylum appeals by:

(a) abolishing the two-tier structure of adjudicators and Immigration Appeal Tribunal originally created by the Immigration Appeals Act 1969;

(b) establishing a new, single-tier body, the Asylum and Immigration Tribunal (AIT).

The 2004 Act adapts the existing mechanisms of review by the High Court (intro- **7.02** duced by the Nationality, Immigration and Asylum Act 2002) and appeal to the Court of Appeal (introduced by the Asylum and Immigration Appeals Act 1993). Under the new scheme, the first AIT decision on a case is subject to review (and not appeal), unless it was made by a panel of three or more members. If the court decid-ing the review application directs the AIT to reconsider, any challenge to the further decision can only be made by appeal to the Court of Appeal. A decision of a panel of three or more members can only be appealed. The result is a complicated sequence of remedies (see flowchart opposite).

7.03   The 2004 Act also:

(a) empowers the AIT to decide on public funding of an application for review;

(b) removes the right to appeal before removal from the United Kingdom from certain refusals of leave to enter;

(c) allows the Home Secretary to remove rights of appeal from certain entry clearance refusals;

(d) gives a right of appeal to certain crew-members of ships and aircraft;

(e) makes minor changes to the system of denying repeat appeals by certification.

B. BACKGROUND

7.04   The Immigration Appeals Act 1969 created a right of appeal to an adjudicator from certain immigration decisions. A further right of appeal lay to the Immigration Appeal Tribunal, with permission of an adjudicator or of the Tribunal. The Tribunal sat in panels of three, almost always consisting of a single legally-qualified member and two lay members. There was no right of appeal from the Tribunal, but its decisions were subject to judicial review by the High Court (in Scotland, Court of Session (Outer House)), with a right of appeal to the Court of Appeal (in Scotland, Court of Session (Inner House)).

7.05   The Immigration Act 1971 maintained that system. The Tribunal was required by rules to grant permission where there was a point of law, and had a discretion to do so in other cases.

7.06   The Asylum and Immigration Appeals Act 1993 gave a right of appeal from a final immigration decision concerning an asylum claimant to a special adjudicator (who was drawn from the ranks of adjudicators). The 1993 Act also provided for a right of appeal from a final decision of the Immigration Appeal Tribunal to the Court of Appeal (in Scotland, Court of Session (Inner House)). Judicial review was only required where the Tribunal refused permission to appeal.

7.07   The Immigration and Asylum Act 1999 consolidated the titles of adjudicator and special adjudicator. It also provided for a right of appeal from a final immigration decision on human rights grounds.

7.08   The Nationality, Immigration and Asylum Act 2002 limited appeals to the Tribunal to those raising a point of law. Instead of judicial review of Tribunal decisions on permission to appeal, the 2002 Act introduced a system of review by the High Court (in Scotland, Court of Session (Outer House)) on the papers, without a hearing or a right of further appeal.

7.09   The 2002 Act provides a right of appeal to an adjudicator from the following decisions:

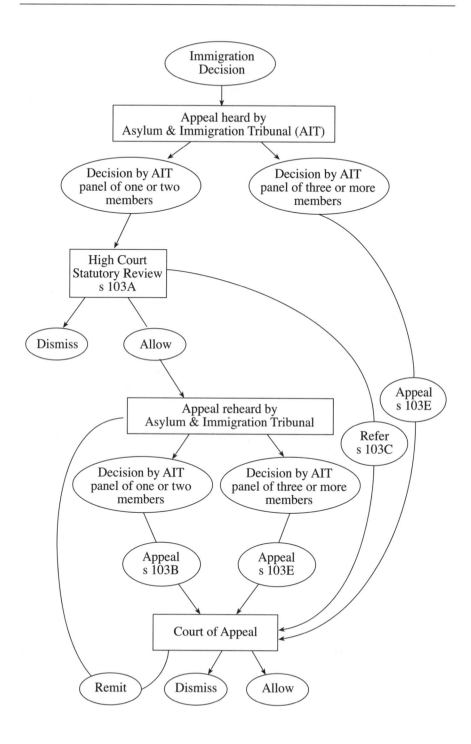

(a) a decision to refuse leave to enter;[1]

(b) a decision to refuse entry clearance;[2]

(c) a decision to refuse a certificate of entitlement of right of abode;[3]

(d) a decision not to vary leave to enter or remain;[4]

(e) a decision to curtail leave to enter or remain;[5]

(f) a decision to revoke indefinite leave to remain;[6]

(g) a decision to remove;[7]

(h) a decision to remove an illegal entrant;[8]

(i) a decision to remove a family member of an illegal entrant being removed;[9]

(j) a decision to make a deportation order;[10]

(k) a decision refusing to revoke a deportation order;[11]

(l) a decision to grant leave to enter or remain whilst refusing asylum.[12]

7.10   The Government's initial Bill proposed radical changes to the structure of the appellate authority, most notably the reduction of the appeal system to a single tier system and, more controversially,[13] an 'ouster clause' purporting to exclude all immigration decisions from review by, or appeal to, the courts. On 15 March 2004, at the Bill's Second Reading in the House of Lords, the Government announced that it had withdrawn the 'ouster clause' from the Bill.

7.11   In its place a Government amendment was introduced[14] which would permit access to the courts, albeit to a limited extent. During the introduction of this amendment in the House of Lords, the Government indicated that the restructuring of the appellate authority was aimed at reducing abuse, increasing speed and preserving judicial oversight to ensure that the system remains independent, thorough and fair.[15]

7.12   The two-tier appellate authority (previously consisting of adjudicators at first instance and the Immigration Appeal Tribunal on appeal) has been replaced with a

---

[1] Nationality, Immigration and Asylum Act 2002, s 82(2)(a).

[2] ibid, s 82(2)(b).

[3] ibid, s 82(3)(c).

[4] ibid, s 82(3)(d).

[5] ibid, s 82(3)(e).

[6] ibid, s 82(3)(f).

[7] ibid, s 82(3)(g).

[8] ibid, s 82(3)(h).

[9] ibid, s 82(3)(i).

[10] ibid, s 82(3)(j).

[11] ibid, s 82(3)(k).

[12] ibid, s 83.

[13] In a letter to the Lord Chancellor, Lord Falconer, dated 29 April 2004 the Lord Chief Justice, Lord Woolf described the ouster clause as 'fundamentally in conflict with the rule of law', a view shared by many other commentators.

[14] cl 14 of HL Bill 66 (53/3), which is now s 26(6) of the Asylum and Immigration (Treatment of Claimants, etc) Act 2004.

[15] Lord Chancellor, Lord Falconer, *Hansard*, HL col 995 (4 May 2004).

single appellate body called the Asylum and Immigration Tribunal.[16] Any appeals against an 'immigration decision' or an appeal against a decision to refuse asylum while granting leave to enter or remain will now be made to the AIT instead of an adjudicator.[17]

The new framework remains controversial. The Joint Committee on Human Rights (JCHR) took the view that **7.13**

> removal of the right to appeal to a second tier tribunal, and at the same time severely restricting the right of access to the higher courts, without replacing these rights of appeal with any other effective mechanism for detecting errors, will mean that, at best, the present level of errors will go undetected; at worst it may mean that the error rate increases in the absence of the availability of effective scrutiny of the rightness or wrongness of the decisions concerned.[18]

The JCHR remained unconvinced that 'the restrictions on the right of access to the higher courts . . . are proportionate to the legitimate aim asserted' and that 'in some respects (notably the five day time limit and the legal aid proposals) they come very close to impairing the very substance of the right itself'.[19] The Committee concluded that, following the restructuring of the appellate authority and the restrictions placed upon access to the courts, 'wrong decisions will continue to be made' and 'are more likely to go uncorrected'.[20] **7.14**

C. THE NEW ASYLUM AND IMMIGRATION TRIBUNAL

Section 26 of the 2004 Act replaces adjudicators and the Immigration Appeal Tribunal with the new AIT (by amending Nationality, Immigration and Asylum Act 2002, s 81). A new Sch 4 to the Nationality, Immigration and Asylum Act 2002 contains the detailed provision for the new AIT.[21] **7.15**

---

[16] Nationality, Immigration and Asylum Act 2002, s 81(1)–(5) (as amended by s 26 of the Asylum and Immigration (Treatment of Claimants, etc) Act 2004). The main reason provided by the Government for this restructuring is that '97% of adjudicators' initial decisions are actually ultimately upheld' (evidence of Beverley Hughes to the Home Affairs Select Committee, 19 November 2003). However some commentators have viewed this figure as misleading as it fails to attach appropriate weight to the significant proportion of appeals (44% for the year 1 October 2002 to 30 September 2003) to the Immigration Appeal Tribunal which, although not allowed outright, were remitted to an adjudicator for rehearing.

[17] Nationality, Immigration and Asylum Act 2002, s 81(2) and (3) as amended by the Asylum and Immigration (Treatment of Claimants, etc) Act 2004.

[18] Thirteenth Report of Session 2003–04 (HL Paper 102, HC Paper 640) para 1.100.

[19] ibid, para 1.101.

[20] ibid, para 1.102.

[21] See Asylum and Immigration (Treatment of Claimants, etc) Act 2004, Sch 1.

1. Membership of the AIT

7.16 Members of the AIT are appointed by the Lord Chancellor.[22] They may serve until they are 70, or exceptionally, 75.[23]

7.17 The Act distinguishes between legally qualified and non-legally qualified members of the AIT:

(a) the requirements for appointment as a legally qualified member are that the person must have seven years experience as a solicitor or barrister in England, Wales or Northern Ireland, or as an advocate in Scotland, or have legal experience which makes her suitable as such a person;[24]

(b) the requirements for appointment as a non-legally qualified member, are that the person has non-legal experience which makes her suitable.[25]

7.18 Persons serving as adjudicators and members of the Immigration Appeal Tribunal at commencement of the new provisions automatically become members of the AIT.[26] Only persons appointed as legally qualified members of the Immigration Appeal Tribunal automatically become legally qualified members of the AIT.[27] An adjudicator with a seven-year legal qualification is treated as a non-legally qualified AIT member, though the Lord Chancellor can appoint her as a legally-qualified member instead.

7.19 Persons serving as members of staff of adjudicators or of the Immigration Appeal Tribunal at commencement of the new provisions are treated as members of staff of the AIT.[28]

2. Structure of the AIT

7.20 Like the Immigration Appeal Tribunal, the AIT is to have a President. The President must be a serving or former judge of the High Court (or its Scottish or Northern Irish equivalent).[29] The AIT will also have a Deputy President (or Deputy Presidents).[30]

7.21 The Lord Chancellor may create additional levels of this hierarchy, and direct which level of AIT member is to deal with certain kinds of case.[31] It seems that this power will be used to maintain some of the existing features of the appellate system, including the practice that lay members of the Immigration Appeal Tribunal only sit on panels which include at least one legally qualified member.

---

[22] Nationality, Immigration and Asylum Act 2002, Sch 4, para 1.
[23] ibid, Sch 4, para 3.
[24] ibid, Sch 4, para 2(1)(a)–(d) and (2).
[25] ibid, Sch 4, para 2(1)(e).
[26] Asylum and Immigration (Treatment of Claimants, etc) Act 2004, Sch 2, paras 27–28.
[27] ibid, Sch 2, para 28(b).
[28] ibid, Sch 2, para 29.
[29] Nationality, Immigration and Asylum Act 2002, Sch 4, para 5(a).
[30] ibid, Sch 4, para 5(b).
[31] ibid, Sch 4, paras 4, 7 and 8.

3. Three-member panels

The most important distinction in the new AIT will be the size of the panel which **7.22** hears the appeal. An appeal determined by a panel of three or more members cannot be challenged on statutory review, but only on appeal to the Court of Appeal.[32] This rule applies regardless of the number of legally qualified members on the panel.

4. Powers of the AIT

The AIT has all the powers that are presently exercised by adjudicators and the **7.23** Immigration Appeal Tribunal:

(a) determining appeals from immigration decisions (see para 7.09 above);
(b) granting bail to those in administrative detention under immigration powers.[33]

D. REVIEW BY THE HIGH COURT (IN SCOTLAND, COURT OF SESSION)

Where the appeal is decided by the AIT (a) for the first time (and not after remittal **7.24** by a higher court) and (b) by a single member (or two-member panel), then the AIT decision can be challenged on review by the High Court or, in Scotland, the Court of Session (Outer House).[34] The AIT itself will filter applications as a transitional measure: see paras 7.49–7.53 below.

There is no oral hearing (see para 7.36 below). **7.25**

The decision can only be challenged by review if it determines the appeal itself **7.26** and is not merely a decision on a preliminary, procedural or ancillary issue.[35]

The decision can only be challenged on grounds of error of law.[36] It should be **7.27**

---

[32] ibid, s 103A(8).

[33] Immigration Act 1971, Sch 2, paras 22(1A) and 29(3) and Sch 3, para 2(4A).

[34] Nationality, Immigration and Asylum Act 2002, s 103A(1) and (8)–(10).

[35] ibid, s103A(7)(a).

[36] ibid, s 103A(1). In *CA v Secretary of State for the Home Department* [2004] EWCA Civ 1165, the Court of Appeal (Mummery LJ, Laws LJ, Sir Martin Nourse) held that the IAT was not entitled to interfere with an adjudicator's determination under the 2002 Act on the basis of a change of circumstances or fresh evidence unless *an error of law* in the adjudicator's determination was established. Laws LJ stated that s 101(1) of the Nationality, Immigration and Asylum Act 2002 permits appeals against adjudicators' determinations promulgated since 9 June 2003 to be brought on points of law only. Both *Ravichandran v Secretary of State for the Home Department* [1996] Imm AR 97, CA and the recent IAT starred determination of *BD (Application of SK and DK) (Croatia)* [2004] UKIAT 32 were concerned with the IAT's historical jurisdiction to consider appeals on points of fact and law. Neither governs the new jurisdiction although if an error of law in the adjudicator's determination is established and the IAT decides to assess the merits, it will do so as of the present date. The Secretary of State argued that the IAT could look at the up-to-date position on the merits even if he could not show an error of law in the adjudicator's determination so long as there was an arguable error of law. Laws LJ said that it was quite impossible to find any such proposition in the wording of s 101. *Ravichandran* was concerned with appeals on the facts. The

noted, however, that an error of law is not limited to cases where the AIT has misunderstood the relevant law. It also includes: perverse factual findings; failing to have proper regard to evidence; failing to give adequate reasons; and breaches of natural justice.

7.28 The court has power to order the AIT to reconsider if the court 'thinks that the AIT may have made an error of law'.[37] The wording indicates a low hurdle of arguability.

7.29 In some cases the AIT acts correctly on the material before it but unwittingly denies justice to a party. The typical case is where the appellant is absent from the AIT hearing without explanation and the appeal is dismissed. It then comes to light that the appellant did not know of the hearing, or that she sent an explanation for her absence which did not reach the AIT. In such cases, the decision can be quashed on judicial review as a denial of justice.[38] It is suggested that 'error of law' should be interpreted to encompass such a non-culpable denial of justice. If that is wrong, then judicial review of the AIT's decision will lie.

1. Application for review: time-limit and late applications

7.30 The application for review must be issued in the appropriate court and not the AIT. The time-limit[39] is very short:

(a) five days from receipt of the AIT decision in all cases, except

(b) where the applicant is outside the United Kingdom and was the appellant before the AIT, the period is 28 days. (Applications by entry clearance officers must thus be made within five days of receipt.)

7.31 The court has power to admit an application made late if the application could 'not reasonably practicably have been made' within the time-limit.[40] In *Wall's Meat Co Ltd v Khan*,[41] a similar provision for extending time to make a claim to an industrial tribunal was considered. The Court of Appeal held that reasonable ignorance of one's rights or a reasonable mistake about how to exercise them meant it was 'not reasonably practicable' to make the claim.

7.32 The Court in the *Wall's Meat* case also held that receipt of bad legal advice is not a basis for holding that it was not reasonably practicable to present the employment claim. It may be that a different approach should apply to applications for review of the AIT. Unlike employment cases, where loss is almost always quantified in monetary terms, return to face persecution cannot be adequately compensated. In *R (Q) v*

---

reasoning in *Ravichandran* could not be read across to the IAT's new limited jurisdiction. Section 101 forbids the IAT from determining the merits itself unless it identifies an error of law.

[37] Nationality, Immigration and Asylum Act 2002, s 103A(2).
[38] *R (Tataw) v Immigration Appeal Tribunal* [2003] EWCA Civ 925, [2003] INLR 585 at [19]–[20].
[39] Nationality, Immigration and Asylum Act 2002, s 103A(3).
[40] ibid, s 103A(4)(b).
[41] [1979] ICR 52, CA.

Secretary of State for the Home Department,[42] the Court of Appeal observed that the rationale for this part of the *Wall's Meat* case 'may be by reason of principles of the law of agency, or considerations of policy, or a combination of the two'.[43] It is suggested that, in cases where the AIT may have erred in law in a decision affecting the applicant's fundamental rights, policy considerations should lead to an interpretation of 'reasonably practicable' which focuses on the applicant's state of knowledge and belief, including any based on mistakes of his advisers.

The five-day time-limit has been severely criticized. The JCHR concluded that   7.33
the time-limit was so short as to render the completion of all the steps that need to be taken by a representative before lodging an application for reconsideration 'a physical impossibility for most asylum-seekers'[44] and thus 'render[s] most individuals dependent on an exercise of discretion to proceed with their right of access to the higher courts'.[45]

The UN High Commissioner for Refugees stated that the five-day time-limit   7.34
'falls short of international standards of fairness by seriously compromising the ability of asylum applicants to access their rights of appeal', 'does not fulfil the standard of reasonableness' and 'does not accord with the UNHCR's view of basic procedural practices required by the Convention'.[46] The UNHCR referred to the European Court of Human Rights jurisprudence on time-limits in ECHR, Art 6(1) cases, in particular *Perez de Rada Cavanilles v Spain*[47] where it was held that a three-day time-limit violated the complainant's right to access to the courts.

The time-limits are contained in the Act, but can be altered by the Lord   7.35
Chancellor.[48]

2. The application for review

The application is considered on the papers—no oral hearing is permitted.[49] The   7.36
detail of the procedure has yet to be announced but will be in the Civil Procedure Rules. It is understood that the court will normally consider the application on the basis of the applicant's bundle only. However, the court may have power to direct the other party to file written submissions and/or evidence.[50]

It is essential that the written submissions fully argue each of the points of law   7.37
which the applicant claims arises from the AIT determination. There will be no opportunity to add to them or express them more persuasively.

---

[42] [2003] EWCA Civ 364, [2004] QB 36, CA.
[43] ibid, 65.
[44] Thirteenth Report, n 18 above, para 1.77.
[45] ibid, para 1.80.
[46] UNHCR Press Notice, Asylum and Immigration (Treatment of Claimants, etc) Bill, 2004—Briefing for the House of Lords at Report Stage (13 May 2004), paras 3–9.
[47] (1998) 29 EHRR 109, para 45.
[48] Asylum and Immigration (Treatment of Claimants, etc) Act 2004, s 26(8)(a).
[49] Nationality, Immigration and Asylum Act 2002, s 103A(5).
[50] ibid, s 103A(5)(b).

7.38   It is suggested that written submissions should include the following:

(a) A short statement of the grounds of challenge, with each ground drafted so that it is clear what error of law is claimed. Where it is the AIT's decision on facts or the AIT's reasons which give rise to the error, it is particularly important that the ground should be drafted to make clear that an error of law is being alleged, and not merely a disagreement with the factual conclusions.

(b) Detailed submissions in support of each of the grounds setting out the factual findings relevant to the ground. The submissions should include references to the relevant parts of the adjudicator's decision and to any relevant evidence contained in the application bundle (see para 7.42 below).

(c) Submissions explaining why the grounds, individually or cumulatively, are material errors of law. If an error made no difference to the result, then there is no reason why it should lead to reconsideration of the case by the AIT.

7.39   The application bundle should contain all material relevant to the application which was before the AIT. The court does not have the AIT file. In asylum cases, relevant country material which was before the AIT may need to be included. For example, if it is alleged that the AIT failed to have any regard to media reports of attacks on supporters of a particular political group, those reports should be included in the application bundle, together with relevant extracts from the other material relating to that group (whether they support or detract from the applicant's case).

7.40   Only relevant material should be included. If the AIT dismissed a marriage appeal because of inadequate maintenance and accommodation, but accepted that the applicant intends to live with the sponsor as his wife, then there is no need for the application bundle to include photographs of the wedding and the correspondence showing intervening devotion.

7.41   In some cases an error of law cannot be made out by reference only to the AIT decision and the papers before it. Two typical cases where further evidence should be submitted are:

(a) The error arises from what happened at the hearing, which the AIT has failed adequately to record in its decision. For example, the Home Office representative may make a concession with which the AIT appears content and the applicant therefore advances no further evidence or submissions on that point. If the AIT fails to record that concession and reaches a decision on a basis which is inconsistent with it, the applicant should include in the material filed with the court a witness statement from a person present at the hearing (preferably the representative) setting out what happened at the hearing.

(b) The importance of the error is demonstrated by material which was not before the AIT. For example, the adjudicator disbelieves the applicant's claimed religion (for perverse reasons) while also reasonably rejecting his case that members of that religion are persecuted. By the time the AIT issues the decision, there is clear evidence of such persecution. That evidence shows that the AIT's error of law on the applicant's own history is a highly material one.

The bundle should be paginated and indexed, with every item identified. It is not **7.42** enough for the index to state 'newspaper reports', or 'correspondence'. Before the bundle is submitted, it should be checked to see that every page is paginated and fully legible. There will not be a hearing at which better copies can be handed up. It is suggested that the detailed guidance on preparation of bundles for the Court of Appeal should be used as a guide.[51]

3. Decision on the review application

The court can make one of three decisions on the application: **7.43**

(a) dismiss the application;

(b) refer the application to the Court of Appeal (or, in Scotland, the Court of Session (Inner House)), see paras 7.44–7.45 below;

(c) direct the AIT to reconsider the appeal (see paras 7.47–7.48 below).

4. Reference to the appellate court

On an application for statutory review, the court may consider that the appeal before **7.44** the AIT raises a question of law of such importance that it should be referred to the Court of Appeal (or, in Scotland, the Court of Session (Inner House)).[52]

The decision to refer is one for the court to make of its own motion. It is likely **7.45** to be exercised rarely and only where the court considers that the issue of law raised requires guidance of the Court of Appeal (or Court of Session). If the applicant considers that this may be the case and wants to avoid the delay and expense of AIT reconsideration, a reference can be suggested in the application for review.

For the appellate court's powers on review, see paras 7.57 and 7.58 below. **7.46**

5. Reconsideration by the AIT

The AIT's procedure rules can make special provision for reconsideration.[53] At the **7.47** time of writing, no draft rules had been published.

The AIT's decision on reconsideration can be challenged, but only by appeal to **7.48** the Court of Appeal (or, in Scotland, the Court of Session (Inner House)), see paras 7.54–7.57 below. There can be no further application for review of a decision made on reconsideration of that appeal.

---

[51] CPR PD52.15.4.

[52] Nationality, Immigration and Asylum Act 2002, s 103B(1).

[53] ibid, s 106(2)(x).

6. Transitional provision: filter by AIT

7.49 The AIT will have power to 'filter' applications for review.[54] This will not affect the right to apply to the court for review.

7.50 According to the Government, the purpose of the 'filter' is to 'meet concerns about the potential volume of cases reaching the High Court' and relieve pressure on that court.[55] The Lord Chancellor has remarked that this transitional mechanism may be necessary 'for the foreseeable future'.[56]

7.51 The filter will work in this way:[57]

(a) The application will be made to the High Court (or Court of Session).

(b) The application will be considered by a member of the AIT.[58] This will be a senior member.[59]

(c) The AIT member can grant the application (including any extension of time).[60]

(d) If the AIT member proposes to refuse the application (or an extension of time), the member will notify the court and the applicant.[61]

(e) An applicant notified of a proposed refusal can ask the court to consider the application. The time-limit for making this request is five days from receipt of the AIT member's decision, which can be extended if it was not reasonably practicable to make the request within that time period.[62]

(f) The court itself will then consider the request.

7.52 Where the AIT member proposes to refuse, the application considered by the court will remain that originally issued and the subject will be the AIT's decision on the appeal, not the AIT member's decision on the application for review. However, where the AIT member gives reasons for proposing to refuse the application, it is important that the applicant ensures those reasons are addressed before the court considers the application, if need be, by submitting supplementary written submissions and further evidence.

7.53 The AIT member cannot refer the appeal to the Court of Appeal.[63]

---

[54] Asylum and Immigration (Treatment of Claimants, etc) Act 2004, Sch 2, para 30(1) and (8).

[55] Letter of 2 May 2004 from Lord Chancellor, Lord Falconer to the JCHR, published as Appendix 1b in Thirteenth Report of Session 2003–04 (HL Paper 102, HC 640) 56.

[56] Letter, n 13 above.

[57] See Asylum and Immigration (Treatment of Claimants, etc) Act 2004, Sch 2, para 30.

[58] ibid, para 30(2).

[59] Letter, n 55 above.

[60] ibid, para 30(4)(a).

[61] ibid, para 30(4)(b).

[62] ibid, para 30(5); this five-day period can be varied by order, see Asylum and Immigration (Treatment of Claimants, etc) Act 2004, s 26(8)(b), where the reference to para 29(5)(b) of Sch 2 to that Act must be understood as a reference to para 30(5)(b).

[63] Asylum and Immigration (Treatment of Claimants, etc) Act 2004, Sch 2, para 30(7).

E. APPEAL TO THE COURT OF APPEAL (IN SCOTLAND, COURT OF SESSION)

An AIT decision on an appeal can reach an appeal court—the Court of Appeal (or, in **7.54** Scotland, Court of Session (Inner House))—in one of three ways:

(a) the first AIT decision on the appeal is made by a panel of three or more AIT members;[64]

(b) the AIT decision appealed is the second or subsequent AIT decision on the appeal, i.e. made after an order for reconsideration by the High Court (in Scotland, Court of Session (Outer House)) or after a remittal by an appeal court;[65]

(c) on an application for review to the High Court (in Scotland, Court of Session (Outer House)), the court referred the appeal to an appeal court:[66] see paras 7.44–7.45 above.

An appeal may only be brought on a point of law.[67]   **7.55**

An appeal may only be made directly from the AIT (rather than arising from an **7.56** application for review) with permission of the AIT or of the appeal court itself.[68] The AIT considers applications for permission on the papers. The appeal court also considers the application on the papers, but if permission is refused the applicant has a right to reconsideration by the appeal court at an oral hearing.

If permission is granted (where required), the appeal court will hold a hearing of **7.57** the appeal (unless the parties otherwise consent). The court has power to:[69]

(a) affirm the AIT decision;

(b) give any decision on the appeal which the AIT could have given;

(c) remit the appeal to the AIT.

Where the appeal came before the appeal court on a reference by a court arising from **7.58** an application for review, the appeal court may order that the application for review be restored before the court which made the reference.[70]

If the appeal court remits the case to the AIT, then any challenge to the AIT's **7.59** decision on remittal would be made by way of appeal back to the appellate court.[71]

Either party to the appeal to the appeal court can petition for leave to appeal to the **7.60** House of Lords on the ground that there is a point of law of general public importance.

---

64 Nationality, Immigration and Asylum Act 2002, s 103E.
65 ibid, s 103B(1)–(2).
66 ibid, s 103C(1).
67 ibid, ss 103B(1), 103C(1) and 103E(2).
68 ibid, ss 103B(3) and 103E(3).
69 ibid, ss 103B(4), 103C(2) and 103E(4).
70 ibid, s 103C(2)(g).
71 ibid, ss 103B(2)(b), 103E(2).

F. JUDICIAL REVIEW

7.61 The possibility of judicial review of AIT decisions remains in three cases:

(a) where the AIT decision is a preliminary, procedural or ancillary one;

(b) where there are grounds for judicial review which cannot be raised on review under s 103A;

(c) where statutory review has been refused (see paras 7.69–7.70 below).

1. Preliminary, procedural and ancillary decisions

7.62 Review and appeal are not available where the AIT decision is a preliminary, procedural or ancillary one.[72]

7.63 It is unclear when decisions will be classified as preliminary. It is suggested that the question will be one of substance, and not of the label attached to it by the AIT. However, the terms of the new scheme do not indicate a clear policy intention about where the courts should draw the line.

7.64 The terms of the new scheme are different from those of Nationality, Immigration and Asylum Act 2002, s 101, but two cases under that section show divergent judicial views on the policy it sought to promote. In *MM (Burundi)*,[73] the Immigration Appeal Tribunal considered what kinds of adjudicator determination could be appealed to that Tribunal under Nationality, Immigration and Asylum Act 2002, s 101(1). The Tribunal held that any determination disposing of an appeal can be further appealed to the Tribunal.[74] The Tribunal considered that Parliament's evident policy was to avoid judicial review and to bring all final decisions of adjudicators within the Tribunal's appellate jurisdiction.[75]

7.65 However, in *R (Erdogan) v Secretary of State for the Home Department*,[76] the Court of Appeal rejected that policy argument in a slightly different context: the correct remedy for a refusal of the Immigration Appeal Tribunal to extend time for permission to appeal to the Tribunal. Reversing Davis J, the Court held that the remedy is judicial review and not 'statutory review' under Nationality, Immigration and Asylum Act 2002, s 101(2).

7.66 Where a decision is classified as preliminary, procedural or ancillary, then judicial review is the correct remedy. Bail is one obvious case of an ancillary decision. If the adjudicator acts unlawfully in refusing (or granting) bail, judicial review is available.

7.67 Where the decision is arguably not preliminary, an application for review or

---

[72] ibid, ss 103A(7)(a), 103E(7)(a).
[73] [2004] UKIAT 182, 7 July 2004, Ouseley P presiding.
[74] ibid at [25]–[30].
[75] ibid at [30].
[76] [2004] EWCA Civ 1087.

appeal can be made, together with a claim for judicial review in an appropriate case. If the court decides that there is no jurisdiction to entertain the application for review or the appeal, then a claim for judicial review should be considered (if not already issued).

2. Power to quash on judicial review

It is suggested above (para 7.29) that statutory review is available where the AIT unwittingly denies justice. If that is wrong and review is confined to 'culpable' errors of law, then judicial review is available in other cases where justice is denied. The 2004 Act does not exclude judicial review of a decision of the AIT. **7.68**

3. Judicial review where review has been refused

The court's decision on review is expressed to be 'final'.[77] **7.69**

The same provision was made for High Court statutory review of decisions of the Immigration Appeal Tribunal on permission to appeal from an adjudicator.[78] However, in *R (G) v Immigration Appeal Tribunal*,[79] Collins J considered two judicial review claims brought on grounds which had failed to persuade judges to grant statutory review of the Immigration Appeal Tribunal. He held that the description of statutory review as 'final' did not oust the court's jurisdiction in judicial review over the Tribunal's decision.[80] He held, however, that statutory review is an alternative remedy and must be pursued, and that it would be an abuse to claim judicial review on grounds which were, or could have been, advanced on statutory review.[81] He refused to consider the judicial review claims on their merits because the grounds were the same as those of the statutory review applications.[82] At the time of writing, the Court of Appeal had not given judgment on the applicants' appeals. **7.70**

G. PUBLIC FUNDING OF REPRESENTATION FOR REVIEW OF AIT AND RECONSIDERATION

The introduction of a new funding regime has also proved controversial. Except with an appeal decided in Scotland,[83] where the High Court has granted review under 2002 Act, s 103A and ordered the AIT to reconsider its decision, the High Court can **7.71**

---

[77] Nationality, Immigration and Asylum Act 2002, s 103A(6).

[78] ibid, s 101(3)(c).

[79] [2004] EWHC 588 (Admin), [2004] 3 All ER 286.

[80] ibid at [10].

[81] ibid at [20].

[82] ibid at [22].

[83] Nationality, Immigration and Asylum Act 2002, s 103D(8), as inserted by Asylum and Immigration (Treatment of Claimants, etc) Act 2004, s 26(6).

direct that the applicant's costs in respect of the application to the High Court for reconsideration be paid out of the Community Legal Service Fund.[84] Similarly, where the AIT reconsiders its decision after such a High Court order, the AIT may also order the appellant's costs be paid out of the Fund in respect of the application for reconsideration (presumably if the High Court has not made such an order already) and/or the actual reconsideration.[85]

7.72   Provided that the Secretary of State consults 'such persons he thinks appropriate',[86] he may make regulations about the exercise of the power of the AIT to order costs to be paid out of the LSC funds[87] and those regulations may specify or determine the amount of payments to be made, the person to whom the payments are to be made, and restrict the exercise of the power.[88]

7.73   The net result of these provisions is that the 2004 Act permits a regime which would amount to, for all practicable purposes, a 'no win, no fee' scheme in applications for High Court review and actual reconsideration by the AIT. The High Court, and more significantly, the AIT, will decide at the end of the application for reconsideration, or the actual reconsideration itself, whether funding is appropriate, presumably having regard not only to the merits of the application but also to the final outcome.

7.74   During the debate on the Bill in the House of Lords, Lord Kingsland, for the Opposition, commented that 'a conditional fee approach is wholly inappropriate in asylum cases', because first 'the outcome in asylum cases is particularly difficult to predict because of the central role credibility plays', secondly 'in a conditional fee system, the client insures himself against losing a case so as to reimburse the solicitor for his expenses in the event of losing' and asylum-seekers will not be in such a position, and, thirdly and 'perhaps the most fundamental objection of all', 'conditional fees are not appropriate to human rights cases, which require, as the judges have repeatedly reminded us in the High Court and above, the most anxious scrutiny'.[89]

7.75   The provisions could have a serious effect on the just determination of appeals because there is a high risk of representatives being deterred from pursuing meritorious applications to the High Court or pursuing the reconsideration after a successful application to the High Court. Prior to the 2004 Act, Government reliance on the availability of 'no win, no fee' arrangements was essentially confined to cases involving pecuniary benefit, most notably those involving personal injury.

7.76   The implicit pressure placed on representatives by this funding regime coupled

---

[84] Nationality, Immigration and Asylum Act 2002, s 103D(1), as inserted by Asylum and Immigration (Treatment of Claimants, etc) Act 2004, s 26(6).

[85] Nationality, Immigration and Asylum Act 2002, s 103D(2) and (3), as inserted by Asylum and Immigration (Treatment of Claimants, etc) Act 2004, s 26(6).

[86] Nationality, Immigration and Asylum Act 2002, s 103D(6).

[87] ibid, s 103D(4).

[88] ibid, s 103D(5).

[89] Lord Kingsland; *Hansard*, HL col 36 (7 June 2004).

with the short time-limit for claiming High Court review of the AIT means that there is serious risk that individuals seeking international protection may not, in practice, have an effective remedy so far as their ECHR rights are concerned as they may have significant difficulty in obtaining representation. As the JCHR put it, 'the effect of the proposed conditional fee legal aid regime for the High Court reviews from the Tribunal will be that meritorious cases do not get brought because of lack of representation'.[90]

H. REMOVAL OF RIGHT OF APPEAL BEFORE REMOVAL IN SOME ENTRY CASES

Under the Nationality, Immigration and Asylum Act 2002, a person refused leave to enter may only appeal before removal from the United Kingdom on asylum, ECHR or EC grounds, or if he has an entry clearance or work permit. **7.77**

Section 28 of the Asylum and Immigration (Treatment of Claimants, etc) Act 2004 withdraws this right of appeal from most work permit holders and some entry clearance holders. Persons affected will only be able to appeal from abroad. **7.78**

1. Work permit holders

Under the new scheme, a person who has a work permit but not an entry clearance only has a right of appeal in the United Kingdom from refusal of leave to enter if he has British nationality (but not the right of abode), i.e. he is a:[91] **7.79**

(a) British overseas territories citizen;
(b) British Overseas citizen;
(c) British National (Overseas);
(d) British protected person;
(e) British subject.

2. Leave to enter granted before arrival

Where a person arrives in the United Kingdom with leave to enter granted before arrival, the immigration officer can cancel leave on the grounds that there has been a change of circumstance; the leave was obtained by deception or non-disclosure; or there are medical grounds for cancellation.[92] Where leave is cancelled, the person is treated as having been refused leave to enter at a time when he had a current entry clearance.[93] **7.80**

---

[90] Thirteenth Report, n 18 above, para 1.87.
[91] See Nationality, Immigration and Asylum Act 2002, s 92(3D).
[92] Immigration Act 1971, Sch 2, para 2A(2).
[93] ibid, Sch 2, para 2A(9).

7.81   Under the new scheme, a person whose leave to enter is cancelled on these grounds has a right of appeal only from abroad.[94]

3. Entry clearance holders

7.82   An immigration officer may refuse leave to enter on the ground that the leave is sought for a purpose other than that specified in the entry clearance. Under the new scheme, a person refused leave to enter on this ground has a right of appeal only from abroad.[95]

I. OTHER CHANGES TO APPEAL SYSTEM

1. Entry clearance: power to remove right of appeal

7.83   Section 13 of the Immigration Act 1971 gave a general right of appeal from a refusal of entry clearance. Subsequent Acts severely reduced the categories of those who could exercise this right.

7.84   Under the Nationality, Immigration and Asylum Act 2002 the right of appeal from a refusal of entry clearance[96] cannot be exercised where the applicant would be in the United Kingdom as:

(a) a visitor (unless the purpose is to visit a family member);[97]

(b) a student on a course of less than six months or one for which the applicant has not yet been accepted.[98]

7.85   The right of appeal is also denied[99] where the ground of refusal is that the requirements of the immigration rules are not met in respect of:

(a) the age, nationality or citizenship of the applicant or dependant;

(b) a passport or work permit;

(c) the period for which leave to enter is sought;

(d) the purpose for which leave to enter is sought.

7.86   The right of appeal on human rights or race discrimination grounds remains in these cases.[100] However, unlike the other rights of appeal, the person refused is not notified of the existence of these rights of appeal unless and until he claims that the decision is unlawful on these grounds.[101]

---

[94] Nationality, Immigration and Asylum Act 2002, s 92(3B).
[95] ibid, s 92(3C).
[96] ibid, s 82(2)(b).
[97] ibid, s 90.
[98] ibid, s 91.
[99] ibid, s 88.
[100] ibid, ss 88(4), 90(4), 91(2).
[101] Immigration (Notices) Regulations 2003, reg 5(6)–(7).

In 2004, the Home Secretary's Independent Monitor of decisions on visitor and **7.87** student applications found 10 per cent of cases (or 10,000 persons) had been wrongly denied a right of appeal.[102]

Section 29 of the 2004 Act inserts a new s 88A into the Nationality, Immigration **7.88** and Asylum Act 2002. This enables the Home Secretary to prescribe that decisions made on other grounds under the Immigration Rules are also not appealable. During the passage of the Bill, the Government said that this power would only be used for grounds 'based on objective criteria' but did not say what these might be.[103]

The right of appeal on human rights or race discrimination grounds will not be **7.89** affected.[104]

The JCHR commented that 'the removal of rights of appeal against entry clear- **7.90** ance decisions raises issues of compatibility with the right to an effective remedy in respect of Convention violations under Article 13 ECHR and the right not to be discriminated against under Article 14 ECHR in conjunction with Article 13 and Article 6(1) (right of access to court)'.[105] The power has been criticized as 'breath-takingly wide' because it gives the Government carte blanche to remove appeal rights in respect of all entry clearance refusals.[106]

2. Right of appeal of certain crew-members of ships and aircraft

A person who comes to the United Kingdom to join the crew of a ship or aircraft, can **7.91** be granted leave to enter limited to requiring that person to leave the United Kingdom in the ship or aircraft concerned.[107] A person who does not leave in that ship or aircraft overstays their leave to enter the United Kingdom and the immigration officer can decide that the person should be removed from the United Kingdom in the vessel concerned.[108]

Section 31 of the 2004 Act provides for a right of appeal to the AIT from a deci- **7.92** sion to remove a person in those circumstances, by inserting a new para (ia) in Nationality, Immigration and Asylum Act 2002, s 82(2).

There remains no right of appeal against a decision to remove: **7.93**

(a) a person who overstays in the circumstances described in para 7.91 above, but whose removal is to take place in some other vessel;[109]

---

[102] Report by the Independent Monitor, Fiona Lindsley, June 2004.
[103] Lord Rooker; *Hansard*, HL col 708 (15 June 2004).
[104] Nationality, Immigration and Asylum Act 2002, s 88A(2)(a).
[105] Fourteenth Report of Session 2003–04 (HL Paper 130, HC Paper 828) para 79.
[106] Immigration Law Practitioners Association, Briefing, 15 June 2004. See also Fourteenth Report, n 105 above, para 80.
[107] Immigration Act 1971, Sch 2, para 12(1).
[108] ibid, Sch 2, para 12(2).
[109] ibid, Sch 2, para 14.

(b) a person who arrived as a member of a crew and who was given leave to enter on condition that he leaves with the vessel, or for the duration of medical treatment, and has overstayed that leave.[110]

There is no clear rationale for providing a right of appeal in the first case and not in the other two.

3. Certification of repeat appeals

7.94 Section 96 of the Nationality, Immigration and Asylum Act 2002 has also been amended by s 30 of the 2004 Act, with the intention of clarifying and simplifying procedure. Prior to the 2004 Act, s 96 allowed the Secretary of State, by means of certification, to remove the right of appeal in circumstances where, 'in the opinion of the Secretary of State or the immigration officer' a claim raised in circumstances where that claim could have been raised at an earlier stage in an earlier appeal or in a 'one stop notice' issued prior to the new claim being raised.

7.95 Before the Secretary of State could lawfully certify under s 96(1) of the 2002 Act he had to (rationally) conclude that the new claim or application had been raised 'in order to delay . . . removal from the United Kingdom'[111] and there was 'no other legitimate purpose for making the claim or application'.[112] Similarly, the Secretary of State could only certify a claim not raised in an earlier 'one stop notice' if the claim 'should have' been included in the notice.

7.96 The new s 96 simplifies the position. It removes the 'no other legitimate purpose' aspect of the pre-amendment s 96, and precludes the Secretary of State from certifying under s 96 unless 'in the opinion of the Secretary of State or the immigration officer, there is no satisfactory reason for that matter not having been raised' either in the earlier appeal or in the one stop notice statement.

---

[110] ibid, Sch 2, para 13(2).

[111] Nationality, Immigration and Asylum Act 2002, s 96(1)(b) prior to amendment by the Asylum and Immigration (Treatment of Claimants, etc) Act 2004, s 30(2).

[112] Nationality, Immigration and Asylum Act 2002, s 96(1)(c) prior to amendment by the Asylum and Immigration (Treatment of Claimants, etc) Act 2004, s 30(2).

8

UNFOUNDED CLAIMS
(SECTION 27)

A. The present law	8.02
B. The new law: removal of the accession states	8.20
C. The new law: extension of the power to designate	8.21
D. Quality of Home Office assessments of countries of origin	8.39
E. Other provisions	8.45

Section 27 of the Asylum and Immigration (Treatment of Claimants, etc) Act 2004 **8.01** amends s 94 of the Nationality, Immigration and Asylum Act 2002 with the aim of extending the Secretary of State's power to certify claims as 'clearly unfounded' and so deny in-country rights of appeal. This chapter sets out the current law relating to 'clearly unfounded' certificates then considers the amendments to s 94 and the extent to which the power (and duty) to certify has been extended. References to the new law are given in terms of the amended s 94 of the 2002 Act.

A. THE PRESENT LAW

The effect of a 'clearly unfounded' certificate under s 94 of the 2002 Act is that the **8.02** claimant is denied any in-country appeal before being expelled to his country of origin. He may bring an appeal from his home country but the Court of Appeal noted in *R (L) v Secretary of State for the Home Department*[1] that this is 'scant consolation' when he has already been removed to the country where he fears persecution and human rights abuses.

The only means of preventing the Secretary of State removing the claimant with- **8.03** out an effective appeal on the merits is to judicially review the certificate. If the claimant is from a designated country, the Home Office is required by s 93(3) to issue a certificate if the claim is clearly unfounded. For other countries, the Secretary of State has a discretion whether or not to certify a claim that is clearly unfounded.

---

[1] [2003] EWCA Civ 25, [2003] 1 WLR 1230.

8.04   Section 94(4) originally designated only the EU accession countries: Cyprus, Czech Republic, Estonia, Hungary, Latvia, Lithuania, Malta, Poland, Slovak Republic, and Slovenia. Section 94(5) provides that:

> (5) The Secretary of State may by order add a State, or part of a State, to the list in subsection (4) if satisfied that—
>
> > (a) there is in general in that State or part no serious risk of persecution of persons enti-tled to reside in that State or part, and
> >
> > (b) removal to that State or part of persons entitled to reside there will not in general contravene the United Kingdom's obligations under the Human Rights Convention.

8.05   The following additional countries have been designated: Albania, Bulgaria, Serbia and Montenegro, Jamaica, Macedonia, Moldova, and Romania;[2] Brazil, Ecuador, Bolivia, South Africa, Ukraine, Sri Lanka and Bangladesh.[3]

8.06   In *L*, the Court of Appeal held that the threshold test for determining whether a claim is clearly unfounded should be applied in the same way whether or not the country is designated:

> Assuming that decision-makers—who are ordinarily at the level of executive officers—are sensible individuals but not trained logicians, there is no intelligible way of applying [the 'clearly unfounded' test to a claim from a designated state] except by a similar process of inquiry and reasoning to [a claim from a non-designated state]. In order to decide whether they are satisfied that the claim is not clearly unfounded, they will need to consider the same ques-tions. If on at least one legitimate view of the facts or the law the claim may succeed, the claim will not be clearly unfounded. If that point is reached, the decision-maker cannot conclude otherwise. He will by definition be satisfied that the claim is not clearly unfounded . . .[4]

8.07   That was confirmed by *Bagdanavicius v Secretary of State for the Home Department*,[5] Auld LJ noting that the 'rather bumpy structure' of the certification provisions:

> might suggest a different approach to certification according to whether the Secretary of State is exercising the power to certify . . . or the significantly qualified duty to do so . . . However, as Lord Phillips, giving the judgment of this Court in [*L*] has indicated at paras 57 and 58, the threshold for certification in each case is much the same, namely, that if the claim cannot on any legitimate view succeed, it is clearly unfounded.

8.08   The test for certifying a human rights claim as 'clearly unfounded' pursuant to ss 93 and 94 of the 2002 Act is no different from the test for certifying a third country human rights claim as 'manifestly unfounded' under s 72(2) of the 1999 Act. The authorities interpreting the earlier phrase therefore also govern the meaning of 'clearly unfounded'.[6]

---

[2]   Asylum (Designated States) Order 2003 SI 2003/970.

[3]   Asylum (Designated States) (No 2) Order 2003 SI 2003/1919.

[4]   [2003] EWCA Civ 25, [2003] 1 WLR 1230 at [58].

[5]   [2003] EWCA Civ 1605, [2004] 1 WLR 1207.

[6]   *R (Kurtolli) v Secretary of State for the Home Department* [2003] EWHC 2744 (Admin), [2004] INLR 198 at [11]; *Bagdanavicius v Secretary of State for the Home Department* [2003] EWCA Civ 1605, [2004] 1 WLR 1207 at [58].

In *R (Razgar) v Secretary of State for the Home Department*,[7] the Court of Appeal **8.09** said that:

[28] As the House of Lords explained in *R (Yogathas) v Secretary of State for the Home Department*; *R (Thangarasa) v Secretary of State for the Home Department* [2002] UKHL 36, [2003] 1 AC 920, the Secretary of State is entitled to certify a claim as manifestly unfounded if, after carefully considering the allegation, the grounds on which it is made and any material relied on in support of it, 'he is reasonably and conscientiously satisfied that the allegation must clearly fail' (Lord Bingham of Cornhill, at para [14]) or the allegation is 'so clearly without substance that the appeal [to the adjudicator] would be bound to fail' (Lord Hope of Craighead, at para [34]), or 'it is plain that there is nothing of substance in the allegation' (Lord Hutton, at para [72]). Lord Millett and Lord Scott of Foscote agreed with the reasoning of Lord Bingham of Cornhill, Lord Hope of Craighead and Lord Hutton. ... The test to be applied by the Secretary of State in certifying a claim as 'manifestly unfounded' is a 'screening process' rather than a 'full blown merits review' (at paras [14] and [34]) . . .[8]

[30] ... There is no difference between the various formulations suggested by their Lordships.

The Court emphasized the 'very high threshold' that had to be met before a claim **8.10** could be certified, explaining that:

The Secretary of State cannot lawfully issue such a certificate unless the claim is bound to fail before an adjudicator. It is not sufficient that he considers that the claim is likely to fail on appeal, *or even that it is very likely to fail*. Moreover, as the House of Lords explained in *Yogathas*,[9] the court will subject the decision of the Secretary of State to the most anxious scrutiny.[10] (emphasis added)

The House of Lords' dismissal of the Secretary of State's appeal in *Razgar*[11] further **8.11** emphasized the high threshold required for certification as clearly unfounded. Lord Carswell stated that while there were strong indicators in favour of the Secretary of State, 'I could not be fully satisfied, however, that the case is so clear in favour of upholding the decision to remove the respondent that no reasonable adjudicator could hold otherwise'.[12]

In *L*, the Court of Appeal concluded that a decision on whether a claim is clearly **8.12** unfounded 'is one which the court is as well placed as the Home Secretary to take, and we go on to review the evidence in that light'.[13] The Court further stated that:

... the test is an objective one: it depends not on the Home Secretary's view but upon a criterion which a court can readily re-apply once it has the materials which the Home Secretary

---

7 [2003] EWCA Civ 840, [2003] Imm AR 529 at [28] and [30].
8 See also [2004] UKHL 27, [2004] 3 WLR 58 at [16] *per* Lord Bingham.
9 [2002] UKHL 36, [2003] 1 AC 920.
10 [2003] EWCA Civ 840, [2003] Imm AR 529 at [111].
11 [2004] UKHL 27, [2004] 3 WLR 58.
12 ibid at [77].
13 [2003] EWCA Civ 25, [2003] 1 WLR 1230 at [29].

had. A claim is either clearly unfounded or it is not . . . If . . . the claim cannot on any legitimate view succeed, then the claim is clearly unfounded; if not, not.[14]

8.13 In *Atkinson v Secretary of State for the Home Department*,[15] Scott Baker LJ stated:

44. There is a further point that requires clarification. Essentially this court has to consider the correctness of the judge's decision when reviewing the Secretary of State's certification. The judge had to decide whether the certification was lawful. He decided that it was. The judge decided that the appellant's claim in respect of Article 3 could not on any legitimate view succeed and that it was therefore clearly unfounded. In the course of argument we asked Mr Fordham about the judge's finding at paragraph 30 that he, like the Secretary of State, was satisfied that the claims were clearly unfounded. Did the judge have to stand in the shoes of the Secretary of State and ask himself whether this was a view to which the Secretary of State was entitled to come, albeit he himself might not have come to the same conclusion, or was it up to the judge to look at the matter afresh and form his own view? Mr Fordham told us that for the purposes of the present case he was prepared to proceed on the latter basis. He referred us to *Bagdanavicius* at para 58 where Auld L.J said:

'The question is a narrow one and the threshold for certification is high; see *Razgar* [2003] Imm AR 529, per Dyson L.J giving the judgment of the court, at para 111. It is one in which the courts, when they have the same material as that put before the Secretary of State, are in as good a position to determine as he is.'

Whilst we have not heard argument on the point, I consider that the speech of Lord Bingham of Cornhill in *Razgar* [2004] UKHL 27 (see paras 16,17) confirms that Mr Fordham was right to make this concession. The judge had to ask himself how an appeal to an adjudicator would be likely to fare.

45. Accordingly, as it seems to me, it is necessary to ask whether in the light of all the present information the appellant's Article 3 claim was bound to fail. More specifically, was the appellant's contention that the Jamaican State was unwilling or unable to provide him with sufficiency of protection bound to fail or could the claim on a legitimate view succeed?[16]

8.14 The fact that the court is as well placed to apply, and therefore does apply the 'clearly unfounded' test for itself means that it will consider evidence that post-dates the certificate and has not been considered by the Secretary of State. The Court of Appeal concluded in *L* that the fast-track procedure was fair in the context of what the claimant must do to avoid certification:

We would emphasise once again that the object of the fast-track procedure is to give applicants the chance to demonstrate that they have, or may have, an arguable case. [17]

8.15 The Court noted that:

. . . in some cases medical evidence will be required to support a protection claim and that, in such circumstances, it is likely to prove impossible to bring a suitably qualified medical expert

---

[14] [2003] EWCA Civ 25, [2003] 1 WLR 1230 at [56] and [57].
[15] [2004] EWCA Civ 846.
[16] ibid at [44]–[45].
[17] [2003] EWCA Civ 25, [2003] 1 WLR 1230 at [51].

onto the site in the time available. In such cases, and in analogous cases, we would expect it to be recognised that the fast-track procedure is not appropriate and the decision deferred. [18]

It also stated that: **8.16**

in a case where the authenticity of documents remains in doubt and the issue of their authenticity is critical, we do not see how a claim can properly be declared clearly unfounded. [19]

As to country expert evidence, the Court of Appeal accepted that it would not be **8.17** possible for a claimant himself to obtain and adduce expert evidence in the time permitted by the fast-track process. However, it was influenced by the fact that representation from the Refugee Legal Centre (RLC) and Immigration Advisory Service (IAS) is available on-site during the fast-track process at Oakington and that these organizations collate expert evidence as an 'ongoing process' and it is not simply driven by individual applications.[20] Different considerations may apply to claims certified outside the Oakington procedure.

It will not ordinarily be possible for the Home Office to say that an adjudicator **8.18** would be bound to reach one credibility finding or another after hearing oral evidence. The Court of Appeal pointed out, in response to concerns about the time required to obtain expert evidence on country conditions, that:

The individual's own experience may raise a question as to whether, at least in the part of the country from which he has come, persecution is occurring . . . In such a case the applicant's claim will not be clearly unfounded and the claim should not be certified.[21]

As well as the individual assessment of whether the claim is 'clearly unfounded', the **8.19** designation of a country may be challenged by judicial review on the ground that the criteria in s 94(5) are not satisfied. This is discussed further at paras 8.24 et seq below.

B. THE NEW LAW: REMOVAL OF THE ACCESSION STATES

Section 27(4) removes the accession countries from the list of designated states for **8.20** the purposes of s 94. This was described to Parliament as a 'regularisation and tidying-up exercise, because from 1 May [2004], nationals of the 10 states will benefit from free movement rights under European law. Individuals from those countries are unlikely to apply for asylum after 1 May, given that they would gain no extra benefit to that to which they are already entitled under EU law.'[22] (This is, of course, not necessarily true since entitlement to benefits may be inferior for refugees relying upon EU law.)

---

[18] ibid at [49].
[19] ibid at [50].
[20] ibid at [48]–[51].
[21] ibid at [51].
[22] Statement of Minister for Immigration, Beverley Hughes, HC Standing Committee B, col 338 (22 January 2004).

C. THE NEW LAW: EXTENSION OF THE POWER TO DESIGNATE

8.21 The current s 94 provides a power to designate only countries or parts of countries that are generally free from persecution and relevant human rights abuses. They must be designated for all claimants from these areas or for none. The intention of the amendment is to enable the Secretary of State to designate countries or parts thereof as safe for particular categories of claimant even though they are accepted to be unsafe for other categories.

8.22 The list of categories includes five that reflect the five Refugee Convention reasons, together with gender, language, and a catch-all, 'any other attribute or circumstance that the Secretary of State thinks appropriate'. The Minister told the Commons Standing Committee that:

> We have listed seven specific examples of the circumstances and attributes that we think most likely to be relevant. We expect to use the provision in relation to those seven examples. The list may not be exhaustive, and it is not easy to give now the sort of situations that we have in mind. For example, factors such as age, employment status and shared history may be relevant in some countries and may not necessarily be caught by the other listed examples. In seeking assurances about the way in which we shall operate, the Committee must remember that every claim will be considered on its merits . . . We shall continue to use [the system] in a way that identifies people who do not fall into the category that we are discussing and that gives us the flexibility to ensure that we have an efficient system and can return people whose claims are not well founded.[23]

8.23 MPs complained that they were being asked to sign a 'blank cheque' in relation to the 'catch-all' category. It may be possible to challenge whether the criteria used to describe a category of claimant designated by the Secretary of State fall within the type of 'descriptions' that Parliament envisaged the provision might encompass.

8.24 The designation of a particular category of claimants may also be challenged (in the same way as the designation of the country, or part thereof) on the ground that the Secretary of State was unjustified in concluding that the criteria in s 94(5) were satisfied in respect of that particular category of claimant.

8.25 The approach the courts will take to challenges to designation (as opposed to challenges to the certificate itself) under the 2002 Act has yet to be clarified. At the time of writing, no challenge to designation under the 2002 Act has been considered beyond the permission stage, and no substantial consideration has been given to the test to be applied.

8.26 Under earlier and different 'White List' provisions in the 1996 Act, the Court of Appeal held that the Secretary of State's designation of Pakistan as a country in which there was 'in general no serious risk of persecution' was irrational in light of the evidence of the risk of persecution to women and Ahmadis: *R (Asif Javed) v*

---

[23] Statement of Minister for Immigration, Beverley Hughes, HC Standing Committee B, col 336 (22 January 2004).

Secretary of State for the Home Department.[24] The Secretary of State's argument that the designation of a country as 'safe' was not ordinarily susceptible to judicial review since it required approval by Parliament was rejected by the Court. The Court also, however, declined the claimants' invitation to apply the heightened level of scrutiny demanded where fundamental human rights are at stake. Its approach in this regard was based upon the fact that certification under the 1996 Act had limited procedural consequences.

On the one hand, certification is now a far more serious matter under the 2002 **8.27** Act than it was under the 1996 Act because it precludes any appeal on the merits prior to removal. On the other hand, unlike the 'White List' produced by the 1996 Act, designation does not have the legal effect of determining whether a claim will be certified or not if it is refused. The test for certification is the same whether or not the country has been designated: either way, the Secretary of State must show that the appeal is bound to fail.

However, while designation determines as a matter of law simply whether the **8.28** Secretary of State has a duty to certify a claim which is in any event bound to fail, the practical effect of designation is far more significant. Experience suggests that the Secretary of State certifies nearly all claims that he refuses from designated states, whereas he certifies virtually no claims from non-designated states. This creates grave dangers for claimants, particularly those without the expert legal representation required to bring emergency judicial review proceedings to prevent removal before an appeal is heard.

In *R (Gibson) v Secretary of State for the Home Department,*[25] Stanley Burnton J **8.29** considered an application for permission to bring a judicial review claim challenging the designation of Jamaica under s 94. He considered that: 'On the basis of the material reviewed in [the Court of Appeal's decision in *A v Secretary of State for the Home Department*[26]], there was a strong argument that Jamaica's inclusion on the White List was inappropriate'. He nevertheless accepted that the Secretary of State had answered these concerns in his Country Information and Policy Unit's 'April 2003 Country Assessment' of Jamaica to the extent that the designation was both rational and the judge agreed with it. (See paras 8.39–8.45 below for concerns about the accuracy of the Secretary of State's 'country assessments' that form the basis of designation under s 94.)

In the more recent Court of Appeal decision of *Atkinson,* however, also address- **8.30** ing a 'clearly unfounded' certificate from Jamaica, Scott Baker LJ said that:

We were referred briefly to *R (Gibson) v Secretary of State for the Home Department* [2003] EWHC 1919 Admin . . . where leave to apply for judicial review of the Secretary of State's decision to include Jamaica on the 'white list' (that is those countries included in section 94(4) of the 2002 Act to which removal would not in general involve a serious risk of persecution or

---

[24] [2001] EWCA Civ 789, [2002] QB 129.
[25] [2003] EWHC 1919 Admin.
[26] [2003] EWCA Civ 175, [2003] INLR 249.

breach of human rights) . . . was refused. The court in that case does not, however, appear to have been invited to consider any expert evidence.[27]

8.31 The designation of Jamaica was not specifically challenged in *Atkinson*, simply the certificate. But as is commonly the case, the certificate was based primarily on a generalized proposition that claims of this sort were clearly unfounded because the Jamaican authorities provided a sufficiency of protection to its citizens, including perceived informers. (The Secretary of State necessarily bases his certificates on such generalizations as it is usually not possible to say that an adjudicator would be bound to reach a particular view on factual disputes individual to the case.)

8.32 Scott Baker LJ noted that:

> In the present case, therefore, the question is whether the state of Jamaica is both willing and able to provide reasonable protection to the appellant. The evidence does not raise any real doubt about willingness to provide such protection: the real focus is on its ability to do so. The difficult question is where to draw the line that defines what is an appropriate standard. It is not enough that some individuals will be failed by the state's criminal justice system, not enough that the state has not been effective in removing risk. There has in my judgment to be a systemic failure that relates at the very least to a category of persons of whom the individual under consideration is one. In this case the focus is on informers or perceived informers or those who in some way are the target of the gangs or the dons who head them. In my view it is no answer that a state is doing its incompetent best if it nevertheless falls below the appropriate standard. One has to ask whether the state is failing to perform its basic function of protecting its citizens. Does the writ of law run or not?[28]

8.33 Scott Baker LJ concluded in light of the expert evidence challenging the Secretary of State's country assessment that on at least one legitimate view, it does not. The other members of the Court agreed. On the basis of the 'clearly unfounded' test and the court's obligation to apply the test for itself, the fact that an adjudicator would not be bound to agree with the Secretary of State on sufficiency of protection rendered the certificate unlawful.

8.34 It is notable that Scott Baker LJ's comments on *Gibson* gave no hint that he considered that the failure of the designation challenge in *Gibson* was based on the application of a different standard of review from that which applied to the certification challenge in *Atkinson*. On the contrary, he distinguished *Gibson* on the basis that the judge in that case did not have the benefit of expert evidence contradicting the Secretary of State's country information.

8.35 It is theoretically possible to apply quite different approaches on judicial review to challenges to designation and challenges to the 'clearly unfounded' certificate. The utility of doing so is however doubtful. If the Court of Appeal has made clear that there is adequate evidence for an adjudicator to disagree with the Secretary of State's assessment of sufficiency of protection for an important category of

---

[27] [2004] EWCA Civ 846 at [29].
[28] ibid at [22].

claimants (as *Atkinson* did)—and both the designation and most certificates are based on a claim that there is a sufficiency of protection—there is little purpose in applying a less intrusive standard of review to designation so as to permit the Secretary of State to designate a country where the basis for a large proportion of his certificates is flawed.

There is the additional question of whether the claimant falls within the desig-   **8.36** nated category. The statutory wording refers to certifying the claim 'only if the Secretary of State is satisfied that he is within that description (as well as being satisfied that he is entitled to reside in the State or part)'. Once again, it may be argued that by analogy to the approach established by *L* to reviewing the question of whether the claim is clearly unfounded—and in light of the fact that the court is in as good a position as the Secretary of State to assess such matters—the courts should approach the question either as one of precedent fact or by asking whether an adjudicator would be bound to agree with the Secretary of State.

The Secretary of State will always have to establish that an adjudicator would be   **8.37** bound to dismiss the appeal, even if different tests are held to apply to judicial review challenges relating to designation, membership of the designated category and the clearly unfounded test. It could then be the case that the Secretary of State's designation is lawful in the sense that it is not irrational, that he has lawfully concluded that the claimant falls within the designated category, but that his certificate is nevertheless unlawful because an adjudicator could reasonably find one of the following:

(a) members of the designated category were at risk (despite the Secretary of State having reasonably concluded that they were not);

(b) the claimant did not fall within the designated category (despite the Secretary of State having lawfully concluded that he did) but instead fell within a different category that was at risk;

(c) while the claimant fell within the designated category and that category was not generally at risk, the claimant was at risk based either on particular circumstances relating to his membership of the designated category, or on factors unconnected to his membership of the designated category.

The power to designate a state in respect only of a particular category of claimant   **8.38** may be significant when a court is asked to consider the justification for the designation of that state for *all* claimants. In respect of states already designated for all claimants, the Secretary of State is given a new power[29] to remove the designation for certain categories of claimant for whom the country is not safe, but retain it for other categories for whom it remains safe. His refusal to comply with a request to do so would be susceptible to judicial review.

---

[29] Nationality, Immigration and Asylum Act 2002, s 94(6)(b).

D. QUALITY OF HOME OFFICE ASSESSMENTS OF
COUNTRIES OF ORIGIN

8.39 The different approaches to sufficiency of protection in *Gibson* and *Atkinson* high-light the importance in s 94 challenges of disputes about the accuracy of the Secretary of State's country information. The fact that the Secretary of State and the courts will now be called upon to assess the safety of categories of claimants from countries which (it is agreed) are not generally safe is hardly likely to diminish the significance of the manner in which the Secretary of State collates and presents such information.

8.40 During the passage of the 2004 Act, the Opposition expressed concern about how the Secretary of State would operate his new power to designate categories of claimants as safe, and in particular about the safety of his own country information upon which he would exercise this power. The Minister assured MPs that:

> Clearly, the way in which we make judgments about safety on those criteria is very important. I am grateful for the comments about improvements in the quality of country information. There is further to go, which is why we have set up the advisory panel. When I was concerned about some cases that crossed my desk I asked for the country information. I had fairly recently assumed responsibility for this policy area and, given what had been said about country information, I was surprised at the detail and depth of the package that I received from the website. It was the package used by caseworkers and contained a wealth of information drawn from a variety of independent sources across the world.[30]

8.41 Concerns had been raised in Parliament about the controversial nature of the countries which had already been designated as 'safe' under s 94 for all claimants and especially about the fact that such states had been designated before the statutory Advisory Panel on Country Information (APCI) had been established.

8.42 The Secretary of State was required to establish the APCI pursuant to s 142 of the 2002 Act. This provision was introduced into that Act in response to criticisms of the quality of the country information upon which the Secretary of State would exercise his powers under s 94. Moving the new clause in the House of Lords, the Home Office Minister said that: 'I believe that the establishment of an independent panel of external people to provide scrutiny and oversight of the quality and content of the biannual country assessments should help to overcome any adverse perception of [the Home Office CIPU] that is held by some external stakeholders'.[31] However, the same Minister subsequently had to give an 'apology' to Parliament for the 'impression' both Houses had been given that the advice of the Panel would be sought before the Secretary of State designated any further states under s 94—whereas, in fact, he designated more states before the APCI was even formed.[32] He was compelled to express further regret three months later in the face of vigorous parliamentary

---

[30] HC Standing Committee B, col 334 (22 January 2004).

[31] *Hansard*, HL col 414 (31 October 2002).

[32] *Hansard*, HL col 1117 (31 March 2003).

concern that he was designating yet more states while still having failed to fulfil the commitment to establish the APCI. The Minister assured the House of Lords on that occasion that the APCI 'needs to be [established], because that is part of an informed process as to whether we are making fair judgments as a government on those countries and that process'.[33] Following the first meeting of the APCI in September 2003, another Home Office Minister was reported as announcing that '[t]he Country Information Advisory Panel will play a valuable role in helping us to ensure the information we provide and use in the asylum process meets the very highest standards . . . We are satisfied that our country information material is accurate and impartial. But we believe that it can only be enhanced by the additional input of independent expert advice.'[34]

The APCI recently produced its first report on a country designated as a safe country of origin, Sri Lanka. The summary findings of the report include the following: **8.43**

. . . the [CIPU] Report does not adequately represent the rather complicated human rights situation in Sri Lanka. This is mainly due to the fact that it glosses over many facts and events, often abbreviating them in a manner which suggests across-the-board improvements where a more cautious assessment would have been appropriate. This results in a rather one-sidedly optimistic view of Sri Lanka as a 'safe' country—a view which is not supported by other sources, sometimes including those used by the Home Office IND in the drafting of this report.

It has to be acknowledged that the overall quality of this specific Country Report has increased when compared to its previous editions, probably in large part due to the criticism voiced by organisations such as the Immigration Advisory Service (IAS) and others before.

Nonetheless, these improvements lack the necessary consistency. Hence, the representation of the facts is still sometimes unbalanced, thus questioning the reliability of the author(s)' assessment on the whole. The following factors contribute to this impression:

Selective quoting: On many occasions, the Report uses the sources it draws on very selectively, emphasising positive developments in the human rights situation, while omitting any comments which could be interpreted as casting doubts on these improvements . . .

Use of outdated source material: Some paragraphs show a lack of interest in following up stories and cases which occurred some time, sometimes years, ago. Combined with ignoring alternative source material which alleges the persistence of problems in the reported area, this creates a partial picture of events.

Lack of analytical substance: On too many occasions, developments are simply reported without inquiring into their consequences for the actual situation on the ground. While the Report is good at tracking certain legal changes and official statements, it is often implied that improvements will follow; but no additional evidence is given, and adverse information is sometimes ignored . . .

Reliance on government sources: Too often, information is gleaned exclusively from government sources, including the Home Office's own fact-finding missions, which show themselves to be content with receiving official reassurances and take these at face value.

---

[33] *Hansard*, HL col 1213 (4 July 2003).
[34] Beverley Hughes, quoted in The Source Public Management Journal, 17 September 2003 (www.sourceuk.net/indexf.html?03851).

Misrepresentation of the sequence of events: Some paragraphs reverse the chronology of events by citing positive news which in reality occurred at an earlier date and has been superseded or qualified by the other source quoted in the same paragraph; even if not intentional, . . . this seriously undermines the credibility of the account given.

Partial reporting: . . . .

Citation problems: The Report is beset by problems relating to the citation system used, which lacks both clarity and consistency . . .[35]

8.44 The Chair of the APCI has stated that in the Sir Lanka assessment

the overwhelming majority of errors seemed to lead to an overly optimistic picture about Sri Lanka. This suggested that the errors may not be completely random, and that some other factors may be at work . . . [O]n the basis of this evaluation . . ., it seemed that the Sri Lanka Report did not provide a sufficient basis to say with confidence that Sri Lanka was a safe country . . .[36]

E. OTHER PROVISIONS

8.45 Section 27(2) of the 2004 Act inserts a new s 94(1A) in the 2002 Act. This relates to a Secretary of State's certificate of an asylum/human rights claim as clearly unfounded. Such a certificate denies the right of suspensive appeal from an immigration decision revoking, varying or refusing to vary leave to enter or remain or refusing a certificate of entitlement of the right of abode. It seems that such a certificate also prevents appeal on other grounds, such as under the Immigration Rules regardless of the merits of those grounds.

8.46 Section 27(3) of the 2004 Act amends s 94(2) of the 2002 Act so that certification of a claim does not affect the right of appeal of an EEA national or family member of such a national where a ground of appeal is that the decision breaches the appellant's EC law rights. In such a case the person has a suspensive right of appeal on that and any other grounds raised.

8.47 Section 27(7) of the 2004 Act inserts a new s 94(6A) which provides that in the case of a person subject to extradition proceedings there is no s 94(3) duty to certify the claim as clearly unfounded. The power under s 94(2) to certify a claim is unaffected.[37]

8.48 Section 27(8) of the 2004 Act inserts a new s 112(5A) in the 2002 Act so that, where a particular statutory instrument makes provision under both s 94(5) and (6) of the 2002 Act, only the positive resolution procedure applies to its approval by Parliament.

---

[35] APCI.2.3 (www.apci.org.uk/PDF/APCI_2_3.pdf).
[36] Minutes of APCI meeting of 2 March 2004, paras 4.4, 4.9, 4.10 (www.apci.org.uk/PDF/APCI_2_minutes.pdf).
[37] Contrary to the Explanatory Notes to the 2004 Act, para 131.

9

THIRD COUNTRY REMOVALS
(SECTION 33 AND SCHEDULE 3)

A. The present law	9.02
B. The new provisions: the structure of Sch 3	9.12
C. The deeming provisions	9.14
D. Scope of human rights deeming provision	9.24
E. ECHR compatibility of human rights deeming provision	9.29
F. Amendment of lists of safe third countries	9.40
G. Introduction of duty to certify clearly unfounded claims	9.52

Section 33 of and Sch 3 to the Asylum and Immigration (Treatment of Claimants, **9.01** etc) Act 2004 now contain all the 'safe third country' provisions which were previously dispersed between the 1999 and 2002 Acts (as amended by secondary legislation). This chapter starts by noting the present law. It then explains the new scheme being introduced by Sch 3, and compares it to the present provisions. It concludes by examining the correlation between Sch 3 and the Asylum Procedures Directive.

A. THE PRESENT LAW

The primary legislative provisions dealing with third country cases are as follows. **9.02**

Section 11 of the Immigration and Asylum Act 1999 (as amended by s 80 of the **9.03** Nationality, Immigration and Asylum Act 2002) provides:

(1) In determining whether a person in relation to whom a certificate has been issued under subsection (2) may be removed from the United Kingdom, a member State is to be regarded as—

(a) a place where a person's life and liberty is not threatened by reason of his race, religion, nationality, membership of a particular social group, or political opinion; and

(b) a place from which a person will not be sent to another country otherwise than in accordance with the Refugee Convention.

(2) Nothing in section 77 of the Nationality, Immigration and Asylum Act 2002 prevents a person who has made a claim for asylum ('the claimant') from being removed from the United Kingdom to a member State if the Secretary of State has certified that—

    (a) the member State has accepted that, under standing arrangements, it is the responsible State in relation to the claimant's claim for asylum; and

    (b) in his opinion, the claimant is not a national or citizen of the member State to which he is to be sent.

(3) Subsection (4) applies where a person who is the subject of a certificate under subsection (2)—

    (a) has instituted or could institute an appeal under section 82(1) of the Nationality, Immigration and Asylum Act 2002 (immigration appeal), and

    (b) has made a human rights claim (within the meaning of section 113 of that Act).

(4) The person may not be removed from the United Kingdom in reliance upon this section unless—

    (a) the appeal is finally determined, withdrawn or abandoned (within the meaning of section 104 of that Act) or can no longer be brought (ignoring any possibility of an appeal out of time with permission), or

    (b) the Secretary of State has issued a certificate in relation to the human rights claim under section 93(2)(b) of that Act (clearly unfounded claim).

(5) In this section 'standing arrangements' means arrangements in force between two or more member States for determining which State is responsible for considering applications for asylum.

9.04 Section 12, as amended by the Nationality, Immigration and Asylum Act 2002 (Consequential and Incidental Provisions) Order 2003,[1] provides that:

12. (1) Subsection (2) applies if the Secretary of State intends to remove a person who has made a claim for asylum ('the claimant') from the United Kingdom to—

    (a) a member State, or a territory which forms part of a member State, otherwise than under standing arrangements; or

    (b) a country other than a member State which is designated by order made by the Secretary of State for the purposes of this section.

(2) Nothing in section 77 of the Nationality, Immigration and Asylum Act 2002 prevents the claimant's removal if—

    (a) the Secretary of State has certified that, in his opinion, the conditions set out in subsection (7) are fulfilled . . .

(4) Subsection (5) applies if the Secretary of State intends to remove a person who has made a claim for asylum ('the claimant') from the United Kingdom to a country which is not—

    (a) a member State; or

    (b) a country designated under subsection (1)(b).

(5) Nothing in section 77 of that Act prevents the claimant's removal if—

    (a) the Secretary of State has certified that, in his opinion, the conditions set out in subsection (7) are fulfilled . . .

(6) For the purposes of subsection (5)(c), an appeal under section 65 is not to be regarded as pending if the Secretary of State has issued a certificate under section 72(2)(a) in relation to the allegation on which it is founded.

---

[1] SI 2003/1016.

(7) The conditions are that—
    (a) he is not a national or citizen of the country to which he is to be sent;
    (b) his life and liberty would not be threatened there by reason of his race, religion, nationality, membership of a particular social group, or political opinion; and
    (c) the government of that country would not send him to another country otherwise than in accordance with the Refugee Convention.

(7A) Subsection (7B) applies where a person who is the subject of a certificate under subsection (2) or (5)—
    (a) has instituted or could institute an appeal under section 82(1) of the Nationality, Immigration and Asylum Act 2002 (immigration appeal), and
    (b) has made a human rights claim (within the meaning of section 113 of that Act).

(7B) The person may not be removed from the United Kingdom in reliance upon this section unless—
    (a) the appeal is finally determined, withdrawn or abandoned (within the meaning of section 104 of that Act) or can no longer be brought (ignoring any possibility of an appeal out of time with permission), or
    (b) the Secretary of State has issued a certificate in relation to the human rights claim under section 93(2)(b) of that Act (clearly unfounded claim).

(8) 'Standing arrangements' has the same meaning as in section 11.

9.05 Section 82(1) of the Nationality, Immigration and Asylum Act 2002 provides that: 'Where an immigration decision is made in respect of a person he may appeal to an adjudicator'.

9.06 Section 93 of the 2002 Act provides that:

(1) A person may not appeal under section 82(1) while he is in the United Kingdom if a certificate has been issued in relation to him under section 11(2) or 12(2) of the Immigration and Asylum Act 1999 (c.33) (removal of asylum claimants to 'third country').
(2) But subsection (1) does not apply to an appeal if—
    (a) the appellant has made a human rights claim, and
    (b) the Secretary of State has not certified that in his opinion the human rights claim is clearly unfounded.

9.07 Essentially, three levels of certification are available pursuant to ss 11, 12 and 93:

(a) *Section 11 certification*: deemed to be safe in respect of the Refugee Convention, but not the European Convention on Human Rights (ECHR). There is a power to certify a human rights claim as 'clearly unfounded' but no presumption in favour of such certification (although in practice, the Secretary of State appears to certify most human rights claims).

(b) *Section 12(2) certification*: no suspensive appeal on Refugee Convention grounds but no deeming provision either, so that the Secretary of State's certification that removal will not breach the Refugee Convention can be challenged by judicial review.

(c) *Section 12(5) certification*: the claimant may raise Refugee Convention grounds in an in-country appeal provided he has made a human rights claim.

9.08 Section 94 also contains powers to curtail third country appeals:

(7) A person may not bring an appeal to which this section applies in reliance on section 92(4) if the Secretary of State certifies that—

    (a) it is proposed to remove the person to a country of which he is not a national or citizen, and

    (b) there is no reason to believe that the person's rights under the Human Rights Convention will be breached in that country.

(8) In determining whether a person in relation to whom a certificate has been issued under subsection (7) may be removed from the United Kingdom, the country specified in the certificate is to be regarded as—

    (a) a place where a person's life and liberty is not threatened by reason of his race, religion, nationality, membership of a particular social group, or political opinion, and

    (b) a place from which a person will not be sent to another country otherwise than in accordance with the Refugee Convention.

9.09 This certification power is on its face wider than s 93 in that it is not a condition of certification of the human rights claim that a certificate has been issued under s 11 or s 12(2). Instead, certification of the human rights claim under s 94(7) has the effect of triggering a separate deeming provision in respect of the Refugee Convention pursuant to s 94(8).

9.10 The Secretary of State does not appear to have utilized this provision. This is not surprising as it sits uncomfortably with the graded statutory scheme created by ss 11, 12 and 93: why would Parliament have limited 'clearly unfounded' certificates to cases where an asylum certificate can be issued under ss 11 and 12(2) if the same effect can be obtained in other cases through using s 94(7)? If s 94(7) was utilized, one would expect that in order to retain a sensible legislative scheme, the phrase 'there is no reason to believe that the person's rights under the Human Rights Convention will be breached in that country' would be interpreted as representing the same test as the s 93(2) test of whether the human rights claim is clearly unfounded.

9.11 The case law on the interpretation and application of the 'clearly unfounded' test applies both to claims certified under s 93(2) and those certified under s 94 (in relation to direct claims from countries of origin). It is dealt with in the preceding chapter at paras 8.08–8.18. The case law on the deeming provision under s 11 of the 2002 Act is addressed at paras 9.14–9.21 below.

B. THE NEW PROVISIONS: THE STRUCTURE OF SCH 3

9.12 Schedule 3 now contains four categories of third countries to which removals may be effected, these categories supposedly reflecting varying levels of confidence in the safety of the particular third country. They are as follows:

    (a) *First List*: deemed to be safe in respect of the Refugee Convention, and also in respect of the ECHR in so far as the complaint concerns indirect refoulement. For other human rights challenges, 'the Secretary of State shall certify [as clearly unfounded] a human rights claim to which this sub-paragraph applies unless satisfied that the claim is not clearly unfounded'.

(b) *Second List*: deemed to be safe in respect of the Refugee Convention, but not in respect of the ECHR, even where the complaint concerns indirect refoulement. The same duty to certify as 'clearly unfounded' applies to any human rights claim as that which applies in relation to First List countries.

(c) *Third List*: deemed to be safe in respect of the Refugee Convention, but not the ECHR. There is a power to certify a human rights claim as 'clearly unfounded' but, unlike First and Second List countries, there is no duty to certify such a claim.

(d) *Individual certification*: this reflects the power in s 12 of the Immigration and Asylum Act 1999, save that it is available for any third country rather than restricted to designated countries and there is no out of country appeal. There is again a power to certify a human rights claim as 'clearly unfounded' but no presumption in favour of certification.

In Committee, the Home Office Minister, Beverley Hughes, described the rationale **9.13** for the different categories as follows:

We are attempting to acknowledge that not all countries are the same in relation to potential human rights claims. We can have a graduated approach on a statutory basis to how we deal with human rights claims from the countries listed in the existing part 2 that are party to Dublin. We can make safe assumptions about how those countries would deal with a person who was removed to them with relation to article 3 and potential removal onwards. In other words, we can assume that they will not remove somebody in breach of article 3. Following from that, we take a progressively more cautious approach, in relation to the other groups of countries, to how human rights challenges may be dealt with under the law. The amendments split the initial first group into two, to ensure that, with the new second group of people, all human rights claims are subject to certification if a non-suspensive appeal is to apply.[2]

We believe [the human rights deeming provision] to be reasonable, because removal to countries on [the First List] would take place within the context of a specific EU legislative framework—Dublin 2—and because claimants in those states will have access to remedies under the ECHR in those states, and also under general EU provisions.[3]

C. THE DEEMING PROVISIONS

All three lists provide for a deeming provision in respect of the Refugee Convention **9.14** but only the First List includes one in respect of the ECHR. A deeming provision was first introduced for the Refugee Convention by s 11 of the Immigration and Asylum Act 1999.

---

[2] HC Standing Committee B, col 351 (22 January 2004).
[3] ibid, col 354.

9.15 In *R (Mohammed) v Secretary of State for the Home Department*,[4] the Secretary of State initially argued that the deeming clause in respect of the Refugee Convention in s 11 also operated as a deeming provision in respect of human rights where the human rights claim was based on the same facts as the asylum claim. The argument essentially was that if the claimant's case is that both the Refugee Convention and Art 3 ECHR would be violated by indirect refoulement to a third country, and the Refugee Convention claim must fail as a result of the deeming provision, the Art 3 claim must fall with it. He abandoned the argument at the hearing in the face of a submission from the claimants that if the Secretary of State's interpretation was the only possible interpretation, a declaration of incompatibility would be appropriate.

9.16 The claimants argued in *Mohammed* that s 11 amounted to a disguised and impermissible ouster clause in respect of the Refugee Convention. This was because there was nothing to suggest that Parliament had intended to prevent the Secretary of State acting upon evidence which he considered established a risk of refoulement. The only potential effect of the clause was therefore to oust the jurisdiction of the court to review the Secretary of State's assessment.

9.17 Having regard to the special rules of construction applicable to ouster clauses, the claimants argued that it was possible to construe s 11 so that it did not preclude the court from reviewing the Secretary of State's assessment of whether removal would violate the Refugee Convention. This was because the deeming provision, s 11(1), was directed to whether someone in respect of whom a certificate had been issued should be removed; it did not restrict the matters that the Secretary of State could consider in deciding whether to exercise his discretion to issue a certificate on safe third country grounds in the first place.

9.18 Turner J dismissed the application. He held[5] that the Secretary of State had an unfettered discretion as to whether or not to remove a person if the conditions in s 11(2) were met, but was not required to form any opinion on the safety of the country to which the asylum applicant was to be sent under the Dublin Convention, and since he was not required to form an opinion in that respect there was no basis for judicial review.

9.19 In refusing a renewed judicial review permission application in *R (Ibrahim) v Secretary of State for the Home Department*,[6] the Court of Appeal reached a similar view to the effect that there was a discretion to certify but that it was unfettered.

9.20 During the proceedings in *Mohammed*, the Secretary of State appeared in two minds as to whether the effect of the deeming provision was to prevent *him* from considering evidence that a country was unsafe or merely to prevent a court from

---

[4] [2002] EWHC 57 (Admin).
[5] ibid at [55].
[6] [2001] EWCA 519, [2001] Imm AR 430.

reviewing his own decision. Although his decision letter claimed that he had assessed whether Germany would be safe for the claimants before issuing the certificate, his later evidence in the case contradicted this, stating that:

Notwithstanding the view the Courts have taken as to the safety of Germany and the primacy of one construction of the Geneva Convention, the Defendant is at least entitled by reason of s 11 of the 1999 Act to regard Germany as a place where a person's life and liberty is not threatened by reason of a Geneva Convention matter, and as a place from which a person will not be sent to another country otherwise than in accordance with the Geneva Convention. *He cannot choose to regard Germany otherwise than as a safe third country, whatever the fear expressed by a claimant.* (emphasis added)

The claimants repeatedly invited the Secretary of State to state whether—faced with **9.21** serious evidence of a Convention breach—he felt that s 11 permitted *him* to act on such evidence so as to conclude that the country would be unsafe, whether generally or for a particular claimant. No clear answer was forthcoming.

Schedule 3 does on its face prevent the Secretary of State from having regard to **9.22** such evidence. Paragraph 3 of Sch 3 (applying to First List countries) is set out below by way of example and for ease of reference. The same formulation is used in relation to the Refugee Convention ouster clauses for the Second and Third Lists:

(1) This paragraph applies *for the purposes of the determination by any person, tribunal or court whether a person who has made an asylum claim or a human rights claim may be removed*—
    (a) from the United Kingdom, and
    (b) to a State of which he is not a national or citizen.
(2) A State to which this Part applies shall be treated in so far as relevant to the question mentioned in sub-paragraph (1), as a place—
    (a) where a person's life and liberty are not threatened by reason of his race, religion, nationality, membership of a particular social group or political opinion, and
    (b) from which a person will not be sent to another State in contravention of his Convention rights, and
    (c) from which a person will not be sent to another State otherwise than in accordance with the Refugee Convention. (emphasis added)

By subpara (1), both the Secretary of State *and* the courts would therefore appear to **9.23** be prohibited from recognizing that removal would violate the Refugee Convention or the ECHR, even if the evidence established this. The inclusion of the Secretary of State in the prohibition may be with an eye to the arguments advanced in *Mohammed* concerning disguised ouster clauses.

D. SCOPE OF HUMAN RIGHTS DEEMING PROVISION

The Bill as originally presented to Parliament stated[7] that: **9.24**

---

[7] para 5(3).

The person may not bring an immigration appeal by virtue of section 92(4)(a) of that Act (appeal from within United Kingdom: asylum or human rights) in reliance on . . .

> (b) a human rights claim in so far as it asserts that to remove the person to a specified State to which this Part applies would, because of circumstances of or relating to that State, be unlawful under section 6 of the Human Rights Act 1998.

9.25 At Committee stage, the Government moved an amendment to restrict the deeming provision to allegations of indirect refoulement. The scope of the provision as enacted is therefore that the third country is deemed to be a country 'from which a person will not be sent to another State in contravention of his Convention rights'. This has the effect that challenges are not excluded where they relate to the treatment or circumstances that the claimant would face in the territory of the third country.

9.26 The Home Office Minister told Parliament that:

> . . . the listed countries are deemed safe on human rights grounds only in the limited sense that they would not remove an asylum seeker to another country in contravention of article 3 of the ECHR—the narrow, so-called refoulement issue. For that group, any other ECHR challenge to removal will be certified, unless the Secretary of State is satisfied that the claim is not clearly unfounded. Such challenges could be based on article 3, in that the applicant could face inhuman or degrading treatment in that safe third country, or on article 8, in that removal from the UK could interfere with his or her private life. Judicial review is also possible on those grounds.[8]
>
> In the new first group . . . it is not the case . . . that all the human rights challenges possible would be deemed safe, and therefore not have to go through the certification process that is required by law of the Secretary of State before a non-suspensive appeal mechanism could be applied. It is simply the very limited challenge that someone could make, that removal to the safe third country would be in breach of article 3, because they could not trust that country to exercise its obligations under the ECHR and not move them on to somewhere that was unsafe.
>
> All other possible human rights claims and ECHR challenges, in relation both to any concerns about treatment inside the third country, including any article 3 concerns, and to any claims in relation to the situation of the person in the UK—article 8 on family issues—would have to go through the certification process that applies now under the law, in that the Secretary of State could remove that person only if he was satisfied that the claim, having been refused, was clearly unfounded. It therefore does not change the situation in relation to any other possible ECHR challenges, apart from that very narrow claim that it would be in breach of article 3 because that country might not properly meet its ECHR obligations and not remove the person to somewhere that was not safe.[9]

9.27 The Government's decision to narrow the scope of the deeming provision will reduce the number of cases in which its compatibility with the ECHR will be in issue. On several recent occasions, the courts have permitted challenges to removals

---

[8] HC Standing Committee B, col 351 (22 January 2004).

[9] ibid, col 354.

to EU member states on human rights grounds relating to the circumstances the claimant will face in the third country.[10]

However, under the 1996 Act, the courts quashed safe third country certificates in respect of several Dublin signatory states (including Denmark, France and Germany) on the ground that the Secretary of State had not shown that they would not refoule the claimant. The most likely scope for an indirect refoulement challenge may relate to accession states which do not yet have safe status determination procedures, particularly where there is doubt as to the opportunity for effective recourse to Strasbourg prior to refoulement.

9.28

E. ECHR INCOMPATIBILITY OF HUMAN RIGHTS DEEMING PROVISION

In *TI v United Kingdom*,[11] the European Court of Human Rights rejected the UK Government's argument that the Court should be unwilling to find that removal to another ECHR contracting state could pose a real risk of onward removal to a country where there was a real risk of Art 3 ill-treatment. The Court was unimpressed by the UK Government's argument that *TI* would be protected by his right in Germany to apply to the European Court if he considered that his removal from there would be contrary to Art 3 and that it would undermine the effective operation of the Dublin Convention if Art 3 challenges were permitted concerning indirect refoulement from a Dublin signatory.[12] The UK Government had argued that the Court:

9.29

. . . should be slow to find that the removal of a person from one Contracting State to another would infringe Article 3 of the Convention, as in this case, the applicant would be protected by the rule of law in Germany and would have recourse, if any problems arose, to this Court, including the possibility of applying for a Rule 39 indication to suspend his deportation. It would be wrong in principle for the United Kingdom to have to take on a policing function of assessing whether another Contracting State such as Germany was complying with the Convention. It would also undermine the effective working of the Dublin Convention, which was brought into operation to allocate in a fair and efficient manner State responsibility within Europe for considering asylum claims.[13]

The Court concluded that:

9.30

In the present case, the applicant is threatened with removal to Germany, where a deportation order was previously issued to remove him to Sri Lanka. It is accepted by all parties that the applicant is not, as such, threatened with any treatment contrary to Article 3 in Germany. His

---

[10] See *R (Razgar) v Secretary of State for the Home Department* [2004] 3 WLR 58, HL; [2003] Imm AR 529, CA; *R (Kurtolli) v Secretary of State for the Home Department* [2003] EWHC 2744 (Admin) [2004] INLR 198; *R (Ahmadi) v Secretary of State for the Home Department* [2002] EWHC 1897 (Admin), [2003] ACD 14; *R (Bardiqi) v Secretary of State for the Home Department* [2003] EWHC 1788 (Admin).
[11] [2000] INLR 211.
[12] See UK Government's argument at ibid, 225–226 and the Court's response at 228.
[13] ibid, 226.

removal to Germany is however one link in a possible chain of events which might result in his return to Sri Lanka where it is alleged that he would face the real risk of such treatment.

The Court finds that the indirect removal in this case to an intermediary country, which is also a Contracting State, does not affect the responsibility of the United Kingdom to ensure that the applicant is not, as a result of its decision to expel, exposed to treatment contrary to Article 3 of the Convention. Nor can the United Kingdom rely automatically in that context on the arrangements made in the Dublin Convention concerning the attribution of responsibility between European countries for deciding asylum claims. Where States establish international organisations, or *mutatis mutandis* international agreements, to pursue co-operation in certain fields of activities, there may be implications for the protection of fundamental rights.

It would be incompatible with the purpose and object of the Convention if Contracting States were thereby absolved from their responsibility under the Convention in relation to the field of activity covered by such attribution (see e.g. *Waite and Kennedy v. Germany* judgment of 18 February 1999, Reports 1999, § 67). The Court notes the comments of the UNHCR that, while the Dublin Convention may pursue laudable objectives, its effectiveness may be undermined in practice by the differing approaches adopted by Contracting States to the scope of protection offered. The English courts themselves have shown a similar concern in reviewing the decisions of the Secretary of State concerning the removal of asylum-seekers to allegedly safe third countries . . .[14]

9.31 The House of Lords has now established that the United Kingdom's obligations may be engaged under any substantive article of the ECHR should the claimant's treatment in the receiving state amount to a flagrant denial or gross violation of the relevant right.[15]

9.32 The House of Lords' decision in *Yogathas*[16] also suggests that to preclude individual human rights challenges is incompatible with the ECHR. Lord Bingham, discussing the present legislation, stated that:

The first legal problem is that Parliament has enacted, in section 11(1)(b) of the 1999 Act, a statutory presumption that a member state (such as Germany) is to be regarded as a place from which he will not be sent to Sri Lanka otherwise than in accordance with the Geneva Convention. Thus the argument which succeeded in Ex p Adan [2001] 2 AC 477 is effectively blocked. But this does not deprive the subject or proposed subject of a removal order of all redress. *The possibility of a challenge on human rights grounds is preserved by section 65 of the 1999 Act, as was no doubt necessary if that Act was to be compatible with the obligations of the United Kingdom under the European Convention on Human Rights.* The breach of human rights must, in this case, relate to the return of (or the decision to return) the appellant to Germany. Since it is not suggested that the appellant will be at risk of ill-treatment in Germany, he must in practice show that there are substantial grounds for believing that if he is sent back to Germany there is a real risk that he will be sent back to Sri Lanka in circumstances giving rise to a real risk of a breach of article 3 of the European Convention.[17] (emphasis added)

---

[14] ibid, 228.
[15] *R (Ullah) v Special Adjudicator* [2004] UKHL 26, [2004] 2 AC 323.
[16] [2002] UKHL 36, [2003] 1 AC 928.
[17] ibid at [11].

In the Immigration Appeal Tribunal's response to the Government's consultation on **9.33** the Bill, Ouseley P stated that:

If section 3 of the Human Rights Act 1998 is to remain in force, no public authority (including Courts and Tribunals as well as Government officials) can make, affirm or allow a decision which breaches the scheduled human rights. However good a country's human rights records may be, it is difficult to see that there could not be scope for an individual to show that he or she is, individually, at risk. No doubt, provisions could properly be adopted, which would have the effect of preventing spurious points from being raised in individual cases. We have grave doubts, however, whether it can be lawful (either under the Convention or the 1998 Act) to remove the right to invoke Article 3 [EHCR].[18]

During the passage of the Bill through Parliament, the Joint Committee on Human **9.34** Rights reported that:

We consider that there is a significant risk of incompatibility with the UK's obligations under the ECHR in enacting an automatic statutory deeming provision, precluding any individual consideration of the facts of a particular claimant's case and conclusively ousting the jurisdiction of the courts to hear a claim that removal to a third country on the First List would breach the claimant's Convention rights because of the risk of onward removal.[19]

The Secretary of State already has a power to certify a human rights claim as 'clearly **9.35** unfounded'.[20] The effect of the Secretary of State issuing such a certificate is that the claimant is denied an in-country right of appeal (unless the Administrative Court finds the certificate to have been issued unlawfully). The power to certify as clearly unfounded is reproduced in Sch 3.[21] The purpose of the further deeming provision in para 3 in respect of human rights claims involving indirect refoulement seems then to be to defeat *meritorious* human rights claims.

It would be incompatible with human rights for the Secretary of State to argue **9.36** that the deeming provision mandated him to shut his eyes to any evidence—of whatever strength—that may emerge at any time to the effect that the removal of any particular claimant will place the United Kingdom in breach of the ECHR. The result of such a construction would be that Parliament had prohibited the Secretary of State from acting upon evidence that the proposed removal would lead to indirect refoulement and therefore prohibited him from acting in accordance with the ECHR.

In the joint Home Office/Department of Constitutional Affairs *Report on the* **9.37** *responses to the consultation to the new legislative proposals on Asylum Reform*,[22] and clearly with Ouseley P's comments in mind (para 9.33 above), the sponsoring Departments explained the provision as follows:

---

[18] 17 November 2003.

[19] Thirteenth Report of Session 2003–04 (HL Paper 102, HC Paper 640).

[20] Nationality, Immigration and Asylum Act 2002, s 93.

[21] Asylum and Immigration (Treatment of Claimants, etc) Act 2004, Sch 3, paras 5(4), 10(4), 15(4) and 19(c).

[22] December 2003.

We cannot simply assume that our obligation, in relation to Article 3, will be met by another State. That is, another State would have procedures in place to ensure that a person would not be removed improperly from that state to another country . . . However, provided we are satisfied as a matter of fact, after detailed and diligent enquiry that the procedures and situation in another State are such that there is no real risk that a breach of the individual's Convention rights will occur, we believe that the provision is lawful.[23]

9.38 As to how they would deal with circumstances particular to a specific claimant in the face of a blanket assumption of safety, the Departments said that the state could not be certified as safe if someone was at risk on the basis of individual factors:

For a state to be considered as a safe third country or state it would have to satisfy a legal test. If a real risk of treatment contrary to our international obligations was identified based on particular factors, the state could not properly be said to be safe.[24]

9.39 They therefore accept that in order to comply with human rights standards, a country cannot be included in the First List (and so subject to the human rights deeming provision) unless that country will be safe for everyone in human rights terms. That would appear on any view to require a willingness to consider evidence to the contrary.

F. AMENDMENT OF LISTS OF SAFE THIRD COUNTRIES

9.40 As indicated above (see para 9.13), the promoting Minister emphasized that the First List was made up entirely of member states participating in the Dublin II mechanism. She stated that the rationale for not including a human rights deeming provision in relation to the Second List was that 'as states on that list will not be party to the Dublin arrangements, there will be no automatic safety provision relating to onward removal in breach of article 3'.[25]

9.41 She added that:

On the limited issue of whether those countries would be likely to act in breach of article 3, for the reasons that I have outlined, any European country removing someone to them under Dublin 2 would then be likely to be in breach of article 3. These are all countries that, under Dublin 2, will have fully to operate the ECHR. On the specific issue, we believe that the Dublin regulations and the EU legislative framework that surrounds them, assure us that we can deem all those countries to be safe. For all other aspects of potential human rights claims, our legislation will require the Secretary of State to certify the cases as clearly unfounded.[26]

9.42 There is nothing on the face of the Act limiting the First List to member states (but see para 9.46 below). Indeed, unlike the provisions relating to 'safe countries of origin'

---

[23] para 21.
[24] para 22.
[25] HC Standing Committee B, col 350 (22 January 2004).
[26] ibid, col 355.

(see Chapter 8 above), there are no express criteria for determining inclusion in or exclusion from the list. However, as indicated above (para 9.37), the Home Office and Department of Constitutional Affairs accepted that to operate the deeming provision would require them to be satisfied that the country was safe for all claimants.

The original version of the Bill[27] did permit the Secretary of State to keep the **9.43** factual situation in the member state under review and to remove a state from the First List should evidence emerge that it was no longer safe for all claimants. An individual with evidence that he faced indirect refoulement would have been able to present his case in the first place as a request to remove the country from the First List. If that request was refused, the refusal could have been subject to judicial review where appropriate.

However, the effect of Government amendments tabled at Commons Committee **9.44** stage was to *delete* the power to remove a state from the First List (it remains in respect of the Second and Third Lists). It is difficult to understand why the Secretary of State should no longer wish to possess this power, nor what measures he would now take were evidence to emerge that a country in the First List was no longer safe.

In the Commons Standing Committee, the Home Office Minister stated that: **9.45**

If we had evidence that a country was not operating to the letter of the human rights convention, I think that that would mean that we would consider the provisions of part 2 of schedule 3 and the inclusion of that country on the list . . . For refugee convention purposes and for the narrow human rights issue, we are deeming all those countries to be safe. If there was evidence that one was not safe for this purpose, we would consider that and amend the legislation.[28]

During Committee Stage in the House of Lords, the Home Office Minister Baroness **9.46** Scotland said:

[W]e do not consider it necessary to provide a similar order-making power in relation to the removal of a state from the list at Part 2. I should reiterate that we intend that the list at Part 2 should be limited to European Union member states which are party to the Dublin arrangements for determining the state responsible for examining an asylum application, and other states, such as Norway and Iceland, which are associated with those arrangements.

I hear what the noble Lord, Lord Avebury, says about new states which may join the Union, but he will remember that all new states seeking to join will still have to comply with the acquis in order to be accepted. In the very unlikely event that such a state deteriorated to a point where it no longer generally met the tests set out in Part 2, we would consider bringing forward new primary legislation to recognise that. This would also apply should any agreements between the Community and other states associating them with the Dublin arrangements be terminated or renounced.[29]

The Earl of Onslow intervened with the following comment: **9.47**

---

[27] para 15(1).

[28] HC Standing Committee B, col 355 (22 January 2004).

[29] *Hansard*, HL col 721 (27 April 2004).

In 1967, Greece was a functioning, squabbling, shrieking democracy when along came a bunch of colonels who kicked out the democrats. I am not saying that that will happen in any of the new Balkan states or Turkey if, peradventure, it should join, but there will always be that risk. Should we not have a quicker method than primary legislation to deal with the problem that the noble Lord, Lord Avebury, has shown could theoretically exist?[30]

9.48 Baroness Scotland's response was:

I of course recognise the noble Lord's anxiety about that. However, he should bear in mind that the deterioration of a member state would be a considerable issue for all other member states. It would be a very serious issue and, in order to act in this way against a fellow member state, primary legislation would be necessary.

Of course, if there were an emergency, it is possible for the parliamentary procedure to be accelerated to meet it. But we hope that that will not be necessary. We are keeping such legislation in reserve for a situation which may very well either never occur or occur in extremis.[31]

9.49 The First List is the only list to include a human rights deeming provision, and therefore the one to which uniquely severe consequences attach. By contrast, the power remains to remove countries from the Second and Third Lists, notwithstanding the implications of inclusion in these lists being less significant.

9.50 While it is predictable that the Secretary of State would consider it unlikely that evidence will emerge indicating a member state to be unsafe, that hardly explains his moving an amendment to deprive himself of a power—which he had originally wished to possess—to remove a state from the First List in that unlikely eventuality, and to justify that amendment on the express basis that he will have primary legislation in reserve. The recognition that such legislation might have to be 'accelerated' in an 'emergency' would seem to arise from the fact that, following the amendment, there is no scope whatsoever in the scheme of the Act for the Secretary of State to take account of even the strongest danger of indirect refoulement when deciding whether to remove someone to a First List state.

9.51 The amendment raises the prospect of a claimant who presents substantial evidence of an individual risk of indirect refoulement—perhaps from an accession state to another transit state without a practical or effective opportunity to obtain intervention from Strasbourg—having to seek judicial review of the Secretary of State's refusal to promote emergency legislation deleting that state from the First List before the claimant would otherwise fall to be removed.

G. INTRODUCTION OF DUTY TO CERTIFY CLEARLY UNFOUNDED CLAIMS

9.52 In the original Bill presented to Parliament, there was no duty to certify clearly unfounded claims. There were therefore only two lists, the first list with a human

---

[30] *Hansard*, HL col 721 (27 April 2004).
[31] ibid.

rights deeming provision (and a power to certify 'clearly unfounded' claims which did not fall within the deeming provision), and the second list omitting the human rights deeming provision but with the same power to certify a 'clearly unfounded' claim.

Government amendments at Committee stage in the Commons introduced a duty **9.53** to certify unfounded claims in relation to the First List and split the original second list into new Second and Third Lists, the only distinction between the two being the duty to certify 'clearly unfounded' claims in relation to Second List but not Third List countries. The Minister said that:

As regards the potential to make human rights claims, the general effect of the Government amendments is that schedule 3 will more closely mirror the approach taken in the safe country of origin provisions in part 5 of the 2002 Act.[32]

Comparing the Second List with the Third List (where there is a power, but no duty **9.54** to certify), the Minister stated that:

To continue the graduated theme, however, there would be a case-by-case consideration of any ECHR challenge, to see whether the claim could be certified as clearly unfounded. That is a different approach to consideration of ECHR challenges.[33]

However, the Court of Appeal has already considered the effect of the corresponding **9.55** distinction between a duty to certify, compared with a simple power to certify 'clearly unfounded' claims from countries of origin (which the Minister said she wished to 'mirror' by her amendment (para 9.53 above)). In its decisions in *L* and *Bagdanavicius,* the Court confirmed that the application of the 'clearly unfounded' test under s 94 of the 2002 Act was the same regardless of whether there was a duty to certify or merely a power to do so, and that the same case-by-case consideration was required to determine whether the claim was 'clearly unfounded' (see quotations at paras 8.06–8.07 above).

The introduction of the duty to certify clearly unfounded claims in the First and **9.56** Second Lists is therefore of limited legal significance. (This is unsurprising given that a claim will only be clearly unfounded in the first place, and therefore susceptible to either a power or duty to certify, if it is bound to fail on appeal.) It is also of limited practical significance in third country cases. Whereas the Secretary of State's practice in relation to 'safe' countries of origin is to certify nearly all claims from designated states and almost no claims from non-designated states, his practice is already to certify nearly all third country claims where he has the power (although at present no duty) to do so. It is therefore not apparent why the Home Office went to the trouble of creating an entirely new list by Government amendment to create a distinction between states where there was and was not a duty to certify clearly unfounded claims.

---

[32] HC Standing Committee B, col 351 (22 January 2004).
[33] ibid.

10

DETENTION
(SECTIONS 32 AND 34–36)

A. Overview   10.01

B. The power to detain under present legislation   10.04

C. Limits on power to detain   10.07

D. Bail under present legislation   10.15

E. Bail from the Special Immigration Appeals Commission   10.20

F. Changes introduced by the 2004 Act   10.22

G. Appeal against a bail decision by the Special Immigration
   Appeals Commission   10.23

H. Detention pending deportation   10.32

I. Failing to co-operate with the obtaining of a travel document 10.39

J. Electronic monitoring   10.53

A. OVERVIEW

As of December 2003, 1,285 persons who had claimed asylum were in administrative immigration detention in the United Kingdom. Most were held in removal centres but 120 people were detained solely under immigration powers in prisons,[1] notwithstanding a Government commitment to end the routine use of prisons for immigration detention.[2] Despite Home Office policies to the contrary, immigration detainees, including the mentally vulnerable and chronically ill, are being held for long periods.   **10.01**

Immigration detention is subject to far fewer checks than detention within the criminal justice system. There is no statutory time-limit on immigration detention and there is also no right to automatic bail hearings for a court to determine whether   **10.02**

---

[1] Home Office Asylum Statistics: 4th Quarter 2003. These figures are only for persons who at some point claimed asylum. The figures do not include other immigrants; persons in 'dual' immigration and criminal detention; or persons held in police cells.

[2] White Paper, *Fairer, Faster and Firmer* (July 1998).

persons in immigration detention should be released.[3] In practice, the onus is on the immigration detainee to apply for bail. This is not as simple as it might seem: an investigation by HM Prison Inspectorate into five British removal centres found that detainees in all removal centres save Oakington lacked reliable information about why they were detained and the progress of their case, and did not have access to competent independent legal advice.[4]

10.03   This chapter summarizes current law on detention, temporary admission and bail before examining the changes introduced by the new legislation. This chapter does not deal with challenges to the lawfulness of detention (via habeas corpus, judicial review or actions for damages).

B. THE POWER TO DETAIN UNDER PRESENT LEGISLATION

10.04   The main provisions on detention are still contained in Schs 2 and 3 to the Immigration Act 1971, though these provisions have been amended and added to by the Immigration Act 1999 and the Nationality, Immigration and Asylum Act 2002.

10.05   Very broadly, powers of immigration detention can be summarized as follows:

(a) Persons subject to immigration control can be detained pending examination and a decision on whether to grant, cancel or refuse leave to enter.[5] This power can be exercised by an immigration officer or by the Secretary of State for the Home Department.

(b) Persons subject to immigration control who have been refused leave to enter, or whose leave has been cancelled; or illegal entrants or overstayers; and persons reasonably suspected of falling in these categories can be detained pending a decision over whether to remove, and pending removal.[6] Similarly, persons who have not observed a condition attached to their limited leave to enter; persons who have used deception in seeking leave to remain; persons whose indefinite leave to remain has been revoked; and their family members who are not British citizens; and persons reasonably suspected of falling within these categories can be detained pending a decision over whether to remove, and pending removal.[7] This power can be exercised by an immigration officer or by the Secretary of State for the Home Department.[8]

---

[3] Immigration and Asylum Act 1999, s 44 had introduced a right to two automatic references to the magistrates' court for bail. These provisions were never brought into force and were repealed by the Nationality, Immigration and Asylum Act 2002, s 68.

[4] HM Prison Inspectorate, *Inspection of Five Immigration Service Custodial Establishments* (April 2003).

[5] Immigration Act 1971, Sch 2, para 16(1) and (1A).

[6] ibid, Sch 2, paras 8, 9, 12–14 and 16(2).

[7] Immigration and Asylum Act 1999, s 10(1) and (7).

[8] The powers of immigration officers are contained in Immigration Act 1971, Sch 2, para 16. The Secretary of State now has parallel powers under the Nationality, Immigration and Asylum Act 2002, s 62.

(c) Persons whom the Secretary of State considers should be excluded for the public good or who are the subject of a criminal court's recommendation for deportation can be detained pending steps in the deportation procedure.[9] This power can only be exercised by the Secretary of State for the Home Department.

The alternative to detention pending examination or administrative removal is **10.06** temporary admission or (where a person has already been detained) temporary release, subject to such residence, employment, occupation or reporting restrictions as may be imposed by an immigration officer or the Secretary of State.[10] The alternative to detention pending deportation is in practice identical—the person is released subject to such restrictions as may be imposed by the Secretary of State.[11]

C. LIMITS ON POWER TO DETAIN

Significant limits have been imposed on the power to detain by the common law, Art **10.07** 5 of the European Convention on Human Rights (ECHR), and Home Office policy.

1. Common law

In immigration detention as in other forms of detention, there is a common law **10.08** presumption of liberty[12] and the statutory power to detain must be narrowly construed.[13] Detention must be for a specific lawful purpose.[14] In removal and deportation cases, the power to detain is implicitly limited to the period reasonably necessary for removal or deportation.[15]

2. Art 5 ECHR

Immigration detention generally falls within the ambit of Art 5(1)(f) ECHR which **10.09** permits 'the lawful arrest or detention of a person to prevent his effecting an unauthorised entry into the country or of a person against whom action is being taken with a view to deportation or extradition'. However, detention will breach Art 5 if the detention is not in accordance with a procedure defined by law;[16] or if the law

---

[9] Immigration Act 1971, Sch 3, para 2(1)–(3).

[10] ibid, Sch 2, paras 21 and 22; Nationality, Immigration and Asylum Act 2002, s 62(3) and (4).

[11] ibid, Sch 3, para 2(5) and (6).

[12] *R (Abbasi) v Secretary of State for Foreign and Commonwealth Affairs* [2002] EWCA Civ 1598, [2003] UKHRR 76: 'The underlying principle, fundamental in English law, is that every imprisonment is prima facie unlawful . . . This principle applies to every person, British citizen or not, who finds himself within the jurisdiction of the court.'

[13] *R v Governor of Durham Prison, ex p Singh (Hardial)* [1984] 1 WLR 704.

[14] *Tan Te Lam v Superintendent of Tai A Chau Detention Centre* [1997] AC 97; *R v Special Adjudicator, ex p B* [1998] INLR 315.

[15] ibid; and *Re Mahmood (Wasfi)* [1995] Imm AR 311.

[16] Art 5(1) ECHR.

is not sufficiently clear and precise;[17] if the detention is arbitrary; or if the detention is disproportionate, i.e. other, less severe measures should have been considered before detention.[18] Under Art 5(2), reasons must be given for detention. Under Art 5(4), 'everyone who is deprived of his liberty by arrest or detention shall be entitled to take proceedings by which the lawfulness of his detention shall be decided speedily by a court and his release ordered if his detention is not lawful'.

3. Home Office policy

10.10 If detention is contrary to the Home Office's published and accessible policy, the detention will be unlawful at common law and also in breach of Art 5 ECHR.[19]

10.11 The most important source of Home Office policy is Chapter 38 of the *Operational Enforcement Manual*. Chapter 38 states that detention should be used 'only as a last resort'. 'There must be strong grounds for believing that a person will not comply with conditions for temporary admission or temporary release for detention to be justified. All reasonable alternatives to detention must be considered before detention is authorised. Once detention has been authorised, it must be kept under close review to ensure that it continues to be justified.' Detention will only be appropriate in 'very exceptional circumstances' where a person is suffering from serious medical conditions or is mentally ill or there is independent evidence that he has been tortured.

10.12 It is Home Office policy not to treat removal as imminent where proceedings have been initiated that challenge the right to remove: Home Office policy in such cases is normally to grant temporary admission pending the result of the proceedings.[20]

10.13 Somewhat distinct Home Office policies and criteria apply to detention in fast-track cases at the Oakington and Harmondsworth centres. All detainees at Oakington and a pilot group of detainees at Harmondsworth are detained while their claims are processed. Detention at Oakington was initially used only for 'White List' countries, where it was presumed that the claim was likely to be 'clearly unfounded'.[21] Oakington detention has considerably expanded and is now available for persons coming from countries or types of claim which are on the 'Oakington list' of over 60 countries from Afghanistan to Zambia, including major asylum source countries.[22]

---

[17] *Amuur v France* (1996) 22 EHRR 533.

[18] *Litwa v Poland* (2000) 33 EHRR 53—a case on criminal detention.

[19] *Nadarajah v Secretary of State for the Home Department* [2003] EWCA 1768, [2004] INLR 139.

[20] Conceded by the Secretary of State in *Nadarajah and Amirthanathan*, ibid at [28] and [42].

[21] Under Nationality, Immigration and Asylum Act 2002, s 115(7).

[22] For some countries, all nationals are deemed appropriate for detention provided they meet the other Oakington criteria. For other countries, only certain classes of case are deemed appropriate for detention.

Under the Oakington criteria, only cases in which it appears that a quick decision can be reached, and persons who are not likely to abscond[23] are suitable for detention.[24] At present, detention within the fast-track system at Harmondsworth is limited to single males deemed to have a 'straightforward case' and coming from countries on the Oakington list.

In *R v Secretary of State for the Home Department, ex p Saadi*[25] the House of **10.14** Lords held that it was lawful and compliant with Art 5 ECHR to detain persons for the purpose of rapidly processing their claims.

D. BAIL UNDER PRESENT LEGISLATION

All detainees can apply for bail, provided that at least seven days have passed since **10.15** their arrival in the United Kingdom.[26] Earlier restrictions on bail for persons liable to be deported were lifted in 2003.[27] The fact that removal directions have been set is not a bar to applying for bail.[28]

Where a person is being detained pending examination or removal, bail can be **10.16** granted by a chief immigration officer, an immigration adjudicator[29] or the Secretary of State[30] on the person's own recognizance with a condition to appear on a subsequent date given in writing.[31] Further conditions can be imposed[32] and sureties may be taken, though sureties should not be required where they are not necessary to ensure compliance.[33]

Where a person has an appeal pending,[34] bail can be granted by a chief immigra- **10.17** tion officer, a police officer not below the rank of inspector, an adjudicator or (where an application for leave to appeal has been made) the Immigration Appeal Tribunal.[35] Where leave to appeal to the Tribunal is granted, a detainee has a statutory right to

---

[23] Since Oakington has lower security.

[24] Immigration and Nationality Directorate, *Operational Enforcement Manual* Ch 38.3.1.

[25] [2002] UKHL 41, [2002] 1 WLR 3131.

[26] Immigration Act 1971, Sch 2, para 22(1) and (1B); for persons liable to deportation, see also Immigration Act 1971, Sch 3, para 2(4A).

[27] By Immigration and Asylum Act 1999, s 54.

[28] Immigration Act 1971, Sch 2, para 34.

[29] ibid, Sch 2, para 22(1A).

[30] Nationality, Immigration and Asylum Act 2002, s 68(2)(b).

[31] Immigration Act 1971, Sch 2, para 22(1A).

[32] ibid, Sch 2, para 22(2).

[33] *R v Secretary of State for the Home Department, ex p Brezinski and Glowacka* (QBD, 19 July 1996, Kay J); and Guidance Notes for Adjudicators (May 2003) para 2.2.2: 'Adjudicators are reminded that sureties are only required where you cannot otherwise be satisfied that the applicant will observe the conditions you may wish to impose'.

[34] Under Nationality, Immigration and Asylum Act 2002, Pt 5, ie to an adjudicator or the Immigration Appeal Tribunal.

[35] Immigration Act 1971, Sch 2, para 29(1)–(4) as amended by Nationality, Immigration and Asylum Act 2002, Sch 7.

bail.[36] Similar provisions exist for bail for persons applying for permission to appeal to the Court of Appeal.[37] Where a person has been granted leave to appeal to the Court of Appeal, or where the appeal is by the Secretary of State, there is a statutory right to bail.[38] In addition, where an application is made for judicial review, the High Court can exercise its inherent jurisdiction to grant bail,[39] and similarly the Court of Appeal can exercise its inherent jurisdiction in a renewed application for permission to appeal to the Court of Appeal.

10.18   As with persons released on bail pending examination or removal, there are provisions on recognizances, conditions and sureties[40] for persons released pending their appeal.[41]

10.19   If a person fails to comply with the conditions of bail, there are provisions for the forfeiture of the recognizance.[42] Immigration officers and constables have the power to arrest without warrant a person released on immigration bail where there are reasonable grounds to suspect that he has broken or is likely to break a bail condition; or where a surety has provided written notification that a person released on bail is likely to fail to appear and the surety wishes to be released of her obligations as a surety.[43] There are accompanying powers of entry and search of premises and search of persons.[44]

E. BAIL FROM THE SPECIAL IMMIGRATION APPEALS COMMISSION

10.20   There is a distinct bail regime for persons believed to be a threat to national security. A person who has been detained under the Immigration Act 1971 or the Nationality, Immigration and Asylum Act 2002 will need to direct his bail application to the Special Immigration Appeals Commission (SIAC) if:

---

[36] Immigration Act 1971, Sch 2, para 29(4).

[37] Asylum and Immigration Appeals Act 1993, s 9A as amended by Asylum and Immigration Act 1996 and Immigration and Asylum Act 1999.

[38] Asylum and Immigration Appeals Act 1993, s 9A(1)–(3).

[39] *R v Secretary of State for the Home Department, ex p Turkoglu* [1988] QB 398.

[40] Immigration Act 1971, Sch 2, para 29(1)–(6).

[41] ibid, Sch 2, para 30(1) provides that if removal directions are in force or the power to give removal directions is exercisable, a person with a pending appeal cannot be released without the consent of the Secretary of State. Since, under Nationality, Immigration and Asylum Act 2002, s 77(4), removal directions can be given notwithstanding the suspensory effect of a pending appeal, this would have the effect of making many bail decisions by the courts subject to consent by the Secretary of State. It is strongly arguable that such a limitation on the courts' power to grant bail would be contrary to Art 5(4) ECHR.

[42] ibid, Sch 2, paras 23 and 31.

[43] ibid, Sch 2, para 24(1) and (for persons released pending an appeal) para 33(1).

[44] ibid, Sch 2, paras 25A and 25B.

(a) the Secretary of State has certified that detention is necessary in the interests of national security;[45]

(b) the person was detained following a decision to refuse leave to enter on the ground that exclusion is in the interest of national security;[46] or

(c) the person was detained following a decision to deport on national security grounds.[47]

SIAC also hears bail applications from persons detained under the Anti-Terrorism, **10.21** Crime and Security Act 2001.[48] Under that Act, a person who is a 'suspected international terrorist' can be detained under immigration powers[49] even though his removal or departure from the United Kingdom is prevented whether temporarily or indefinitely by a point of law which relates wholly or partly to an international agreement or a practical consideration.[50] This provision enables a person who cannot be removed, for example because removal would breach Art 3 ECHR, to be detained indefinitely without criminal charges. This provision has required a derogation by the United Kingdom from Art 5(1) ECHR.[51]

F. CHANGES INTRODUCED BY THE 2004 ACT

The Asylum and Immigration (Treatment of Claimants, etc) Act 2004 introduces **10.22** four changes in the areas of detention, bail and temporary admission:

(a) there is a new right of appeal on a point of law against a decision by the SIAC on bail;

(b) where a person is liable to be deported, he can be detained by the Secretary of State even though he has been bailed by a court with the power to grant him bail;

(c) a new offence is created of failing to co-operate in the obtaining of a travel document; and

(d) electronic monitoring can now be imposed as a condition of temporary admission or bail.

---

[45] SIAC Act 1997, s 3(2)(a).

[46] ibid, s 3(2)(b).

[47] ibid, s 3(2)(c).

[48] Anti-Terrorism, Crime and Security Act 2001, s 24.

[49] ie under Immigration Act 1971, Sch 2 (detention of persons liable to examination or removal) or Sch 3, para 2 (detention pending deportation) or under Nationality, Immigration and Asylum Act 2002, s 62 (detention by the Secretary of State).

[50] Anti-Terrorism, Crime and Security Act 2001, s 23.

[51] Human Rights Act 1998 (Designated Derogation) Order 2001, SI 2001/3644.

G. APPEAL AGAINST A BAIL DECISION BY THE SPECIAL IMMIGRATION APPEALS COMMISSION

1. Present legislation and case law

10.23 The previous legislation did not provide for an appeal against a decision on bail by the SIAC. Under the previous legislation, the only appeal against a decision by the SIAC was against 'a final determination of an appeal'.[52]

10.24 In the case of *G v Secretary of State for the Home Department*,[53] the Court of Appeal confirmed that there was no statutory right of appeal against a bail decision by the SIAC. In that case, the Secretary of State sought permission to appeal against the SIAC's grant of bail to G. G had been certified and detained as a 'suspected international terrorist' and had lost his appeal against the certification. After a severe deterioration in his mental health, G had been granted bail by the SIAC on conditions akin to house arrest.[54] The Court of Appeal held that bail was not 'a final determination of an appeal' and that it therefore had no jurisdiction to hear an appeal by the Secretary of State against the grant of bail by the SIAC.

2. The new provisions

10.25 Section 32 of the 2004 Act introduces a right of appeal against a decision on bail in the case of a person certified as a 'suspected international terrorist'[55] by the SIAC. The appeal must be on a point of law and will be available for the bail applicant or for 'a person who made representations to the Commission about the application'.[56]

10.26 An appeal against a bail determination in the case of a 'suspected international terrorist' by the SIAC will require leave from the SIAC, or, where the SIAC refuses leave, from the 'appropriate appeal court'.[57]

10.27 Where the determination by the SIAC was made in England or Wales, the 'appropriate appeal court' will be the Court of Appeal. Where the determination was made in Scotland, the 'appropriate appeal court' will be the Court of Session. Where the determination was made in Northern Ireland, the 'appropriate appeal court' will be the Court of Appeal in Northern Ireland.[58]

10.28 The Lord Chancellor may make rules for the procedures for an appeal against a

---

[52] SIAC Act 1997, s 7.

[53] [2004] EWCA Civ 265, [2004] 1 WLR 1349.

[54] The Home Secretary, David Blunkett, complained in the press that the SIAC's decision was 'extraordinary' and might be viewed as 'bonkers'. Lord Donaldson, the former Master of the Rolls, and human rights organizations criticized the Secretary of State for his unusual commentary on a judicial decision.

[55] Under Anti-Terrorism, Crime and Security Act 2001, s 21.

[56] Asylum and Immigration (Treatment of Claimants, etc) Act 2004, s 32(1).

[57] SIAC Act 1997, s 7(2) and Anti-Terrorism, Crime and Security Act 2001, s 24(5) as amended by Asylum and Immigration (Treatment of Claimants, etc) Act 2004, s 32(1).

[58] SIAC Act 1997, s 7(3) and Anti-Terrorism, Crime and Security Act 2001, s 24(5) as amended by Asylum and Immigration (Treatment of Claimants, etc) Act 2004, s 32(1).

TABLE 13-13

THE HEAD-HANGING MANEUVER EVALUATING FOR POSITIONAL NYSTAGMUS

1. The adolescent sits in front of the examiner with eyes directed to the clinician's forehead.
2. The examiner has the teen quickly lie supine while holding the patient's head; have the head turned 30° to one side and then 30° below the exam table. Hold the head firmly but gently!
3. Have the patient sit up.
4. Repeat the procedure on the other side.
5. If positional nystagmus is induced, consider benign paroxysmal positional vertigo.

sclerosis. Brainstem lesions may be evaluated with brainstem evoked potentials.

Benign Paroxysmal Positional Nystagmus

Among three primary vestibular disorders, benign paroxysmal positional vertigo (benign paroxysmal positional nystagmus or cupulolithiasis) is the most common. It is an idiopathic, self-limiting condition in which there are frequent, transient episodes of vertigo, often with head turning, occurring in 1- to 6-week cycles. There is usually an associated positional nystagmus, usually rotatory (with a vertical or horizontal feature), which can be demonstrated with the head-hanging maneuver (Table 13-13). There is usually gradually diminishing severity of symptoms and ultimate clearing over a 6- to 12-month period. It can occur secondary to a viral infection or head trauma, as well as be a normal physiologic variant. Benign positional vertigo may be related to the basilar migraine syndrome. There also is a disorder described in adults, called recurrent vestibulopathy (benign recurrent vertigo or vestibular Meniere's disease) in which patients have intermittent episodes of constant vertigo lasting for minutes or hours.

Labyrinthitis

Labyrinthitis (vestibular neuronitis) is characterized by the sudden onset of vertigo, nystagmus, and ataxia that increases in severity over 8–12 hours and then gradually clears from 4 days to 3 weeks.

The etiology is unknown, but toxin exposure, drug ingestants, and infections of the ear or upper respiratory tract are thought to be contributing factors. The presence of fever, headaches, lethargy, myalgias, leukopenia, and the presence of lymphocytes in CSF all suggest a viral infection. Meniere syndrome is a rare chronic condition characterized by recurrent episodes of vertigo, nystagmus, ataxia, fluctuating hearing loss, and tinnitus. The hearing loss is usually unilateral and there is an increase in semicircular canal fluid. The vertigo can be maximal in certain directions of head and eye movement–as also noted with vestibular neuronitis. Attacks tend to last several hours at a time and occur every 4–8 weeks. The etiology is unknown.

Management

Treatment of these labyrinthine disorders (or vertigo from any cause) is usually symptomatic and employs the following antinauseant drugs alone or in combination with a weak tranquilizer (diazepam).

1. Diphenhydramine HCL (Benadryl—25 or 50 mg capsule): 25–50 mg t.i.d.-q.i.d.
2. Meclizine hydrochloride (Antivert—12.5 mg, 25 mg or 50 mg tabs; Bonine—25 mg tab); 25 mg b.i.d. or q.i.d. p.o.
3. Trimethobenzamide HCL (Tigan 100 mg and 250 mg Caps): 100 mg or 250 mg t.i.d.-q.i.d.

Drug treatment is not always effective in Meniere's disease, and labyrinthectomy may be necessary in particularly resistant and dysfunctional states.

Syncope

Etiology

Syncope, or fainting, is the transient loss of consciousness due to a diminished cerebral blood flow with resultant anoxia. Faintness, also referred to as dizziness, defines the presyncopal period with a sense of impending consciousness loss. Vasovagal syncope is most common, but other possible causes of fainting are listed in Table 13-14. Migraine, hyperventilation, hysteria, orthostatic hypotension, epilepsy, cardiac arrhythmias, aortic stenosis, and heat stroke are noted in adolescents. The thorough history, thoughtful physical examination, and selective laboratory evaluation are primarily directed at the eyes, ears, heart, neurologic system, and psychosocial factors. A detailed history of the events leading up to the syncopal episode(s), including history of any recent medicine or drug use, is important.

Etiology: Cardiac

If the syncope occurs after exercise, consider aortic stenosis, idiopathic hypertrophic subaortic stenosis (IHSS), coronary artery anomaly, cardiac arrhythmias, and illicit drug use. Prolonged ECG monitoring (Holter monitor) may be necessary to pinpoint cardiac arrhythmia as the cause of recurrent syncope. Specialized cardiac catheterization, including transesophageal monitoring and other electrophysiologic studies, may be necessary.

Brain Stem Ischemia: Subclavian Steal Syndrome

Syncope with arm exercise in a teenager with unequal blood pressures in the upper extremities suggests the subclavian steal syndrome. In this unusual syndrome, subclavian artery occlusion results in a reversal of blood flow in the ipsilateral vertebral artery from the basilar artery to the subclavian artery beyond the blocked point; the reduced flow to the brain may cause syncopal symptoms. Other causes of brain stem ischemia, in addition to the subclavian steal syndrome, include basilar artery migraine and transient ischemic attacks (TIAs).

Additional neurologic findings will be present in these cases. Also, syncope while shaving, turning one's head, or wearing a tight collar suggest the carotid sinus syndrome. In this case, a carotid massage for up to 40 seconds can be done while monitoring the blood pressure and ECG to identify the hypersensitive carotid sinus.

Seizure Disorder

Epilepsy and syncope can be difficult to distinguish. See the previous section on epilepsy. Bradycardia, hypotension, and syncope may occur with temporal lobe seizure disorder. Epileptic symptomatology not usually noted with syncope includes mouth frothing, tongue biting, postictal sleepiness, disorientation, and unconsciousness for over 5 minutes. Symptoms suggestive of syncope versus epilepsy include nausea and sweating before the syncopal event as well as orientation after the event.

Other causes of syncope are discussed in the following sections.

Vasovagal Syncope

Etiology

Vasovagal syncope (simple faint; neurocardiogenic syncope; neurallymediated syncope) is a common adolescent phenomenon. Precipitating factors include any set of circumstances that can induce autonomic dysfunction: intense emotion, stress, traumatic injury, pain or the threat of pain, the sight of blood, fasting, medical procedures, fatigue, sudden exposure to cold, coughing, Valsalva maneuver, and others. Vasovagal syncope physiology involves increased stimulation of the mechanoreceptors (C fibers) in the ventricle, with an increase in myocardial contractility, paradoxic decrease in sympathetic activity and increase in parasympathetic tone. There is a resultant bradycardia and hypotension of varying degrees; cerebral vasoconstriction is part of this syncopal mechanism.

Symptomatology: some may not always recall or even wish to recall their specific precipitating factor(s). There is often a positive family and personal history for similar episodes, as well as a

TABLE 13-14

DIFFERENTIAL DIAGNOSIS OF SYNCOPE (SUDDEN LOSS OF CONSCIOUSNESS)

Vasomotor disorders

Simple faint (vasovagal syncope; neurocardiogenic syncope)

Orthostatic hypotension

Hyperventilation (exercise; anxiety)

Situation syncope

    Postmicturition syncope

    Posttussive or cough syncope

    Defecation syncope

    Swallow syncope

Voluntary syncope

CNS disorders

Seizure disorder

Subarachnoid or subdural hemorrhage (spontaneous; traumatic)

Brainstem or spinal cord lesion (paralytic syncope)

Migraine headache

Narcolepsy

Glossopharyngeal neuralgia (related to swallow syncope)

Trigeminal neuralgia

Peripheral neuropathies

Other cerebrovascular disease

Cardiovascular disorders

Idiopathic hypertrophic subaortic stenosis (IHSS)

Aortic stenosis

Tachyarrhythmias

Stokes-Adams syncope (third-degree heart block with asystole)

Mitral valve prolapse with arrhythmia

Other hypertrophic cardiomyopathy

Moyamoya disease (occlusive disease of internal carotid artery and its branches)

Takayasu's arteritis (arteritis of thoracic aorta & branches; also abdominal aorta & branches in some cases)

Pulmonary hypertension

Pulmonary embolism

Carotid sinus hypersensitivity (syndrome)

Subclavian steal syndrome (variant of subclavian artery occlusion)

Myxoma

Behavioral/psychiatric disorders

Conversion disorder

Somatization disorder (hysteria; Briquet syndrome)

Panic disorders

Generalized anxiety disorder

Depression disorders

Others

Miscellaneous

ENT disorders

    Meniere's disease

    Swallow syncope due to esophageal dysfunction

Endocrine disorders

    Hypoglycemia

    Hypocalcemia

    Hyponatremia

Heat stroke

Anemia (severe)

Swimming apnea

Drugs

Tricyclic antidepressants

Monoamine oxidase inhibitors

Phenothiazines

Barbiturates

Calcium channel blockers

ACE inhibitors

Nitrates

Beta-blockers

Hydralazine

Prazosin

Quinidine

Procainamide

Vincristine

Diuretics

Digitalis

Insulin

Alcohol

Cocaine

Marijuana

Others

Others

positive history for migraine headaches and motion sickness. Signs and symptoms are dizziness, weakness, nausea, diaphoresis, blurred vision, salivation, and tachycardia followed shortly by bradycardia. If the individual is sitting or standing, the sudden decrease in cerebral perfusion attendant to the bradycardia results in cerebral anoxia and loss of consciousness for 10 seconds up to several minutes. During this time, the patient is limp, pale, diaphoretic, and unresponsive, with flaccid musculature, bradycardia, and mydriatic but light-reactive pupils. Infrequently, brief tonic-clonic movements or opisthotonus are noted as well, but in these circumstances the diagnosis of vasovagal syncope can only be made after careful exclusion of other possible causes. Confusion with GTCS, simple partial seizures or atonic seizures can occur as noted previously. On return to consciousness, the patient is fully alert without evidencing a postictal state, though symptoms of continued autonomic dysfunction may persist from 5 to 20 minutes; if the patient stands up during this time, syncope may recur.

Laboratory Studies

The upright tilt test has become a useful procedure to identify vasovagal or neurocardiogenic syncope as the cause of approximately 70% of unexplained, recurrent syncope. It can be used to induce vasovagal syncope in the susceptible patient. Blood pressure, heart rate, and ECG monitoring occurs for 15 minutes while the teenager is in the supine position and then while in an upright tilt position (at 60°, 70°, or 90°). If syncope does not occur, the test is repeated after giving intravenous isoproterenol. Syncopal symptoms can occur 2 minutes or more after the position change, including a drop in heart rate, drop in blood pressure (40 mmHg or more), or both. Isoproterenol can sensitize vagal afferent or C fibers involved in the induction of the syncopal event. Standardization of the tilt test in the testing facility used is necessary to produce reliable results.

In general, unless indicated by careful history and physical examination, these tests, though often performed, are usually not helpful in evaluating a patient with recurrent syncope: lumbar puncture, radionuclide brain scan, cerebral angiography, CT,

and MRI. The glucose tolerance test will identify the rare case of hypoglycemia causing the syncope. Tests that are helpful include 24-hour ECG monitoring, tilt testing, carotid sinus message, and possibly EEG monitoring.

Management

Syncope itself may be aborted in the presyncopal phase if the head is placed at or below heart level. This is accomplished by lying the patient down or, if sitting, by placing the head between the knees. During an actual syncopal episode, the patient should be placed on his/her back with legs elevated and the airway cleared. Improvement may occur with attention to known precipitating factors, such as avoiding some of these factors, or even biofeedback treatment to decrease the effect of these factors. Treatment of recurrent vasovagal syncope includes the use of beta-blockers (as metoprolol or atenolol) with reports of 90% efficacy. These medications reduce the contractility of cardiac tissue and inhibit the cardiac receptors that stimulate the syncopal event. It has been shown that the response to intravenous metoprolol during tilt testing does not accurately predict which patient will benefit from the use of beta-blockers.

Another treatment approach has been to increase the intravascular volume by increasing the salt intake, adding a mineral corticoid (fludrocortisone acetate, 0.1–1 mg/day), and have the patient wear an ankle-to-waist support. Other medications reported to help patients with resistant, recurrent syncope include disopyramide phosphate (150 mg t.i.d.), theophylline, fluoxetine HCL (20 mg/day), and transdermal scopolamine (1 patch/3 days). A pacemaker is used for situations that prove resistant to medication, especially if severe bradycardia develops.

Orthostatic Hypotension

Orthostatic (postural) hypotension is a particularly common complaint in adolescents of either sex. Dizziness and light-headedness, with or without actual loss of consciousness, are experienced on standing up rapidly from a sitting or lying position. It can be identified by noting a systolic blood pressure bail decision by the SIAC. The bail applicant[59] will have the right to be legally represented. The rules governing such appeals may provide for the bail applicant not to be given full particulars of the reason for the decision which is the subject of the appeal; and for the proceedings to be held in the absence of any person, including the bail applicant and his legal representatives.[60] The rules may provide for an application for leave to appeal to be heard by a single member of the Commission.[61]

3. Commentary

Section 32 ensures that there will be a possible avenue of appeal, on a point of law, **10.29** for the Secretary of State against the grant of bail to a 'suspected international terrorist' by the SIAC. The Secretary of State will be 'a person who made representations to the Commission about the [original bail] application'.[62] Section 32 therefore adds a further hurdle to a 'suspected international terrorist' obtaining bail.

Section 32 also affords a new avenue of appeal to a 'suspected international **10.30** terrorist' who has been refused bail by the SIAC. An unsuccessful bail applicant who is a 'suspected international terrorist' will now be able to seek leave to appeal, on a point of law, to the appropriate appeal court. However, it should be noted that unsuccessful bail applicants were already able to make repeat applications for bail to the SIAC[63] under the previous legislation.

Section 32 is drafted as an amendment to the provisions on bail in the Anti- **10.31** Terrorism, Crime and Security Act 2001. Section 32 does not cover a person whose bail application must be made to the SIAC, even though he is not certified as a 'suspected international terrorist' (for example, a person who is detained following a decision to deport on national security grounds).[64] This creates an anomaly in which only a bail decision by the SIAC in respect of a 'suspected international terrorist' is subject to appeal. As at the time of writing, the question of whether judicial review is available against a decision of the SIAC had yet to be decided.[65]

---

[59] SIAC Act 1997, s 5 refers to the 'appellant' but this will be taken to refer to the bail applicant. SIAC (Procedure) Rules 2003, SI 2003/1034, r 2(1)(i) clarifies that 'appellant' includes the 'bail applicant'.

[60] SIAC Act 1997, s 5 and Anti-Terrorism, Crime and Security Act 2001, s 27(5)–(6) as amended by Asylum and Immigration (Treatment of Claimants, etc) Act 2004, s 32(2).

[61] SIAC Act 1997, s 8 and Anti-Terrorism, Crime and Security Act 2001, s 27(5)–(6) as amended by Asylum and Immigration (Treatment of Claimants, etc) Act 2004, s 32(2).

[62] Asylum and Immigration (Treatment of Claimants, etc) Act 2004, s 32(1).

[63] Though with an obligation to specify any change of circumstance since a previous refusal: SIAC (Procedure) Rules 2003, r 29(g).

[64] For other classes of person who have to make their bail applications to the SIAC see para 10.20 above.

[65] In *G v Secretary of State for the Home Department* [2004] EWCA Civ 265, [2004] 1 WLR 1349, the Court of Appeal adjourned, for further argument at a subsequent hearing, the question of whether judicial review was available against a decision of the SIAC.

H. DETENTION PENDING DEPORTATION

1. Present legislation

10.32 Section 34 of the 2004 Act amends the Immigration Act 1971, Sch 3, paras 2(1) and 2(2). The Immigration Act 1971, Sch 3 empowers the Secretary of State to detain:

(a) persons in respect of whom a recommendation for deportation has been made by a court which remains in force, pending the making of a deportation order;[66]

(b) persons who have received notice of a decision to make a deportation order pending the making of the deportation order;[67] and

(c) persons against whom a deportation order is in force, pending their removal or departure from the United Kingdom.[68]

10.33 Under the old Sch 3, the Secretary of State could not place a person in immigration detention if he was already in custody or 'for the time being released on bail by a court having power so to release him'. It has been held that the word 'court' in Sch 3, para 2(1) would only refer to a court seised of the issue of deportation.[69] However, this interpretation of 'court' plainly could not extend to a person who had been detained under para 2(2) following an administrative decision by the Secretary of State to deport. The purpose of the amendment therefore appears to be to prevent a situation in which a court, unaware of the deportation order, releases a person on bail, so preventing further detention by the Secretary of State.[70]

2. The new provisions

10.34 The amended para 2(1) will permit a person who is the subject of a court recommendation for deportation to be detained pending the making of a deportation order, even where a court with the power to do so has already granted him bail.

10.35 The amended para 2(2) will permit a person who has received a notice of a decision to make a deportation order against him to be detained pending the making of a deportation order, even where a court with the power to do so has granted him bail.

3. Commentary

10.36 The effect of the new legislation is that the Secretary of State has the power to place a person in immigration detention who has been granted bail by a criminal court (for

---

[66] Immigration Act 1971, Sch 3, para 2(1).
[67] ibid, Sch 3, para 2(2).
[68] ibid, Sch 3, para 2(3), as amended by Immigration and Asylum Act 1999, s 54(3).
[69] *R v Governor of Holloway Prison, ex p Giambi* [1982] 1 WLR 535.
[70] See Explanatory Notes for Bill in House of Lords, para 109.

example, while appealing conviction or sentence[71]) or to re-detain a person liable to deportation who has been bailed from immigration detention.

The new legislation does not specify what will happen where a court has granted **10.37** a person bail being fully aware of the impending deportation. If the Secretary of State re-detained a person where there had been no material change of circumstances since the court's decision to grant bail, it would be strongly arguable that the detention was arbitrary and in breach of Art 5 ECHR.

Unfortunately, the new legislation has not cleared up an anomaly in Immigration **10.38** Act 1971, Sch 3, para 2(1). The wording of para 2(1)[72] appears to reverse the presumption of liberty specifically for persons subject to a court recommendation to deport. However, it has been held that the presumption of liberty applies even where a person is the subject of a recommendation for deportation.[73]

I. FAILING TO CO-OPERATE WITH THE OBTAINING OF A TRAVEL DOCUMENT

1. Present legislation

There are already wide powers to get information to facilitate the obtaining of travel **10.39** documents in order to remove or deport. Under earlier legislation, immigration officers, police, prison officers and anyone else authorized by the Secretary of State can take all such steps as may be reasonably necessary to fingerprint, photograph, measure or otherwise identify immigration detainees[74] and persons liable to immigration detention.[75] Detainees can also be taken in the custody of a constable, or any person acting under the authority of an immigration officer, to any place to ascertain their citizenship or nationality or to make arrangements for their admission to a country other than the United Kingdom.[76] Where a person is to be removed to a country of which he is a national or citizen but does not have a valid passport or travel document for that country, the Secretary of State can provide identification data to the Government[77] but cannot reveal that the person has made a claim for

---

[71] Immigration Act 1971, Sch 3, para 2(1A), added by the Criminal Justice Act 1982, specifies that while a person is appealing against the conviction or the recommendation to deport, the court determining the appeal may direct the person's release without setting aside the recommendation.

[72] ibid, Sch 3, para 2(1) states that persons subject to a court recommendation to deport 'shall' be detained pending the making of a deportation order unless the court making the recommendation or the Secretary of State directs otherwise or unless bail is granted.

[73] *R v Secretary of State for the Home Department, ex p Sedrati, Butraigo-Lopez and Anaghatu* (17 May 2001, Moses J).

[74] Immigration Act 1971, Sch 2, para 18(2) and (2A).

[75] In *R v Secretary of State for the Home Department, ex p Z* [1998] Imm AR 516 these powers were held to apply to persons liable to be detained as well as detainees.

[76] Immigration Act 1971, Sch 2, para 18(3).

[77] Immigration and Asylum Act 1999, s 13.

asylum.[78] (In practice, the fact of applying for a special travel document will often alert the home government that the returnee is a failed asylum seeker.) This data is deemed to be 'a transfer of personal data which is necessary for reasons of substantial public interest',[79] and therefore falls outside the general prohibition in the Data Protection Act 1998[80] on transferring personal data to countries outside the European Economic Area unless there are adequate safeguards on data processing.

10.40   Depending on the person's immigration status, the Secretary of State may be seeking to remove a person to his country of nationality or citizenship or to another country. Overstayers[81] and deportees[82] can be removed to a country of which they are nationals or citizens, or to which there is reason to believe they will be admitted. Illegal entrants and those refused entry can be removed to a country of which they are nationals or citizens; countries in which they obtained a passport or identity documents; countries from which they embarked for the United Kingdom; or to which there is reason to believe they will be admitted.[83]

2. The new provisions

10.41   The 2004 Act creates a new either-way offence of failing to co-operate with the obtaining of a travel document for deportation or removal. The offence—which may be committed by failing to make an appointment or to provide full details on an application for a travel document—carries draconian penalties, and comes with wide powers of arrest, search and entry.

10.42   Under s 35, the Secretary of State may 'require a person to take specified action if the Secretary of State thinks that "(a) the action will enable a travel document to be obtained and (b) the possession of the travel document will facilitate deportation or removal from the United Kingdom"'.[84]

10.43   There is a non-exhaustive list of actions which a person may be required to undertake. A person may be required to provide information or documents to the Secretary of State 'or to any other person';[85] to obtain information or documents;[86] to provide fingerprints, submit to the taking of a photograph or submit to the recording of information about external physical characteristics (including the iris);[87] to make, consent to or co-operate with the making of an application to a representative of a foreign government;[88] to co-operate with a process designed to enable determination

---

[78] Immigration and Asylum Act 1999, s 13(3).
[79] ibid, s 13(4).
[80] Data Protection Act 1998, Sch 1, eighth principle and Sch 4, para 4(1).
[81] Immigration (Removal Directions) Regulations 2000, SI 2000/2243, reg 4(2).
[82] Immigration Act 1971, Sch 3, para 1.
[83] ibid, Sch 2, paras 8(1)(c)(i)–(iv) and 10(1).
[84] Asylum and Immigration (Treatment of Claimants, etc) Act 2004, s 35(1).
[85] ibid, s 35(2)(a).
[86] ibid, s 35(2)(b).
[87] ibid, s 35(2)(c).
[88] ibid, s 35(2)(d).

of an application;[89] to complete a form accurately and completely;[90] to attend an interview and answer questions accurately and completely;[91] and to make an appointment.[92]

If a person 'fails without reasonable excuse' to comply with such a requirement, **10.44** this constitutes an offence.[93] The offence is punishable by up to two years' imprisonment, a fine or both on conviction on indictment;[94] or up to 12 months' imprisonment,[95] a fine up to the statutory maximum (£5,000 at the time of writing) or both on summary conviction.[96]

3. Powers of arrest, search and entry

If a constable or immigration officer reasonably suspects a person of having commit- **10.45** ted an offence under s 35, she may carry out an arrest without warrant.[97]

If a justice of the peace is, by written information on oath, satisfied that there are **10.46** reasonable grounds to suspect that a person liable to be arrested under s 35 is to be found on any premises, she may grant a warrant authorizing any immigration officer or constable to enter the premises, if need be by force, for the purpose of searching for and arresting the suspect.[98]

A justice of the peace may, on an application by an immigration officer, grant a **10.47** warrant for the search of premises for the purpose of seizing material relating to a s 35 offence. There must be reasonable grounds to believe that an offence under s 35 has been committed, and that there is material on the premises likely to be relevant and of substantial value to the investigation of the offence, which is not subject to legal privilege, excluded material or special procedure material. It must be not practicable to communicate with any person entitled to grant entry to the premises; or not practicable to communicate with any person entitled to grant access to the evidence; or entry to the premises will not be granted unless a warrant is produced; or the circumstances must be such that the purposes of the search may be frustrated or seriously prejudiced unless an immigration officer can secure immediate entry.[99]

---

[89] ibid, s 35(2)(e).

[90] ibid, s 35(2)(f).

[91] ibid, s 35(2)(g).

[92] ibid, s 35(2)(h).

[93] ibid, s 35(3).

[94] ibid, s 35(4)(a).

[95] The maximum period of imprisonment on summary conviction for this offence is six months in Scotland and Northern Ireland. The maximum period of imprisonment on summary conviction will remain six months in England and Wales until the commencement of s 154 of the Criminal Justice Act 2003 increases the limits on magistrates' powers of imprisonment to 12 months: Asylum and Immigration (Treatment of Claimants, etc) Act 2004, s 35(9)–(11).

[96] Asylum and Immigration (Treatment of Claimants, etc) Act 2004, s 35(4)(b).

[97] ibid, s 35(4) and (5).

[98] Immigration Act 1971, s 28B as amended by Asylum and Immigration (Treatment of Claimants, etc) Act 2004, s 35(6)(a).

[99] ibid, s 28D as amended by ibid, s 35(6)(a).

10.48   If a person is arrested for a s 35 offence at a place other than a police station, an immigration officer can enter and search any premises in which the person was arrested or in which he was immediately before he was arrested. The power can only be exercised if the officer has reasonable grounds for believing that there is relevant evidence on the premises, and to the extent that it is reasonably required for the purpose of discovering relevant evidence.[100] The immigration officer can also search the arrested person if she has reasonable grounds to suspect that the arrested person may present a danger to himself or to others and search him for anything which he might use to assist his escape from lawful custody or which might be evidence relating to the offence for which he was arrested, but only if there are reasonable grounds to believe that some such thing is concealed on his person and it is reasonably required. Only the removal of outer clothing and the search of a person's mouth is permitted.[101]

10.49   If a person is arrested in police custody for an offence under s 35, he can be searched to see whether he has anything which he might use to cause physical harm to himself or others; damage property; interfere with evidence; or assist his escape; or which the officer has reasonable grounds for believing is evidence relating to the offence. The power can only be exercised to the extent considered necessary by the custody officer for the purpose of discovering the item. This does not permit intimate searches.[102]

10.50   The Secretary of State's immigration powers (of detention, removal and deportation) can still be exercised against a person notwithstanding that proceedings under s 35 have been taken against him.[103]

4. Commentary

10.51   The degree of discretion available under s 35 to the Secretary of State in requiring information is alarming. As the provision is worded, the Secretary of State does not need to have reasonable grounds for his belief that the 'required action' may enable the obtaining of a travel document for removal. The Secretary of State need not even believe that the 'required action' is necessary. The examples of 'required actions' are wide in the extreme. While a person who did not comply with a pointless, unclear, or unduly intrusive requirement might be able to rely on the reasonable excuse defence provided in the statute, there may also be ECHR challenges on the grounds that the law is insufficiently clear and precise.

10.52   Section 35 does not specify what the mental element is for the offence, nor what constitutes a reasonable excuse. Section 35 also does not set out what stage of the appeals, removal or deportation process should have been reached before a person can be 'required to take a specified action' to enable a travel document to be

---

[100] ibid, s 28E as amended by ibid, s 35(6)(b).
[101] ibid, s 28G as amended by ibid, s 35(6)(b).
[102] ibid, s 28H as amended by ibid, s 35(6)(b).
[103] ibid, s 28(4) as amended by ibid, s 35(6)(b).

obtained. Presumably Parliament cannot intend that persons who may yet be found to be at risk on return should be compelled to provide identifying data to the government of their country of origin. Section 35 also does not make specific provision for situations in which there is a dispute over nationality.

J. ELECTRONIC MONITORING

1. The new legislation

Section 36 of the 2004 Act permits the electronic monitoring of persons granted temporary admission or immigration bail and those liable to be detained pending deportation. Initially, electronic monitoring is likely to take the form of wearing an electronic 'tag'. The tag, the size of a large wristwatch and worn on the wrist or ankle, sends a signal to a receiver at a location (usually the person's home address), so that it can be verified that the wearer is there at specified times. Tagging is likely to be attached to a curfew requirement to remain at or near home during certain periods for monitoring purposes. In the future, electronic monitoring may also include requirements to report in by telephone from a fixed landline at a fixed address at a specified time using biometric voice recognition software (so avoiding the need to report physically to a hearing centre or police station). On a more draconian note, electronic monitoring may also, in the future, mean wearing a satellite 'tracking' device which can monitor a person's whereabouts on a continuous basis. **10.53**

The following categories of persons may be subject to electronic monitoring: **10.54**

(a) persons liable to immigration detention or detained pending examination or removal who have had a residence restriction imposed on them as a condition of temporary admission to the United Kingdom;[104]

(b) persons against whom a recommendation for deportation has been made by a court; or who have been given notice of a decision to make a deportation order or against whom a deportation order is in force, while they are not detained and who have had a residence restriction imposed;[105]

(c) persons against whom a reporting condition could have been imposed[106] (ie, persons liable to be detained or detained pending examination or removal and granted temporary admission or temporary release; and persons against whom a recommendation for deportation has been made by a court; or who have been given notice of a decision to make a deportation order or against whom a deportation order is in force, while they are not detained);

---

[104] Asylum and Immigration (Treatment of Claimants, etc) Act 2004, s 36(1)(a) and (2); Immigration Act 1971, Sch 2, para 21.

[105] Asylum and Immigration (Treatment of Claimants, etc) Act 2004, ss 36(1)(a)(ii) and (2); Immigration Act 1971, Sch 3, para 2(5).

[106] Asylum and Immigration (Treatment of Claimants) Act 2004, s 36(3).

(d) persons granted immigration bail on a recognizance or bail bond (in Scotland) by a court, a justice of the peace, the sheriff (in Scotland), the Asylum and Immigration Tribunal, the Secretary of State, an immigration officer or persons granted bail by the SIAC.[107]

10.55 Where electronic monitoring is imposed, the person can be required to wear a device; required to make specified use of the device; prohibited from taking or permitting action which would or might prevent the effective operation of the device; and required to communicate in a specified manner or at specified times or during specified periods.[108]

10.56 Only persons over the age of 18 can be subject to electronic monitoring.[109] No provision is made in the legislation for age dispute cases (in which a person asserts that they are under 18 but this is not accepted by the Secretary of State).

10.57 Electronic monitoring can only be imposed where the Secretary of State has notified those likely to be in a position to exercise powers of electronic monitoring in the area in which the person is residing or is expected to reside.[110] Statutory instruments will contain rules about arrangements for electronic monitoring.[111]

2. Commentary

10.58 No criteria have been set to indicate when imposition of electronic monitoring will be appropriate, or (as the technology develops) which type of monitoring will be appropriate in which circumstances. However, the Minister for Citizenship and Immigration has indicated that:

Tagging will allow those at the lower end of the risk spectrum, who would otherwise have to be detained or would have to report on an onerous basis, to be monitored in other ways. That will free detention space for those whom we believe present a higher risk of absconding . . . the intention is to use the provision in cases where there is a risk of absconding but in which we assess that the risk can be managed by electronic monitoring . . . we shall use the least intrusive option necessary to manage the risk in all cases.[112]

10.59 Electronic monitoring is not subject to time-limits. The lack of checks on the new electronic monitoring powers is of concern: monitoring will potentially affect large numbers; monitoring will restrict the liberty of persons not charged with a criminal offence and the wearing of an electronic device is likely to carry a social stigma. The risk is that electronic monitoring, rather than providing an alternative to detention, will be used for persons who would otherwise have been admitted or released without any conditions, or with less onerous conditions.

---

[107] ibid, s 36(1)(d).
[108] ibid, s 36(6).
[109] ibid, s 36(7).
[110] ibid, ss 36(8)(b) and (10)(b).
[111] ibid, ss 36(8)(a) and (11).
[112] *Hansard*, HC col 364 (22 January 2004).

11

IMMIGRATION SERVICES
(SECTIONS 37–41)

A. Introduction	11.01
B. New power to search and seize evidence	11.08
C. Power to require information from legal professional bodies	11.36
D. New offence of offering prohibited immigration services	11.38
E. Other changes to regulation of immigration services	11.40

A. INTRODUCTION

Sections 37–40 of the Asylum and Immigration (Treatment of Claimants, etc) Act **11.01** 2004 make changes to the scheme of regulation of immigration services (including advice) in the United Kingdom. The main changes are:

(a) the Immigration Services Commissioner is given power to obtain a warrant to enter and search premises and seize material including that which is legally privileged (but not personal material relating to health or counselling);

(b) the Commissioner is also given power to require legal professional bodies to provide information to him and the Secretary of State is given power to remove a body from the approved list if it fails to comply;

(c) the creation of an offence of offering immigration services by a person who would commit an offence by providing such services.

Part V of the Immigration and Asylum Act 1999 came fully into force on 30 October **11.02** 2000.

Part V established an Immigration Services Commissioner. His function is to **11.03** ensure that immigration advisers and representatives are competent and honest:

(a) in the case of members of the legal professions (solicitors, barristers and legal executives), his role is to ensure that their professional bodies adequately supervise the activities and standards of their members;[1]

---

[1] Immigration and Asylum Act 1999, s 86(9).

(b) in the case of immigration advisers who are not members of the legal professions (or working under the supervision of one who is), the Commissioner's role
is to license, supervise and discipline.[2] To that end he is obliged to publish Rules
and a Code of Conduct.[3]

11.04 There are exemptions for employers (in the case of their own employees, prospec-
tive employees and family) and advisers in educational and health establishments.[4]

11.05 It is a criminal offence for a person to provide immigration services or representation if she is not a legal professional or has not been licensed or exempted by the
Commissioner.[5]

11.06 The Immigration Services Tribunal hears appeals from decisions of the
Commissioner to refuse to license or exempt or to impose disciplinary sanctions.[6]

11.07 The Commissioner currently licenses 1,206 organizations and 2,198 individuals
to provide immigration services.[7] In the year ending March 2004, the Commissioner
refused nine applications to continue registration/exemption and 21 new applications.[8] About 500 complaints were received, of which 90 per cent came from the
public.[9] No disciplinary charges were made.[10] There were 12 prosecutions for provision of unauthorized services, which resulted in 11 convictions.[11]

B. NEW POWER TO SEARCH AND SEIZE EVIDENCE

1. Background

11.08 Under the original scheme, the Commissioner has no power to search and seize
evidence and there is no criminal sanction for a refusal to co-operate.

11.09 In cases of complaints about competence or fitness, or of a breach of the
Commissioner's Rules, the Commissioner's staff may:

(a) enter premises being used by a registered person during reasonable hours;

(b) require persons on the premises to provide documents and computer records; and

(c) take copies of those documents and/or records.[12]

---

[2] ibid, ss 83–85 and Sch 5.

[3] ibid, Sch 5, paras 1 and 3.

[4] Immigration and Asylum Act 1999 (Part V Exemption: Educational Institutions and Health Sector
Bodies) Order 2001, SI 2001/1403; Immigration and Asylum Act 1999 (Part V Exemption: Relevant
Employers) Order 2003, SI 2003/3214.

[5] Immigration and Asylum Act 1999, s 91.

[6] ibid, ss 87–88.

[7] Annual Report and Accounts of the Office of the Immigration Service Commissioner 2003–04 (HC
663, 21 July 1994) 8.

[8] ibid, 12–13.

[9] ibid, 18.

[10] ibid, 17.

[11] ibid, 26.

[12] Immigration and Asylum Act 1999, Sch 5, para 7.

Refusal to co-operate with such a visit may result in cancellation of the registration.[13]

There is no power to enter or search premises suspected of being used for immigration services by a person who is not already registered. **11.10**

2. The new power

Section 38(1) of the 2004 Act adds a new s 92A to the Immigration and Asylum Act 1999. Section 92A empowers the Commissioner to apply to a justice of the peace (or, in Scotland, a sheriff) for a warrant to enter and search premises and to seize material there. Premises include a dwelling.[14] **11.11**

Under s 92A(2)–(3), the warrant can only be issued if there are reasonable grounds for believing that each of the following conditions is met: **11.12**

(a) an offence has been committed under Immigration and Asylum Act 1999, s 91, ie immigration services have been provided by a person who is neither a legal professional, nor registered or exempted by the Commissioner;

(b) there is material on the premises which is likely to be of substantial value to the investigation of the offence;

(c) it is not practicable to communicate with a person entitled to grant access or entry to the premises;

(d) entry to the premises will be prevented unless a warrant is produced; and

(e) the purpose of the search may be frustrated or seriously prejudiced unless the Commissioner can secure immediate entry on arrival at the premises.

The terms of these provisions are based in part on those used for 'special procedure material' in the Police and Criminal Evidence Act 1984.[15] However, the Commissioner can also seize material which could not be used as evidence at a trial.[16] **11.13**

A person who obstructs the Commissioner is guilty of an offence punishable by imprisonment.[17] **11.14**

3. Limits on material that can be seized

The Commissioner's power to seize material extends to 'legally privileged material'.[18] This is particularly important since the power can be used to seize material **11.15**

---

[13] ibid, Sch 5, para 7(7).
[14] ibid, s 92A(7)(b).
[15] See Sch 1, paras 2(a)(iii), 14(a) and (b).
[16] Immigration and Asylum Act 1999, s 92A(7)(c)(iii). (Compare with Police and Criminal Evidence Act 1984, Sch 1, para 2(a)(iv) and definition of 'relevant evidence' in s 8(4) of that Act.)
[17] ibid, s 92A(5)–(6).
[18] ibid, s 92A(7)(c)(i) and (8)(b).

from solicitors' offices and barristers' chambers. This could arise if the Commissioner suspects that a solicitor is allowing her offices to be used by unlicensed advisers or if a barrister is suspected of assisting such advisers.

11.16 In England, Wales and Northern Ireland, the Commissioner's power to seize does not extend to 'excluded material' or to 'special procedures material'.[19] These limitations may prove important in some cases where the Commissioner is considering searching premises belonging to an unlicensed adviser.

11.17 *'Excluded material'* (and 'personal records') are defined in Police and Criminal Evidence Act 1984, ss 11 and 12.[20]

(a) It is material which was acquired or created by the adviser concerned in the course of her business as an adviser;

(b) is documentary or other records relating to:
  (i) an identifiable person's physical or mental health;
  (ii) spiritual counselling or assistance given to such a person; or
  (iii) counselling or assistance given to that person for the purposes of his personal welfare by a voluntary organization or by an individual who by reason of her office or occupation has responsibilities for the person's personal welfare;

(c) is held in confidence.

11.18 Excluded material would therefore include: medical reports; reports from counsellors; letters from spiritual figures such as priests relating to counselling or spiritual assistance given to the client; and letters from community leaders relating to counselling or personal welfare assistance. Correspondence with such persons about reports, counselling or assistance is also excluded. The material is excluded even if it is also legally privileged.

11.19 *'Special procedures material'* (and 'journalistic material') are defined in Police and Criminal Evidence Act 1984, ss 13 and 14.[21] It is material which:

(a) was acquired or created by the adviser concerned in the course of her business as an adviser;

(b) is not legally privileged material; but

(c) is held in confidence.

It is suggested that any material provided by a client to his adviser to enable him to be advised or represented is to be presumed to be held in confidence by that adviser.

11.20 'Legally privileged material' is defined in s 10 of the Police and Criminal Evidence Act 1984.[22] It consists of material created by the adviser or the client for

---

[19] ibid, s 92A(7)(c)(ii) and (9).

[20] For Northern Ireland, see Police and Criminal Evidence (Northern Ireland) Order 1989, SI 1989/1341, arts 13–14.

[21] ibid, arts 15 and 16.

[22] ibid, art 12.

the purpose of receiving advice or of bringing legal proceedings. Legal advice has been held to include advice on how best to proceed with conveying title to real property.[23] It seems therefore that advice on how to make or proceed with an immigration application, such as one for leave to enter or remain, is legally privileged.

It follows that the Commissioner is entitled to seize letters of advice, drafts of witness statements, drafts of expert reports and correspondence with potential witnesses (unless the material is excluded: see paras 11.17–11.18 above). **11.21**

However, legal privilege does not extend to documents which are not created for the purpose of legal advice or proceedings.[24] Examples of such documents which may arise in cases investigated by the Commissioner are: marriage and birth certificates; foreign arrest warrants and court documents; political party membership cards; unsolicited letters from abroad; and bank statements. Notes in diaries or on time-sheets about meetings with a client are not legally privileged.[25] **11.22**

'Special procedures material' also includes 'journalistic material', ie material acquired or created for the purposes of journalism, which is still in the possession of the person who acquired it or created it for those purposes, or who received it from someone who intended it to be used for journalistic purposes.[26] **11.23**

Material remains excluded/special procedures material even if it is not held by the adviser personally, but on her behalf (for example by a relative).[27] **11.24**

Material would cease to be excluded/special procedures material if the client to whom it relates waives his right to confidence in those documents, for example by notifying the Commissioner that he does so. **11.25**

In order to have excluded or special procedures material seized, the Commissioner can ask the police to apply to a circuit judge for a warrant under Police and Criminal Evidence Act 1984, Sch 1. This can only be done in respect of material which would be admissible in evidence.[28] **11.26**

4. ECHR compatibility

Legal professional privilege is 'a fundamental human right long established in the common law'.[29] Section 92A(7)(c) and (8)(b) expressly empowers the justice or sheriff to allow the commissioner to override that right. **11.27**

Article 8(1) of the European Convention on Human Rights (ECHR) guarantees **11.28**

---

[23] *R v Inner London Crown Court, ex p Baines and Baines (a firm)* [1988] QB 579, 587 (though the contrary does not seem to have been argued).

[24] *R v Guildhall Magistrates' Court, ex p Primlaks Holdings Co (Panama) Inc* [1990] 1 QB 261, 273–274.

[25] *R v Manchester Crown Court, ex p Rogers* [1999] 1 WLR 832.

[26] Police and Criminal Evidence Act 1984, s 13.

[27] *R v Chief Constable of the Metropolitan Police, ex p Gross* (DC, 24 July 1998) p 12 of transcript.

[28] Police and Criminal Evidence Act 1984, Sch 1, para 2(a)(iv) and definition of 'relevant evidence' in s 8(4) of that Act.

[29] *R (Morgan Grenfell and Co Ltd) v Special Commissioner for Income Tax* [2002] UKHL 21, [2003] 1 AC 563 at [7] *per* Lord Hoffmann.

the right to respect for correspondence, which includes legal professional privilege. Any interference must be 'accompanied by adequate and effective safeguards which ensure minimum impairment of the right to respect for his correspondence'.[30]

11.29   The Government's justification for s 92A is that prosecution of offences under s 91 is necessary to prevent unqualified advisers preying on immigrants, and that the material needed to make good the prosecution will often consist of material which is legally privileged.[31] The Government points to the following factors:[32]

(a) the Commissioner is concerned with prosecuting advisers not their clients;

(b) onward transmission of information obtained is limited by Immigration and Asylum Act 1999, s 93;

(c) the Commissioner must satisfy a justice or sheriff that the warrant should be issued.

It is suggested that these matters may be insufficient to meet the requirements of Art 8 ECHR.

11.30   First, it is unclear what level of protection against onward disclosure is provided. The Commissioner has power to disclose information if necessary for the purpose of discharging his functions under that Act.[33] He is required to exercise his functions to secure that immigration advisers neither 'knowingly mislead any court, tribunal or adjudicator in the United Kingdom' nor 'abuse any procedure operating in the UK in connection with immigration or asylum'.[34] It may be that the Commissioner or a member of staff will consider that these functions entitle the disclosure of legally privileged material to the immigration service in cases where the Commissioner suspects that a procedure may have been abused or a court or tribunal misled. If an early draft of a witness statement or report suggests that a person has changed his account, that might be thought to constitute evidence of an abuse of procedure.

11.31   Secondly, the procedure for obtaining and executing the warrant affords no real protection:

(a) the Commissioner can authorize any member of his staff to apply for a warrant[35] (that compares poorly with the legal restrictions on the police, where an application for a warrant must be supported by a signed written authority from an officer of inspector rank or above[36]);

---

[30] *Foxley v United Kingdom* (2000) 31 EHRR 637, para 43; see also *Campbell v United Kingdom* (1992) 15 EHRR 137.

[31] Letter of 27 January 2004 from Beverley Hughes MP to JCHR, published as Appendix 1 to the Committee's *Scrutiny of Bills: Progress Report*, Third Report of Session 2003–04 (HL Paper 23, HC Paper 252) 47.

[32] ibid, 47–48.

[33] Immigration and Asylum Act 1999, s 93(3)(b).

[34] ibid, s 83(5).

[35] ibid, s 92A(7)(a).

[36] Police and Criminal Evidence Act 1984 Code B 'Code Of Practice For Searches Of Premises By Police Officers And The Seizure Of Property Found By Police Officers On Persons Or Premises', para 3.4.

(b) the application can be made orally (applications by the police must be supported in writing[37]);

(c) refused applications can be renewed before a different justice (the police may only do this if different grounds become available[38]);

(d) there is no statutory requirement to give the occupier of the premises a copy of the warrant or notice of any statutory rights, nor any statutory rules for the conduct of searches.[39]

Thirdly, the requirement to persuade a justice of the peace affords minimal protec- **11.32** tion. A justice of the peace is at the lowest level of the English judiciary. (The Government's lack of concern with this aspect of protection is demonstrated by its reluctance to agree that warrants could not be issued by Scottish justices of the peace, some of whom have no legal training at all.[40])

An application for excluded or special procedures material can only be made to a **11.33** circuit judge (there is no equivalent procedure in Scotland). In *R v Maidstone Crown Court, ex p Waitt*,[41] Lloyd LJ described the special procedure for these kinds of material as 'a serious inroad on the liberty of the subject'. He continued: 'The responsibility for ensuring that the procedure is not abused lies with the circuit judges. It is of cardinal importance that circuit judges should be scrupulous in discharging that responsibility. The responsibility is greatest when the circuit judge is asked to issue a search warrant under [the ex parte procedure] of paragraph 12.'

A warrant under s 92A confers authority to seize legally privileged material, **11.34** which even the special procedure does not permit. It is suggested that Art 8 ECHR requires at least equivalent procedural protection to that given for excluded and special procedure material and that this requires the warrant to be issued by a circuit judge.[42]

5. Extension of power to enter premises

Section 38(2) of the 2004 Act extends the Commissioner's existing power to enter **11.35** premises and require documents (see para 11.09 above). The power is extended to exempt persons[43] and to cases where the complaint only relates to a breach of the Code of Conduct.[44]

---

[37] ibid, para 3.6.
[38] ibid, para 3.8.
[39] Again, compare with ibid, paras 6.7–6.8 and 6.9–6.13 respectively.
[40] *Hansard*, HL col 732 (27 April 2004), col 754 (18 May 2004), col 777 (6 July 2004).
[41] [1988] Crim LR 384.
[42] See Third Report, n 31 above, paras 95–98.
[43] Asylum and Immigration (Treatment of Claimants, etc) Act 2004, s 38(2)(b), (d) and (e).
[44] ibid, s 38(2)(a) and (c).

C. POWER TO REQUIRE INFORMATION FROM LEGAL PROFESSIONAL BODIES

11.36 Section 86 of the Immigration and Asylum Act 1999 designates the professional bodies for solicitors, barristers, advocates and legal executives as those whose members are authorized to provide immigration services. The Secretary of State may by order remove a body from that list if it has consistently failed to provide effective regulation of its members in their provision of immigration services. The effect of such an order would be to require all the members of that body who wished to provide immigration services to become licensed by the Commissioner.

11.37 Section 41 of the 2004 Act amends Immigration and Asylum Act 1999, s 86 so that:

(a) each designated professional body is required to comply with a request of the Commissioner for information;[45]

(b) the Commissioner must report to the Secretary of State if such a body has failed to comply with a request[46] and address that matter in the annual report;[47]

(c) the Secretary of State can by order remove a body from the list if it has failed to comply with a request by the Commissioner for the provision of information.[48]

D. NEW OFFENCE OF OFFERING PROHIBITED IMMIGRATION SERVICES

11.38 Section 39 of the 2004 Act adds a new s 92B to the Immigration and Asylum Act 1999. Section 92B makes it a criminal offence to offer to provide advice or services when that provision would be an offence, ie where the person who would provide them is neither a member of a professional body nor registered with or exempted by the Commissioner.

11.39 A person is regarded as offering to provide services if she arranges an advertisement in which she offers those services or is presented as competent to provide them.[49]

E. OTHER CHANGES TO REGULATION OF IMMIGRATION SERVICES

11.40 The 2004 Act makes some other minor changes to the regulation of immigration services.

---

45 Immigration and Asylum Act 1999, s 86(9A).
46 ibid, s 86(9)(b)(ii).
47 ibid, Sch 5, para 21(2)(b).
48 ibid, s 86(2)(b).
49 ibid, s 92B(2)(b) and (c).

Section 40 of the 2004 Act abolishes the right of appeal to the Immigration **11.41**
Services Tribunal from a decision of the Commissioner to allow a complaint to lie
on the file. Four of the 11 hearings held by the Tribunal in the year to March 2004
concerned such appeals.[50]

Under Immigration and Asylum Act 1999, s 84 a person is licensed if she works **11.42**
under the supervision of a person who is a member of a professional body or is registered with or exempted by the Commissioner. Section 37(1)–(2) of the 2004 Act
amends ss 84 and 85 so that a person is only licensed or exempt if she 'acts on behalf
of and under the supervision of' such a person. Section 37(3) and (4) amends
Immigration and Asylum Act 1999, ss 89 and 90, so that a person who acts on behalf
of a registered person can be disciplined by the Immigration Services Tribunal.
Consequential amendments are made to Immigration and Asylum Act 1999, Schs 5
and 6 by s 37(5) and (6)(b).

Section 37(6)(a) removes the Commissioner's discrete power to require an appli- **11.43**
cation for registration to be accompanied by information and supporting evidence.[51]
However, the Commissioner retains power to require the application to be made in
such form and manner as he determines.[52]

Section 41(5) amends Immigration and Asylum Act 1999, s 166(2) in relation to **11.44**
s 90(1) to make clear that an order by a disciplinary body against an individual is not
required to be made by statutory instrument.

---

[50] Annual Report and Accounts, n 7 above, 17.
[51] Immigration and Asylum Act 1999, Sch 6, para 1(1)(b).
[52] ibid, Sch 6, para 1(1)(a).

12

EUROPEAN ASYLUM PROCEDURES DIRECTIVE

A. Unfounded claims (safe countries of origin)	12.03
B. Third country removals	12.15
C. Rights of appeal	12.34

Final agreement on the text of the Council Directive on minimum standards on **12.01** procedures in Member States for granting and withdrawing refugee status was reached on 29 April 2004, subject to parliamentary scrutiny reservations from the German, Netherlands, Swedish and UK delegations.[1] The European Parliament is also to be re-consulted on the text of the Directive. Its formal adoption is intended to take place in December 2004, requiring a unanimous vote of the 25 current Member States in the Council.

The drafting process proved contentious and has led to a consistent diminution in **12.02** standards. The focus in this chapter is on three aspects that relate directly to the Asylum and Immigration (Treatment of Claimants, etc) Act 2004:[2]

(a) unfounded claims;
(b) third country removals;
(c) appeals.

A. UNFOUNDED CLAIMS (SAFE COUNTRIES OF ORIGIN)

Note that the Directive refers to safe countries of origin as one category of 'third **12.03** country', whereas in the United Kingdom, the term 'third country' usually denotes a

---

[1] The approved draft is document 8771/04, Interinstitutional File 2000/0238 (CNS), 30 April 2004, see http://register.consilium.eu.int/pdf/en/04/st08/st08771.en04.pdf.

[2] This chapter draws extensively on the *Analysis and Critique of the Directive* (July 2004) of the Immigration Law Practitioners' Association (ILPA), the UK's professional association of immigration lawyers, advisers and academics. Available at www.ilpa.org.uk.

country other than the claimant's country of origin. The Preamble to the Directive states that:

The designation of a third country as a safe country of origin for the purposes of this Directive cannot establish an absolute guarantee of safety for nationals of that country. By its very nature, the assessment underlying the designation can only take into account the general civil, legal and political circumstances in that country and whether actors of persecution, torture or inhuman or degrading treatment or punishment are subject to sanction in practice when found liable in the country concerned. For this reason, it is important that, where an applicant shows that there are serious reasons to consider the country not to be safe in his/her particular circumstances, the designation of the country as safe can no longer be considered relevant for him/her.

12.04   Article 30 sets out procedures for drawing up a 'Minimum common list of third countries as safe countries of origin':

1. The third countries designated in the minimum common list of third countries as contained in Annex . . . shall be regarded by Member States as safe countries of origin.

2. The Council may, acting by a qualified majority on a proposal from the Commission and after consultation of the European Parliament, amend the minimum common list by adding or removing third countries, in accordance with Annex II. The Commission shall examine any request made by the Council or by a Member State that it submit a proposal to amend the minimum common list. When making its proposal, the Commission shall make use of information from the Member States, its own information and, where necessary, information from UNHCR, the Council of Europe and other relevant international organisations.

3. Where the Council requests the Commission to submit a proposal for removing a third country from the minimum common list, the obligation of Member States pursuant to Article 30B(2) shall be suspended with regard to this third country as of the day following the Council decision requesting such a submission.

4. Where a Member State requests the Commission to submit a proposal to the Council for removing a third country from the minimum common list, that Member State shall notify the Council in writing of the request made to the Commission. The obligation of this Member State pursuant to Article 30B(2) shall be suspended with regard to the third country as of the day following the notification of the request to the Council.

5. The European Parliament shall be informed of the suspensions under paragraphs 3 and 4.

6. The suspensions under paragraphs 3 and 4 shall end after three months, unless the Commission makes a proposal, before the end of this period, to withdraw the third country from the minimum common list. The suspensions shall end in any case where the Council rejects, a proposal by the Commission to withdraw the third country from the list.

7. Upon request by the Council, the Commission shall report to the Council and the European Parliament on whether the situation of a country on the minimum common list is still in conformity with Annex II. When presenting its report to the Council and the European Parliament, the Commission may make such recommendations or proposals as it deems appropriate.

12.05   The Immigration Law Practitioners' Association's (ILPA) *Analysis and Critique* raises fundamental competency concerns about this provision which requires member states to accept a common list of 'safe countries of origin' and to treat those countries as generally safe even if that is inconsistent with the assessment of those countries by the relevant national authorities. ILPA comments as follows:

Article 30(1)   Mandatory list—competence concerns

The Directive creates a procedure to establish a common list of countries which all Member States must treat as 'safe countries of origin'. The Commission originally proposed that Member States should have an option whether to apply the principle in their asylum law, subject to strict safeguards. However, in October 2003 the Council agreed that Member States would be required to apply this principle, at least for a common list of states deemed 'safe'. Many Member States do not currently operate safe country of origin systems. Accordingly, aside from the clear human rights concerns, this is the first time that EU Member States will be required to dilute their standards of protection by a measure of EC law. This raises serious *competence concerns*, as the EU is only entitled to establish 'minimum standards' in this area. In contrast, Article 30(1) states that countries on the common list 'shall be regarded by the Member States' as safe countries of origin. Thus, they are precluded from adopting higher standards in this field. This is the case notwithstanding Article 30B(3), which provides that 'Member States shall lay down in national legislation further rules and modalities for the application of the safe country of origin concept' and the provision of some individual assessment under Article 30(1). While individual Member States may add to the list, they may not subtract from it, even if the human rights situation in a particular country deteriorates.

Article 30(2)   Procedural Impropriety

The *procedure* for agreeing this common list is suspect. It is to be determined by the Council by QMV, with mere consultation of the European Parliament. There is a legal impediment to creating such an implementation mechanism, as it is not envisaged in Title IV EC. Rather, what the Treaty envisages in Article 67(5) EC, is that once the Council has adopted 'common rules and basic principles' in relation to asylum procedures by unanimity, further measures in this field *must* be adopted under co-decision. Thus, agreeing the common list by QMV with mere consultation would infringe the prerogatives of the European Parliament, and disturb the institutional balance of the Treaty.

Article 30(3)–(6)   Removal of countries from the list

Even if the accuracy of the original list could be assumed, human rights situations can change rapidly. The process is not sufficiently receptive to the possibility of deterioration of human rights standards. Where an individual Member State requests the Commission to propose an amendment to the list, that Member State is then temporarily freed of the requirement to treat applications from that country as unfounded. However, until the Commission proposes the formal amendment to the list, and that amendment is agreed by the Council by QMV, other Member States remain obliged to treat the country as safe. (emphasis in original)

Article 30A deals with 'national designation of third countries as safe countries of **12.06** origin':

1. Without prejudice to Article 30, Member States may retain or introduce legislation that allows, in accordance with Annex II, for the national designation of third countries other than those appearing on the minimum common list, as safe countries of origin for the purpose of examining applications for asylum. This may include designation of part of a country as safe where the conditions in Annex II are fulfilled in relation to that part.

2. By derogation to paragraph 1, Member States may retain legislation in force at the time of adoption of this Directive that allows for the national designation of third countries, other than those appearing on the minimum common list, as safe countries of origin for the purposes of examining applications for asylum where they are satisfied that persons in the third countries concerned are generally neither subject to:

   (a) persecution as defined in Article 9 of Council Directive . . . on minimum standards for the qualification and status of third country nationals or stateless persons as refugees or as persons who otherwise need international protection and the content of the protection granted; nor

   (b) torture or inhuman or degrading treatment or punishment.

3. Member States may also retain legislation in force at the time of the adoption of this Directive that allows for the national designation of part of a country as safe or a country or part of a country as safe for a specified group of persons in that country where the conditions in paragraph 2 are fulfilled in relation to that part or group.

4. In assessing whether a country is a safe country of origin in accordance with paragraphs 2 and 3, Member States shall have regard to the legal situation, the application of the law and the general political circumstances in the third country concerned.

5. The assessment of whether a country is a safe country of origin in accordance with this Article shall be based on a range of sources of information, including in particular information from other Member States, the UNHCR, the Council of Europe and other relevant international organisations.

6. Member States shall notify to the Commission the countries that are designated as safe countries of origin in accordance with the provisions of this Article.

12.07 The United Kingdom may therefore be able to designate countries as safe countries of origin even though they have not been included in the EU common list. However, the article draws a distinction between pre-existing and new legislation. In respect of new national legislation, the test for designation must reflect that set out in Annex II of the Directive (see para 12.13 below). However, the United Kingdom may continue to apply existing domestic legislation (ie, in force when the Directive comes into force) which permits designation of a country or part thereof as 'safe', either for all persons or for 'a specified group of persons' where such persons are 'generally' not subjected to persecution or Art 3 ECHR ill-treatment. This formulation is actually narrower than the test in s 94, which is that removal to the designated state 'will not in general contravene the United Kingdom's obligations under the Human Rights Convention'. In light of the House of Lords' decision in *Ullah*,[3] the Secretary of State is not entitled to restrict his consideration to Art 3 ill-treatment when determining whether to designate a state under s 94, but must consider evidence relating to all substantive articles of the ECHR.

12.08 With respect to Art 30A(5), see also the concerns raised about the quality of country information informing designation of safe countries of origin by the Secretary of State.[4]

---

[3] *R (Ullah) v Special Adjudicator* [2004] UKHL 26, [2004] 2 AC 323.

[4] See paras 8.40–8.46 above.

Article 30B provides as follows: **12.09**

Application of the safe country of origin concept

1. A third country designated as a safe country of origin either in accordance with the provisions of Article 30 or 30A can, after an individual examination of the application, be considered as a safe country of origin for a particular applicant for asylum only if:
   (a) he/she has the nationality of that country or,
   (b) he/she is a stateless person and was formerly habitually resident in that country;
and he/she has not submitted any serious grounds for considering the country not to be a safe country of origin in his/her particular circumstances in terms of his/her qualification as a refugee in accordance with Council Directive . . . on minimum standards for the qualification and status of third country nationals or stateless persons as refugees or as persons who otherwise need international protection and the content of the protection granted.

2. Member States shall, in accordance with paragraph 1, consider the application for asylum as unfounded where the third country is designated as safe pursuant to Article 30.

3. Member States shall lay down in national legislation further rules and modalities for the application of the safe country of origin concept.

Article 30B is somewhat oddly worded. Article 30B(1) appears to confirm that a   **12.10**
country can be treated as a safe country of origin for the particular claimant only if
there are no serious grounds for considering that it is not a safe country of origin for
that claimant in light of his individual circumstances. If that is interpreted as asking
whether the claim is arguable, then the provision is capable of being read consistently with the domestic case law on the 'clearly unfounded' test.

In that case, though, it is unclear how Article 30B(2) fits. If it were the case that   **12.11**
countries from the common list of safe countries of origin were to be assumed to be
safe regardless of the facts of the individual case then that would be plainly inconsistent with s 94 and the relevant case law.

Paragraph 2 is, however, expressly to be applied 'in accordance with paragraph   **12.12**
1'. The better view therefore is that the presumption is in law no more significant
than the distinction between designated and non-designated states under s 94 (see
paras 8.06–8.07 above): the overriding issue is whether or not there is an arguable
claim, rather than how the claim is treated if it is not arguable.

Annex II sets out the criteria for inclusion in the common list of safe countries of   **12.13**
origin:

Designation of safe countries of origin for the purposes of Articles 30 and 30A(1)

A country is considered as a safe country of origin where, on the basis of the legal situation, the application of the law within a democratic system and the general political circumstances, it can be shown that there is generally and consistently no persecution as defined in Article 9 of Council Directive . . . on minimum standards for the qualification and status of third country nationals or stateless persons as refugees or as persons who otherwise need international protection and the content of the protection granted; no torture or inhuman or degrading treatment or punishment; and no threat by reason of indiscriminate violence in situations of international or internal armed conflict.

In making this assessment, account shall be taken inter alia of the extent to which protection is provided against persecution or mistreatment through:

(a) the relevant laws and regulations of the country and the manner in which they are applied;

(b) observance of the rights and freedoms laid down in the European Convention for the Protection of Human Rights and Fundamental Freedoms and/or the International Covenant for Civil and Political Rights and/or the Convention against Torture, in particular the rights from which derogation cannot be made under Article 15(2) of the said European Convention;

(c) respect of the non-refoulement principle according to the Geneva Convention;

(d) provision for a system of effective remedies against violations of these rights and freedoms.

12.14 The Council also adopted the following statement:

The Council considers, having regard to the preparatory work already conducted, that apart from Romania and Bulgaria, the following countries may also be suitable for inclusion on a minimum common list of safe countries of origin to be adopted as part of this Directive: Benin, Botswana, Cape Verde, Chile, Costa Rica, Ghana, Mali, Mauritius, Senegal, Uruguay.

The Council undertakes, prior to the date on which the European Parliament will be re-consulted with regard to this draft Directive, to conduct during the coming months an in-depth assessment of these countries to ensure that they fulfil the criteria in Annex II. When conducting this assessment, regard shall be had to a range of information sources, including information from the Member States, the UNHCR, the Council of Europe and other international organisations. Where, following this assessment, a country is considered not to fulfil the criteria in Annex II, that country shall not be included on the minimum common list of safe countries of origin.

It will be apparent that the proposed list bears little resemblance to the list presently operated in the United Kingdom.

B. THIRD COUNTRY REMOVALS

1. The European third country scheme

12.15 The Directive (together with the Dublin II Regulation which is already in force) will create a detailed legislative scheme at EU level governing third country removals by member states, both to other member states and to states outside the EU. Reflecting to some degree the 'graded' categories of 'safe third countries' created by Sch 3 of the 2004 Act, the EU scheme will create three categories of safe third country: first, member states; secondly, 'supersafe' non-EU third countries in the European region; thirdly, ordinary 'safe' third countries which do not qualify under the first two categories. The correlation between the respective categorizations under Sch 3 and at EU level is discussed further at paras 12.31–12.33.

(a) *Removal to member states*

Procedures for third country transfers within the European Union and Iceland and **12.16**
Norway are now covered by the Dublin II Regulation.[5] Paragraph 8 of the Preamble
states that Iceland and Norway will be treated as member states for the purposes of
the Dublin Convention and references in this text to 'member states' include them.

Dublin II (like its predecessor, the Dublin Convention) does not address issues **12.17**
about the safety of the member state to which a transfer is made. Neither does the
Asylum Procedures Directive. The Preamble to the Directive states that:

This Directive does not deal with procedures governed by Council Regulation (EC) No
343/2003 of 18 February 2003 establishing the criteria and mechanisms for determining the
Member State responsible for examining an asylum application lodged in one of the Member
States by a third country national.

In domestic terms, these member states will constitute the First List under Sch 3. **12.18**
(See Chapter 9 for issues relating to human rights challenges to removal to First List
states.)

(b) *The Supersafe Third Country concept*

The next category, consisting of the so-called 'supersafe countries', was added late **12.19**
in the drafting negotiations at the behest of some member states. The aim is to reduce
the scope for challenging removals to some countries in the European region outside
the European Union. (The concept cannot be applied outside the Council of Europe
as ratification of the ECHR is a necessary although not a sufficient criterion.)

The criteria for membership of this category, and the implications of member- **12.20**
ship, are governed by Art 35A of the Directive. This states as follows:

1. Member States may provide that no, or no full, examination of the asylum application and
of the safety of the applicant in his/her particular circumstances as described in Chapter II
takes place in cases where a competent authority has established, on the basis of the facts, that
the applicant for asylum is seeking to enter or has entered illegally into its territory from a safe
third country according to paragraph 2.

2. A third country can only be considered as a safe third country for the purpose of paragraph
1 where:
   (a) it has ratified and observes the provisions of the Geneva Convention without any
       geographical limitations; and
   (b) it has in place an asylum procedure prescribed by law; and
   (c) it has ratified the European Convention for the Protection of Human Rights and
       Fundamental Freedoms and it observes its provisions, including the standards relating
       to effective remedies; and
   (d) it has been so designated by the Council in accordance with paragraph 3.

---

[5] Council Regulation (EC) 343/2003 of 18 February 2003 establishing the criteria and mechanisms
for determining the Member State responsible for examining an asylum application lodged in one of the
Member States by a third-country national [2003] OJ L50/1.

3. The Council shall, acting by qualified majority on the proposal of the Commission and after consultation of the European Parliament, adopt or amend a common list of third countries that shall be regarded as safe third countries for the purposes of paragraph 1.

4. Member States concerned shall lay down in national law the modalities for implementing the provisions of paragraph 1 and the consequences of decisions pursuant to those provisions in accordance with the principle of non-refoulement under the Geneva Convention including providing for exceptions from the application of this Article for humanitarian or political reasons or for reasons of public international law.

5. When implementing a decision solely based on this Article, Member States concerned shall:

    (a) inform the applicant accordingly; and

    (b) provide him/her with a document informing the authorities of the third country, in the language of that country, that the application has not been examined in substance.

6. Where the safe third country does not readmit the applicant for asylum in question, Member States shall ensure that access to a procedure is given in accordance with the basic principles and guarantees described in Chapter II.

7. Member States which have designated third countries as safe countries in accordance with national legislation in force at the date of the adoption of this Directive and on the basis of the criteria in paragraph 2(a) to (c), may apply paragraph 1 to these third countries until such time as the Council has adopted the common list pursuant to paragraph 3.

12.21   Unlike the common list of 'safe countries of origin', there does not appear to be any compulsion upon member states to accept all the states on the common list as 'supersafe' for the purposes of this article.

12.22   ILPA comments in its *Analysis and Critique* that:

These provisions are grounded on the assumption that countries in the European region may be assumed to be safer than others—'supersafe'. The criteria are ratification of the Refugee Convention without any geographical limitations; having in place an asylum process and ratification of the ECHR and observing its provisions, including those on effective remedies. The countries potentially at issue, neighbouring the enlarged European Union, include Albania, Belarus, Bulgaria, Croatia, Macedonia, Romania, the Russian Federation, Serbia & Montenegro, Norway, Turkey, Ukraine and Switzerland.

Many of these countries, although they may have adopted asylum laws, implement them only in a very limited fashion and in effect cannot provide access to a proper procedure. As such, transferring applicants to such countries may amount to a denial of international protection. Indeed, there is much evidence to rebut any generalised assumption of safety in relation to these countries. For example, ECRE provides recent examples in relation to Turkey, the Russian Federation and Bulgaria, indicating a failure to provide refugee protection.[6] In 2003, Turkey removed two Uzbek asylum seekers, despite a request to suspend deportation from the European Court of Human Rights. Although Turkey is a party to the ECHR and the Refugee Convention, the applicants' asylum arguments were not heeded. The ECtHR will now examine whether the deportations amounted to a violation of Article 3 ECHR. In the Russian

---

[6] ECRE, *Recommendations to the Justice and Home Affairs Council on the Safe Third Country Concept at its Meeting 22–23 January 2004* (15 January 2004).

Federation, asylum seekers are denied access to the procedure if they are undocumented and may be subsequently removed to third countries which are unsafe. In the case of Bulgaria, the Commission's own accession reports acknowledge serious shortcomings in the asylum system.[7]

12.23 Human rights NGOs across Europe have opposed the Directive on the basis that it would be contrary to international law, citing the third country provisions and in particular the 'supersafe third country concept'. The European Council on Refugees and Exiles (ECRE), Amnesty International, and Human Rights Watch issued a statement on the eve of the Council's agreement to the Directive stating that:

Last month ECRE and nine other European human rights NGOs issued an unprecedented call for the withdrawal of the draft Directive on asylum procedures on the basis that it would be in breach of the commitments of the EU as set out in the Charter of Fundamental Rights and would violate individual Member States' legal obligations under international refugee and human rights law. Today, ECRE, Amnesty International and Human Rights Watch expressed their regret at the fact that this and other calls from the NGO community, the European Parliament, UNHCR, lawyers and leading academics have been completely set aside. In view of this we are extremely disappointed that the European Commission has expressed its satisfaction that the standards due to be agreed are consistent with international obligations.[8]

12.24 The UN High Commissioner for Refugees joined the criticism:[9]

UN High Commissioner for Refugees Ruud Lubbers expressed concerns about the Directive, 'warning that several provisions . . . would fall short of accepted international legal standards . . . [and] . . . could lead to an erosion of the global asylum system, jeopardizing the lives of future refugees.'[10] The day after the Directive's adoption, UNHCR reiterated its concerns, in particular in relation to the Directive's safe third country provisions and those non-suspensory appeals, which would allow Member States to deport asylum seekers whilst their appeals were pending. It noted in particular that the Directive would allow 'a number of . . . restrictive and highly controversial practices that are currently only contained in one or two member states national legislation but could, as of 1 May 2004, be inserted in the legislation of all 25 EU Member States'.[11]

12.25 At the time of writing, the measure has been approved by the Council and is returning to the European Parliament for re-consultation (as required by the EU legislative process). It is unlikely that there will be significant further amendment, but NGOs are already arguing that the European Court of Justice should annul the measure on the basis that it is in violation of EU fundamental rights.

12.26 Antonio Vitorino, the Commissioner for Justice and Home Affairs, responded to

---

[7] European Commission, *2003 Regular Report on Bulgaria's Progress towards Accession*, 104–105.

[8] News Release, 28 April 2004, 'Refugee and Human Rights Organisations Across Europe Express Their Deep Concern At the Expected Agreement on Asylum Measures in Breach of International Law'.

[9] ILPA, *Analysis and Critique*.

[10] UNHCR Press Release, 'Lubbers calls for EU asylum laws not to contravene international law' (29 March 2004).

[11] UNHCR Press Release, 'UNHCR regrets missed opportunity to adopt high EU asylum standards' (30 April 2004).

criticism of the safe third country provisions in a statement to the European Parliament:

> The provisions on the safe third country concept provide an essential safeguard where they ensure that as a minimum in each individual case, a Member State must examine whether the applicant will not run the risk, as stated in article 3 of the European Convention on Human Rights, of being tortured or subject to inhuman treatment or punishment. In this context it is important to underline that the protection ECHR affords to individual applicants against removal in breach of this right is absolute and allows for no exceptions.
>
> The provisions on the supersafe third country concept provide a series of safeguards: strict criteria for designation (observance in full of ECHR and Geneva Convention), Community method for the list (Commission exclusive right of initiative) and the obligation for Member States to introduce a safety net at national level for exceptional individual cases.[12]

12.27 It is unsurprising that there should be argument about the extent to which the super-safe country concept permits individual consideration of safety. On the one hand, Art 35A(1) states that 'member states may provide that no, or no full, examination of the asylum application and of the safety of the applicant in his/her particular circumstances' will take place where the claimant entered illegally and is to be removed to a supersafe third country. Yet, on the other hand, Art 35A(4) renders the supersafe concept expressly subject to international law and requires that states make provision to determine applications according to international law, including the principle of non-refoulement. The international law principle of non-refoulement clearly does require the opportunity for individual consideration of safety issues.

(c) *Other safe third countries*

12.28 The remaining category is the 'ordinary' safe third country concept addressed by Art 27:

> 1. Member States may apply the safe third country concept only where the competent authorities are satisfied that a person seeking asylum will be treated in accordance with the following principles in the third country concerned:
>   (a) life and liberty are not threatened on account of race, religion, nationality, membership of a particular social group or political opinion; and
>   (b) the principle of non-refoulement in accordance with the Geneva Convention is respected; and
>   (c) the prohibition on removal in breach of the right to freedom from torture and cruel, inhuman or degrading treatment as laid down in international law is respected; and
>   (d) the possibility exists to request refugee status and, if found to be a refugee, to receive protection in accordance with the Geneva Convention.
>
> 2. The application of the safe third country concept shall be subject to rules laid down in national legislation, including:
>   (a) rules requiring a connection between the person seeking asylum and the third country concerned based on which it would be reasonable for that person to go to that country;

---

[12] 'Statement on the European Asylum Policy', Speech/04/226 to European Parliament, 5 May 2004 (http://europa.eu.int/rapid/pressReleasesAction.do?reference=SPEECH/04/435).

(b) rules on the methodology by which the competent authorities satisfy themselves that the safe third country concept may be applied to a particular country or to a particular applicant. Such methodology shall include case by case consideration of the safety of the country for a particular applicant and/or national designation of countries considered to be generally safe;

(c) rules, in accordance with international law, allowing an individual examination of whether the third country concerned is safe for a particular applicant which, as a minimum, shall permit the applicant to challenge the application of the safe third country concept on the grounds that he/she would be subjected to torture, cruel, inhuman or degrading treatment or punishment.

3. When implementing a decision solely based on this Article, Member States shall:
   (a) inform the applicant accordingly; and
   (b) provide him/her with a document informing the authorities of the third country, in the language of that country, that the application has not been examined in substance.

4. Where the third country does not permit the applicant for asylum in question to enter its territory, Member States shall ensure that access to a procedure is given in accordance with the basic principles and guarantees described in Chapter II.

5. Member States shall inform the Commission periodically of the countries to which this concept is applied in accordance with the provisions of this Article.

Unlike Art 35A(1), Art 27 does not refer to the possibility of states removing a claimant without individual consideration of safety. However, it does refer to 'national designation of countries considered to be generally safe' as, apparently, a potential alternative to individual consideration. The only specific reference to challenging third country removals on human rights grounds is that member states should provide: **12.29**

. . . rules, in accordance with international law, allowing an individual examination of whether the third country concerned is safe for a particular applicant which, as a minimum, shall permit the applicant to challenge the application of the safe third country concept on the grounds that he/she would be subjected to torture, cruel, inhuman or degrading treatment or punishment.

Such a right is more restrictive than that permitted under UK law, which allows challenges based on substantive rights guaranteed by other ECHR articles.[13] A further matter of concern is that the Directive permits the assessment of the safety of a third country to be made by a different body from that which determines substantive asylum claims: Art 3A(2)(a). **12.30**

2. Correlation between Sch 3 to the 2004 Act and the Asylum Procedures Directive

This section notes the potential correlation between the respective categories of safe third countries created by Sch 3 and at EU level. **12.31**

---

[13] *R (Ullah) v Special Adjudicator* [2004] UKHL 26, [2004] 2 AC 323.

12.32   As indicated in Chapter 9 above, Ministers assured Parliament that the First List was restricted to member states and expressly justified the human rights deeming provision on that basis. It should not therefore be open to the Secretary of State to seek to use the First List to avoid individual examination in relation to non-member states including 'supersafe' third countries. Supersafe third countries could only be included in the Second and Third Lists. The only distinction between them is the duty to certify unfounded claims in relation to Second List countries (see paras 9.52–9.56). Neither list permits removal without individual consideration of human rights claims (and indeed a human rights appeal unless that appeal would be bound to fail).

12.33   Article 27 could also encompass removals falling within the fourth category in Sch 3—countries certified as safe simply for the particular individual.

C. RIGHTS OF APPEAL

1. Article 38: the right to an effective remedy

12.34   The Directive amplifies the current trend towards restricting appeals, and allowing deportation while appeals are pending. Article 38 provides not a right to appeal as such, but rather a 'right to an effective remedy, before a court or tribunal'.

12.35   Article 38(1) sets out a range of negative decisions (a)–(e) against which an individual must have 'the right to an effective remedy before a court or tribunal'.

12.36   Article 38(2) requires Member States to provide for 'time limits and other necessary rules for the applicant to exercise his/her right to an effective remedy' and under Art 38(4) they may lay down time-limits 'for the court or tribunal to examine the decision of the determining authority'.

12.37   Article 38(3) requires Member States 'where appropriate' to adopt rules 'in accordance with their international obligations' dealing with whether the remedy has suspensive effect. The options permitted indicate that, very often, the right to remain will be eroded or illusory. Rules should deal with whether 'the remedy . . . shall have the effect of allowing applicants to remain in the Member State concerned pending its outcome' and 'the possibility of legal remedy or protective measures where the remedy . . . does not have the effect of allowing applicants to remain in the Member State concerned pending its outcome. Member States may also provide for an *ex officio* remedy.' It remains to be seen whether the reference to 'in accordance with their international obligations' is sufficient to ensure compliance with ECHR case law on the requirements of effective remedies.[14]

12.38   Article 38(5) allows applications for the effective remedy to be treated as inadmissible, where the applicant has been granted complementary protection under the

---

[14] eg *Jabari v Turkey* [2001] INLR 136; *Hilal v UK* (2001) 33 EHRR 2.

Qualification Directive.[15] The claim may be rejected as 'inadmissible or unlikely to succeed on the basis of insufficient interest on the part of the applicant in maintaining the proceedings'.

Article 39(6) allows member states to lay down rules on the abandonment of applications for an effective remedy. **12.39**

---

[15] Council Directive (EC) 2004/83 on minimum standards for the qualification and status of third country nationals or stateless persons as refugees or as persons who otherwise need international protection and the content of the protection granted [2004] OJ L304/12.

APPENDIX 1

Asylum and Immigration (Treatment of Claimants, etc.) Act 2004

CONTENTS

Offences   154

 1 Assisting unlawful immigration
 2 Entering United Kingdom without passport, &c.
 3 Immigration documents: forgery
 4 Trafficking people for exploitation
 5 Section 4: supplemental
 6 Employment
 7 Advice of Director of Public Prosecutions

Treatment of claimants   159

 8 Claimant's credibility
 9 Failed asylum seekers: withdrawal of support
10 Failed asylum seekers: accommodation
11 Accommodation for asylum seekers: local connection
12 Refugee: back-dating of benefits
13 Integration loan for refugees

Enforcement powers   166

14 Immigration officer: power of arrest
15 Fingerprinting
16 Information about passengers
17 Retention of documents
18 Control of entry

Procedure for marriage   169

19 England and Wales
20 England and Wales: supplemental
21 Scotland
22 Scotland: supplemental
23 Northern Ireland

151

24 Northern Ireland: supplemental

25 Application for permission under section 19(3)(b), 21(3)(b) or 23(3)(b)

Appeals   173

26 Unification of appeal system

27 Unfounded human rights or asylum claim

28 Appeal from within United Kingdom

29 Entry clearance

30 Earlier right of appeal

31 Seamen and aircrews: right of appeal

32 Suspected international terrorist: bail

Removal and detention   179

33 Removing asylum seeker to safe country

34 Detention pending deportation

35 Deportation or removal: cooperation

36 Electronic monitoring

Immigration services   183

37 Provision of immigration services

38 Immigration Services Commissioner: power of entry

39 Offence of advertising services

40 Appeal to Immigration Services Tribunal

41 Professional bodies

Fees   187

42 Amount of fees

43 Transfer of leave stamps

General   188

44 Interpretation: 'the Immigration Acts'

45 Interpretation: immigration officer

46 Money

47 Repeals

48 Commencement

49 Extent

50 Short title

Schedule 1—New Schedule 4 to the Nationality, Immigration and Asylum Act 2002   191

Schedule 2—Asylum and Immigration Tribunal: Consequential Amendments and
            Transitional Provision   192
    Part 1—Consequential Amendments
    Part 2—Transitional Provision

Schedule 3—Removal of Asylum Seeker to Safe Country 200

    Part 1—Introductory

    Part 2—First List of Safe Countries (Refugee Convention and Human Rights (1))

    Part 3—Second List of Safe Countries (Refugee Convention and Human Rights (2))

    Part 4—Third List of Safe Countries (Refugee Convention Only)

    Part 5—Countries Certified as Safe for Individuals

    Part 6—Amendment of Lists

Schedule 4—Repeals 206

ASYLUM AND IMMIGRATION (TREATMENT OF CLAIMANTS, ETC.)
ACT 2004

Offences

1 Assisting unlawful immigration

(1) At the end of section 25 of the Immigration Act 1971 (c. 77) (offence of assisting unlawful immigration to member State) add—

'(7) In this section—
(a) a reference to a member State includes a reference to a State on a list prescribed for the purposes of this section by order of the Secretary of State (to be known as the "Section 25 List of Schengen Acquis States"), and
(b) a reference to a citizen of the European Union includes a reference to a person who is a national of a State on that list.
(8) An order under subsection (7)(a)—
(a) may be made only if the Secretary of State thinks it necessary for the purpose of complying with the United Kingdom's obligations under the Community Treaties,
(b) may include transitional, consequential or incidental provision,
(c) shall be made by statutory instrument, and
(d) shall be subject to annulment in pursuance of a resolution of either House of Parliament.'

(2) In section 25C(9)(a) of that Act (forfeiture of vehicle, ship or aircraft) for '(within the meaning of section 25)' substitute '(for which purpose "member State" and "immigration law" have the meanings given by section 25(2) and (7))'.

2 Entering United Kingdom without passport, &c.

(1) A person commits an offence if at a leave or asylum interview he does not have with him an immigration document which—
(a) is in force, and
(b) satisfactorily establishes his identity and nationality or citizenship.

(2) A person commits an offence if at a leave or asylum interview he does not have with him, in respect of any dependent child with whom he claims to be travelling or living, an immigration document which—
(a) is in force, and
(b) satisfactorily establishes the child's identity and nationality or citizenship.

(3) But a person does not commit an offence under subsection (1) or (2) if—
(a) the interview referred to in that subsection takes place after the person has entered the United Kingdom, and
(b) within the period of three days beginning with the date of the interview the person provides to an immigration officer or to the Secretary of State a document of the kind referred to in that subsection.

(4) It is a defence for a person charged with an offence under subsection (1)—
(a) to prove that he is an EEA national,
(b) to prove that he is a member of the family of an EEA national and that he is exercising a right under the Community Treaties in respect of entry to or residence in the United Kingdom,
(c) to prove that he has a reasonable excuse for not being in possession of a document of the kind specified in subsection (1),

     (d) to produce a false immigration document and to prove that he used that document as an immigration document for all purposes in connection with his journey to the United Kingdom, or

     (e) to prove that he travelled to the United Kingdom without, at any stage since he set out on the journey, having possession of an immigration document.

(5) It is a defence for a person charged with an offence under subsection (2) in respect of a child—

     (a) to prove that the child is an EEA national,

     (b) to prove that the child is a member of the family of an EEA national and that the child is exercising a right under the Community Treaties in respect of entry to or residence in the United Kingdom,

     (c) to prove that the person has a reasonable excuse for not being in possession of a document of the kind specified in subsection (2),

     (d) to produce a false immigration document and to prove that it was used as an immigration document for all purposes in connection with the child's journey to the United Kingdom, or

     (e) to prove that he travelled to the United Kingdom with the child without, at any stage since he set out on the journey, having possession of an immigration document in respect of the child.

(6) Where the charge for an offence under subsection (1) or (2) relates to an interview which takes place after the defendant has entered the United Kingdom—

     (a) subsections (4)(c) and (5)(c) shall not apply, but

     (b) it is a defence for the defendant to prove that he has a reasonable excuse for not providing a document in accordance with subsection (3).

(7) For the purposes of subsections (4) to (6)—

     (a) the fact that a document was deliberately destroyed or disposed of is not a reasonable excuse for not being in possession of it or for not providing it in accordance with subsection (3), unless it is shown that the destruction or disposal was—

          (i) for a reasonable cause, or

          (ii) beyond the control of the person charged with the offence, and

     (b) in paragraph (a)(i) 'reasonable cause' does not include the purpose of—

          (i) delaying the handling or resolution of a claim or application or the taking of a decision,

          (ii) increasing the chances of success of a claim or application, or

          (iii) complying with instructions or advice given by a person who offers advice about, or facilitates, immigration into the United Kingdom, unless in the circumstances of the case it is unreasonable to expect non-compliance with the instructions or advice.

(8) A person shall be presumed for the purposes of this section not to have a document with him if he fails to produce it to an immigration officer or official of the Secretary of State on request.

(9) A person guilty of an offence under this section shall be liable—

     (a) on conviction on indictment, to imprisonment for a term not exceeding two years, to a fine or to both, or

     (b) on summary conviction, to imprisonment for a term not exceeding twelve months, to a fine not exceeding the statutory maximum or to both.

(10) If a constable or immigration officer reasonably suspects that a person has committed an offence under this section he may arrest the person without warrant.

(11) An offence under this section shall be treated as—

    (a) a relevant offence for the purposes of sections 28B and 28D of the Immigration Act 1971 (c. 77) (search, entry and arrest), and

    (b) an offence under Part III of that Act (criminal proceedings) for the purposes of sections 28(4), 28E, 28G and 28H (search after arrest, &c.) of that Act.

(12) In this section—

'EEA national' means a national of a State which is a contracting party to the Agreement on the European Economic Area signed at Oporto on 2nd May 1992 (as it has effect from time to time), 'immigration document' means—

    (a) a passport, and

    (b) a document which relates to a national of a State other than the United Kingdom and which is designed to serve the same purpose as a passport, and

'leave or asylum interview' means an interview with an immigration officer or an official of the Secretary of State at which a person—

    (a) seeks leave to enter or remain in the United Kingdom, or

    (b) claims that to remove him from or require him to leave the United Kingdom would breach the United Kingdom's obligations under the Refugee Convention or would be unlawful under section 6 of the Human Rights Act 1998 (c. 42) as being incompatible with his Convention rights.

(13) For the purposes of this section—

    (a) a document which purports to be, or is designed to look like, an immigration document, is a false immigration document, and

    (b) an immigration document is a false immigration document if and in so far as it is used—

        (i) outside the period for which it is expressed to be valid,

        (ii) contrary to provision for its use made by the person issuing it, or

        (iii) by or in respect of a person other than the person to or for whom it was issued.

(14) Section 11 of the Immigration Act 1971 (c. 77) shall have effect for the purpose of the construction of a reference in this section to entering the United Kingdom.

(15) In so far as this section extends to England and Wales, subsection (9)(b) shall, until the commencement of section 154 of the Criminal Justice Act 2003 (c. 44) (increased limit on magistrates' power of imprisonment), have effect as if the reference to twelve months were a reference to six months.

(16) In so far as this section extends to Scotland, subsection (9)(b) shall have effect as if the reference to twelve months were a reference to six months.

(17) In so far as this section extends to Northern Ireland, subsection (9)(b) shall have effect as if the reference to twelve months were a reference to six months.

3 Immigration documents: forgery

    (1) Section 5 of the Forgery and Counterfeiting Act 1981 (c. 45) (offences relating to various documents) shall be amended as follows.

    (2) After subsection (5)(f) (passports) insert—

'(fa) immigration documents;'.

    (3) After subsection (8) add—

'(9) In subsection (5)(fa) "immigration document" means a card, adhesive label or other instrument which satisfies subsection (10) or (11).

(10) A card, adhesive label or other instrument satisfies this subsection if it—

    (a) is designed to be given, in the exercise of a function under the Immigration Acts (within the meaning of section 44 of the Asylum and Immigration (Treatment of Claimants, etc.) Act 2004), to a person who has been granted leave to enter or remain in the United Kingdom, and

    (b) carries information (whether or not wholly or partly electronically) about the leave granted.

(11) A card, adhesive label or other instrument satisfies this subsection if it is given to a person to confirm a right of his under the Community Treaties in respect of entry to or residence in the United Kingdom.'

4 Trafficking people for exploitation

(1) A person commits an offence if he arranges or facilitates the arrival in the United Kingdom of an individual (the 'passenger') and—

    (a) he intends to exploit the passenger in the United Kingdom or elsewhere, or

    (b) he believes that another person is likely to exploit the passenger in the United Kingdom or elsewhere.

(2) A person commits an offence if he arranges or facilitates travel within the United Kingdom by an individual (the 'passenger') in respect of whom he believes that an offence under subsection (1) may have been committed and—

    (a) he intends to exploit the passenger in the United Kingdom or elsewhere, or

    (b) he believes that another person is likely to exploit the passenger in the United Kingdom or elsewhere.

(3) A person commits an offence if he arranges or facilitates the departure from the United Kingdom of an individual (the 'passenger') and—

    (a) he intends to exploit the passenger outside the United Kingdom, or

    (b) he believes that another person is likely to exploit the passenger outside the United Kingdom.

(4) For the purposes of this section a person is exploited if (and only if)—

    (a) he is the victim of behaviour that contravenes Article 4 of the Human Rights Convention (slavery and forced labour),

    (b) he is encouraged, required or expected to do anything as a result of which he or another person would commit an offence under the Human Organ Transplants Act 1989 (c. 31) or the Human Organ Transplants (Northern Ireland) Order 1989 (S.I. 1989/2408 (N.I. 21)),

    (c) he is subjected to force, threats or deception designed to induce him—

        (i) to provide services of any kind,

        (ii) to provide another person with benefits of any kind, or

        (iii) to enable another person to acquire benefits of any kind, or

    (d) he is requested or induced to undertake any activity, having been chosen as the subject of the request or inducement on the grounds that—

        (i) he is mentally or physically ill or disabled, he is young or he has a family relationship with a person, and

        (ii) a person without the illness, disability, youth or family relationship would be likely to refuse the request or resist the inducement.

(5) A person guilty of an offence under this section shall be liable—

    (a) on conviction on indictment, to imprisonment for a term not exceeding 14 years, to a fine or to both, or

    (b) on summary conviction, to imprisonment for a term not exceeding twelve months, to a fine not exceeding the statutory maximum or to both.

5 Section 4: supplemental

(1) Subsections (1) to (3) of section 4 apply to anything done—

    (a) in the United Kingdom,

    (b) outside the United Kingdom by an individual to whom subsection (2) below applies, or

    (c) outside the United Kingdom by a body incorporated under the law of a part of the United Kingdom.

(2) This subsection applies to—

    (a) a British citizen,

    (b) a British overseas territories citizen,

    (c) a British National (Overseas),

    (d) a British Overseas citizen,

    (e) a person who is a British subject under the British Nationality Act 1981 (c. 61), and

    (f) a British protected person within the meaning of that Act.

(3) In section 4(4)(a) 'the Human Rights Convention' means the Convention for the Protection of Human Rights and Fundamental Freedoms agreed by the Council of Europe at Rome on 4th November 1950.

(4) Sections 25C and 25D of the Immigration Act 1971 (c. 77) (forfeiture or detention of vehicle, &c.) shall apply in relation to an offence under section 4 of this Act as they apply in relation to an offence under section 25 of that Act.

(5) At the end of section 25C(9)(b), (10)(b) and (11) of that Act add 'or section 4 of the Asylum and Immigration (Treatment of Claimants, etc.) Act 2004 (trafficking people for exploitation).'

(6) After paragraph 2(n) of Schedule 4 to the Criminal Justice and Court Services Act 2000 (c. 43) (offence against child) insert—

    '(o) an offence under section 4 of the Asylum and Immigration (Treatment of Claimants, etc.) Act 2004 (trafficking people for exploitation).'

(7) At the end of paragraph 4 of Schedule 2 to the Proceeds of Crime Act 2002 (c. 29) (lifestyle offences: England and Wales: people trafficking) add—

    '(3) An offence under section 4 of the Asylum and Immigration (Treatment of Claimants, etc.) Act 2004 (exploitation).'

(8) At the end of paragraph 4 of Schedule 4 to the Proceeds of Crime Act 2002 (lifestyle offences: Scotland: people trafficking) add 'or under section 4 of the Asylum and Immigration (Treatment of Claimants, etc.) Act 2004 (exploitation)'.

(9) At the end of paragraph 4 of Schedule 5 to the Proceeds of Crime Act 2002 (lifestyle offences: Northern Ireland: people trafficking) add—

    '(3) An offence under section 4 of the Asylum and Immigration (Treatment of Claimants, etc.) Act 2004 (exploitation).'

(10) After paragraph 2(l) of the Schedule to the Protection of Children and Vulnerable Adults (Northern Ireland) Order 2003 (S.I. 2003/417 (N.I. 4)) (offence against child) insert—

    '(m) an offence under section 4 of the Asylum and Immigration (Treatment of Claimants, etc.) Act 2004 (trafficking people for exploitation).'

(11) In so far as section 4 extends to England and Wales, subsection (5)(b) shall, until the commencement of section 154 of the Criminal Justice Act 2003 (c. 44) (increased limit on magistrates' power of imprisonment), have effect as if the reference to twelve months were a reference to six months.

(12) In so far as section 4 extends to Scotland, subsection (5)(b) shall have effect as if the reference to twelve months were a reference to six months.

(13) In so far as section 4 extends to Northern Ireland, subsection (5)(b) shall have effect as if the reference to twelve months were a reference to six months.

6 Employment

(1) For section 8(4) of the Asylum and Immigration Act 1996 (c. 49) (employment: penalty) substitute—

'(4) A person guilty of an offence under this section shall be liable—
(a) on conviction on indictment, to a fine, or
(b) on summary conviction, to a fine not exceeding the statutory maximum.'

(2) Section 8(9) of that Act (extension of time limit for prosecution) shall cease to have effect.

7 Advice of Director of Public Prosecutions

In section 3(2) of the Prosecution of Offences Act 1985 (c. 23) (functions of Director of Public Prosecutions) after paragraph (eb) insert—

'(ec) to give, to such extent as he considers appropriate, advice to immigration officers on matters relating to criminal offences;'.

Treatment of claimants

8 Claimant's credibility

(1) In determining whether to believe a statement made by or on behalf of a person who makes an asylum claim or a human rights claim, a deciding authority shall take account, as damaging the claimant's credibility, of any behaviour to which this section applies.

(2) This section applies to any behaviour by the claimant that the deciding authority thinks—
(a) is designed or likely to conceal information,
(b) is designed or likely to mislead, or
(c) is designed or likely to obstruct or delay the handling or resolution of the claim or the taking of a decision in relation to the claimant.

(3) Without prejudice to the generality of subsection (2) the following kinds of behaviour shall be treated as designed or likely to conceal information or to mislead—
(a) failure without reasonable explanation to produce a passport on request to an immigration officer or to the Secretary of State,
(b) the production of a document which is not a valid passport as if it were,
(c) the destruction, alteration or disposal, in each case without reasonable explanation, of a passport,
(d) the destruction, alteration or disposal, in each case without reasonable explanation, of a ticket or other document connected with travel, and

      (e) failure without reasonable explanation to answer a question asked by a deciding authority.

(4) This section also applies to failure by the claimant to take advantage of a reasonable opportunity to make an asylum claim or human rights claim while in a safe country.

(5) This section also applies to failure by the claimant to make an asylum claim or human rights claim before being notified of an immigration decision, unless the claim relies wholly on matters arising after the notification.

(6) This section also applies to failure by the claimant to make an asylum claim or human rights claim before being arrested under an immigration provision, unless—

      (a) he had no reasonable opportunity to make the claim before the arrest, or

      (b) the claim relies wholly on matters arising after the arrest.

(7) In this section—

'asylum claim' has the meaning given by section 113(1) of the Nationality, Immigration and Asylum Act 2002 (c. 41) (subject to subsection (9) below),

'deciding authority' means—

      (a) an immigration officer,

      (b) the Secretary of State,

      (c) the Asylum and Immigration Tribunal, or

      (d) the Special Immigration Appeals Commission,

'human rights claim' has the meaning given by section 113(1) of the Nationality, Immigration and Asylum Act 2002 (subject to subsection (9) below),

'immigration decision' means—

      (a) refusal of leave to enter the United Kingdom,

      (b) refusal to vary a person's leave to enter or remain in the United Kingdom,

      (c) grant of leave to enter or remain in the United Kingdom,

      (d) a decision that a person is to be removed from the United Kingdom by way of directions under section 10(1)(a), (b), (ba) or (c) of the Immigration and Asylum Act 1999 (c. 33) (removal of persons unlawfully in United Kingdom),

      (e) a decision that a person is to be removed from the United Kingdom by way of directions under paragraphs 8 to 12 of Schedule 2 to the Immigration Act 1971 (c. 77) (control of entry: removal),

      (f) a decision to make a deportation order under section 5(1) of that Act, and

      (g) a decision to take action in relation to a person in connection with extradition from the United Kingdom,

'immigration provision' means—

      (a) sections 28A, 28AA, 28B, 28C and 28CA of the Immigration Act 1971 (immigration offences: enforcement),

      (b) paragraph 17 of Schedule 2 to that Act (control of entry),

      (c) section 14 of this Act, and

      (d) a provision of the Extradition Act 1989 (c. 33) or 2003 (c. 41),

'notified' means notified in such manner as may be specified by regulations made by the Secretary of State,

'passport' includes a document which relates to a national of a country other than the United Kingdom and which is designed to serve the same purpose as a passport, and

'safe country' means a country to which Part 2 of Schedule 3 applies.

(8) A passport produced by or on behalf of a person is valid for the purposes of subsection (3)(b) if it—

      (a) relates to the person by whom or on whose behalf it is produced,

      (b) has not been altered otherwise than by or with the permission of the authority who issued it, and

      (c) was not obtained by deception.

(9) In subsection (4) a reference to an asylum claim or human rights claim shall be treated as including a reference to a claim of entitlement to remain in a country other than the United Kingdom made by reference to the rights that a person invokes in making an asylum claim or a human rights claim in the United Kingdom.

(10) Regulations under subsection (7) specifying a manner of notification may, in particular—

    (a) apply or refer to regulations under section 105 of the Nationality, Immigration and Asylum Act 2002 (c. 41) (notice of immigration decisions);

    (b) make provision similar to provision that is or could be made by regulations under that section;

    (c) modify a provision of regulations under that section in its effect for the purpose of regulations under this section;

    (d) provide for notice to be treated as received at a specified time if sent to a specified class of place in a specified manner.

(11) Regulations under subsection (7) specifying a manner of notification—

    (a) may make incidental, consequential or transitional provision,

    (b) shall be made by statutory instrument, and

    (c) shall be subject to annulment in pursuance of a resolution of either House of Parliament.

(12) This section shall not prevent a deciding authority from determining not to believe a statement on the grounds of behaviour to which this section does not apply.

(13) Before the coming into force of section 26 a reference in this section to the Asylum and Immigration Tribunal shall be treated as a reference to—

    (a) an adjudicator appointed, or treated as if appointed, under section 81 of the Nationality, Immigration and Asylum Act 2002 (c. 41) (appeals), and

    (b) the Immigration Appeal Tribunal.

9 Failed asylum seekers: withdrawal of support

(1) In Schedule 3 to the Nationality, Immigration and Asylum Act 2002 (withholding and withdrawal of support) after paragraph 7 insert—

'*Fifth class of ineligible person: failed asylum-seeker with family*

7A (1) Paragraph 1 applies to a person if—

    (a) he—

        (i) is treated as an asylum-seeker for the purposes of Part VI of the Immigration and Asylum Act 1999 (c. 33) (support) by virtue only of section 94(3A) (failed asylum-seeker with dependent child), or

        (ii) is treated as an asylum-seeker for the purposes of Part 2 of this Act by virtue only of section 18(2),

    (b) the Secretary of State has certified that in his opinion the person has failed without reasonable excuse to take reasonable steps—

        (i) to leave the United Kingdom voluntarily, or

        (ii) to place himself in a position in which he is able to leave the United Kingdom voluntarily,

    (c) the person has received a copy of the Secretary of State's certificate, and

    (d) the period of 14 days, beginning with the date on which the person receives the copy of the certificate, has elapsed.

(2) Paragraph 1 also applies to a dependant of a person to whom that paragraph applies by virtue of sub-paragraph (1).

(3) For the purpose of sub-paragraph (1)(d) if the Secretary of State sends a copy of a certificate by first class post to a person's last known address, the person shall be treated as receiving the copy on the second day after the day on which it was posted.

(4) The Secretary of State may by regulations vary the period specified in sub-paragraph (1)(d).'

(2) In paragraph 14(1) and (2) of Schedule 3 to the Nationality, Immigration and Asylum Act 2002 (local authority to notify Secretary of State) for 'paragraph 6 or 7' substitute 'paragraph 6, 7 or 7A'.

(3) No appeal may be brought under section 103 of the Immigration and Asylum Act 1999 (asylum support appeal) against a decision—

(a) that by virtue of a provision of Schedule 3 to the Nationality, Immigration and Asylum Act 2002 (c. 41) other than paragraph 7A a person is not qualified to receive support, or

(b) on the grounds of the application of a provision of that Schedule other than paragraph 7A, to stop providing support to a person.

(4) On an appeal under section 103 of the Immigration and Asylum Act 1999 (c. 33) against a decision made by virtue of paragraph 7A of Schedule 3 to the Nationality, Immigration and Asylum Act 2002 the adjudicator may, in particular—

(a) annul a certificate of the Secretary of State issued for the purposes of that paragraph;

(b) require the Secretary of State to reconsider the matters certified.

(5) An order under section 48 providing for this section to come into force may, in particular, provide for this section to have effect with specified modifications before the coming into force of a provision of the Nationality, Immigration and Asylum Act 2002.

10 Failed asylum seekers: accommodation

(1) At the end of section 4 of the Immigration and Asylum Act 1999 (provision of accommodation for failed asylum seekers, &c.) add—

'(5) The Secretary of State may make regulations specifying criteria to be used in determining—

(a) whether or not to provide accommodation, or arrange for the provision of accommodation, for a person under this section;

(b) whether or not to continue to provide accommodation, or arrange for the provision of accommodation, for a person under this section.

(6) The regulations may, in particular—

(a) provide for the continuation of the provision of accommodation for a person to be conditional upon his performance of or participation in community activities in accordance with arrangements made by the Secretary of State;

(b) provide for the continuation of the provision of accommodation to be subject to other conditions;

(c) provide for the provision of accommodation (or the continuation of the provision of accommodation) to be a matter for the Secretary of State's discretion to a specified extent or in a specified class of case.

(7) For the purposes of subsection (6)(a)—

(a) "community activities" means activities that appear to the Secretary of State to be beneficial to the public or a section of the public, and

(b) the Secretary of State may, in particular—

(i) appoint one person to supervise or manage the performance of or participation in activities by another person;

(ii) enter into a contract (with a local authority or any other person) for the provision of services by way of making arrangements for community activities in accordance with this section;

(iii) pay, or arrange for the payment of, allowances to a person performing or participating in community activities in accordance with arrangements under this section.

(8) Regulations by virtue of subsection (6)(a) may, in particular, provide for a condition requiring the performance of or participation in community activities to apply to a person only if the Secretary of State has made arrangements for community activities in an area that includes the place where accommodation is provided for the person.

(9) A local authority or other person may undertake to manage or participate in arrangements for community activities in accordance with this section.'

(2) In section 166(5) of that Act (regulations: affirmative instrument) before paragraph (a) insert—

'(za) section 4(5),'.

(3) In section 103 of the Immigration and Asylum Act 1999 (c. 33) (support for asylum-seekers: appeal) as it has effect before the commencement of section 53 of the Nationality, Immigration and Asylum Act 2002 (c. 41)—

(a) after subsection (2) insert—

'(2A) If the Secretary of State decides not to provide accommodation for a person under section 4, or not to continue to provide accommodation for a person under section 4, the person may appeal to an adjudicator.', and

(b) in subsections (6) and (7) for 'section 95' substitute 'section 4 or 95'.

(4) In section 103 of the Immigration and Asylum Act 1999 (support for asylum-seekers: appeal) as it has effect after the commencement of section 53 of the Nationality, Immigration and Asylum Act 2002—

(a) for subsection (1) substitute—

'(1) This section applies where a person has applied for support under all or any of the following provisions—

(a) section 4,

(b) section 95, and

(c) section 17 of the Nationality, Immigration and Asylum Act 2002.',

(b) in subsection (4)(a) for 'the other provision' substitute 'another of those provisions', and

(c) in subsection (7) for 'subsection (1)(a) or (b)' substitute 'subsection (1)'.

(5) In section 103A of the Immigration and Asylum Act 1999 (appeal about location of support) in subsection (1) (and in the heading) for 'section 95' substitute 'section 4 or 95'.

(6) In an amendment made by this section a reference to providing accommodation includes a reference to arranging for the provision of accommodation.

(7) Regulations under section 4(5)(b) of the Immigration and Asylum Act 1999 (c. 33) (as inserted by subsection (1) above) may apply to persons receiving support under section 4 when the regulations come into force.

11 Accommodation for asylum seekers: local connection

(1) At the end of section 199 of the Housing Act 1996 (c. 52) (local connection) add—

'(6) A person has a local connection with the district of a local housing authority if he was (at any time) provided with accommodation in that district under section 95 of the Immigration and Asylum Act 1999 (support for asylum seekers).

(7) But subsection (6) does not apply—

    (a) to the provision of accommodation for a person in a district of a local housing authority if he was subsequently provided with accommodation in the district of another local housing authority under section 95 of that Act, or

    (b) to the provision of accommodation in an accommodation centre by virtue of section 22 of the Nationality, Immigration and Asylum Act 2002 (c. 41) (use of accommodation centres for section 95 support).'

(2) Subsection (3) applies where—

    (a) a local housing authority would (but for subsection (3)) be obliged to secure that accommodation is available for occupation by a person under section 193 of the Housing Act 1996 (homeless persons),

    (b) the person was (at any time) provided with accommodation in a place in Scotland under section 95 of the Immigration and Asylum Act 1999 (support for asylum seekers),

    (c) the accommodation was not provided in an accommodation centre by virtue of section 22 of the Nationality, Immigration and Asylum Act 2002 (use of accommodation centres for section 95 support), and

    (d) the person has neither—

        (i) a local connection with the district of a local housing authority (in England or Wales) within the meaning of section 199 of the Housing Act 1996 as amended by subsection (1) above, nor

        (ii) a local connection with a district (in Scotland) within the meaning of section 27 of the Housing (Scotland) Act 1987 (c. 26).

(3) Where this subsection applies—

    (a) the duty of the local housing authority under section 193 of the Housing Act 1996 in relation to the person shall not apply, but

    (b) the local housing authority—

        (i) may secure that accommodation is available for occupation by the person for a period giving him a reasonable opportunity of securing accommodation for his occupation, and

        (ii) may provide the person (or secure that he is provided with) advice and assistance in any attempts he may make to secure that accommodation becomes available for his occupation.

12 Refugee: back-dating of benefits

(1) Section 123 of the Immigration and Asylum Act 1999 (c. 33) (back-dating of benefits for refugees) shall cease to have effect.

(2) Accordingly (and without prejudice to any other implied repeal, revocation or amendment) the following (each of which concerns the treatment of refugees) lapse—

    (a) in the Income Support (General) Regulations 1987 (S.I. 1987/1967)—

        (i) regulation 21ZB,

        (ii) paragraph 18A of Schedule 1B, and

        (iii) paragraph 57 of Schedule 9,

    (b) in the Income Support (General) Regulations (Northern Ireland) 1987 (S.R. 1987 No. 459)—

      (i)   regulation 21A,

      (ii) paragraph 18A of Schedule 1B, and

      (iii) paragraph 57 of Schedule 9,

  (c) in the Social Security (Claims and Payments) Regulations 1987 (S.I. 1987/1968)—

      (i)   regulation 4(3C),

      (ii) regulation 6(4D), and

      (iii) regulation 19(8),

  (d) in the Social Security (Claims and Payments) Regulations (Northern Ireland) 1987 (S.R. 1987 No. 465)—

      (i)   regulation 4(3C),

      (ii) regulation 6(4D), and

      (iii) regulation 19(8),

  (e) in the Housing Benefit (General) Regulations 1987 (S.I. 1987/1971)—

      (i)   regulation 7B,

      (ii) Schedule A1,

      (iii) paragraphs 61 and 62 of Schedule 4, and

      (iv) paragraphs 50 and 51 of Schedule 5,

  (f) in the Housing Benefit (General) Regulations (Northern Ireland) 1987 (S.R. 1987 No. 461)—

      (i)   regulation 7B,

      (ii) Schedule A1,

      (iii) paragraphs 62 and 63 of Schedule 4, and

      (iv) paragraphs 48 and 49 of Schedule 5, and

  (g) in the Council Tax Benefit (General) Regulations 1992 (S.I. 1992/ 1814)—

      (i)   regulation 4D,

      (ii) Schedule A1,

      (iii) paragraphs 60 and 61 of Schedule 4, and

      (iv) paragraphs 50 and 51 of Schedule 5.

(3) Regulation 12(1) and (2) of the Social Security (Immigration and Asylum) Consequential Amendments Regulations 2000 (S.I. 2000/636) (which save for transitional purposes the effect of provision made for back-payment of benefits for refugees under section 11(2) of the Asylum and Immigration Act 1996 (c. 49)) shall cease to have effect.

(4) Regulation 11(1) and (2) of the Social Security (Immigration and Asylum) Consequential Amendments Regulations (Northern Ireland) 2000 (S.R. 2000 No. 71) (which make similar transitional savings) shall cease to have effect.

(5) An order under section 48 bringing this section into force may, in particular, provide for this section to have effect in relation to persons recorded as refugees after a specified date (irrespective of when the process resulting in the record was begun).

13 Integration loan for refugees

(1) The Secretary of State may make regulations enabling him to make loans to refugees.

(2) A person is a refugee for the purpose of subsection (1) if the Secretary of State has—

  (a) recorded him as a refugee within the meaning of the Convention relating to the Status of Refugees done at Geneva on 28 July 1951, and

  (b) granted him indefinite leave to enter or remain in the United Kingdom (within the meaning of section 33(1) of the Immigration Act 1971 (c. 77)).

(3) Regulations under subsection (1)—

  (a) shall specify matters which the Secretary of State shall, in addition to other matters appearing to him to be relevant, take into account in determining whether or not to make a loan (and those matters may, in particular, relate to—

    (i) a person's income or assets,

    (ii) a person's likely ability to repay a loan, or

    (iii) the length of time since a person was recorded as a refugee),

  (b) shall enable the Secretary of State to specify (and vary from time to time) a minimum and a maximum amount of a loan,

  (c) shall prevent a person from receiving a loan if—

    (i) he is under the age of 18,

    (ii) he is insolvent, within a meaning given by the regulations, or

    (iii) he has received a loan under the regulations,

  (d) shall make provision about repayment of a loan (and may, in particular, make provision—

    (i) about interest;

    (ii) for repayment by deduction from a social security benefit or similar payment due to the person to whom the loan is made),

  (e) shall enable the Secretary of State to attach conditions to a loan (which may include conditions about the use of the loan),

  (f) shall make provision about—

    (i) the making of an application for a loan, and

    (ii) the information, which may include information about the intended use of a loan, to be provided in or with an application,

  (g) may make provision about steps to be taken by the Secretary of State in establishing an applicant's likely ability to repay a loan,

  (h) may make provision for a loan to be made jointly to more than one refugee, and

  (i) may confer a discretion on the Secretary of State.

(4) Regulations under this section—

  (a) shall be made by statutory instrument, and

  (b) may not be made unless a draft has been laid before and approved by resolution of each House of Parliament.

Enforcement powers

14 Immigration officer: power of arrest

(1) Where an immigration officer in the course of exercising a function under the Immigration Acts forms a reasonable suspicion that a person has committed or attempted to commit an offence listed in subsection (2), he may arrest the person without warrant.

(2) Those offences are—

  (a) the offence of conspiracy at common law (in relation to conspiracy to defraud),

  (b) at common law in Scotland, any of the following offences—

    (i) fraud,

    (ii) conspiracy to defraud,

    (iii) uttering and fraud,

    (iv) bigamy,

     (v) theft, and

     (vi) reset,

(c) an offence under section 57 of the Offences against the Person Act 1861 (c. 100) (bigamy),

(d) an offence under section 3 or 4 of the Perjury Act 1911 (c. 6) (false statements),

(e) an offence under section 7 of that Act (aiding, abetting &c.) if it relates to an offence under section 3 or 4 of that Act,

(f) an offence under section 53 of the Registration of Births, Deaths and Marriages (Scotland) Act 1965 (c. 49) (knowingly giving false information to district registrar, &c.),

(g) an offence under any of the following provisions of the Theft Act 1968 (c. 60)—

     (i)   section 1 (theft),

     (ii) section 15 (obtaining property by deception),

     (iii) section 16 (obtaining pecuniary advantage by deception),

     (iv) section 17 (false accounting), and

     (v)   section 22 (handling stolen goods),

(h) an offence under section 1, 15, 16, 17 or 21 of the Theft Act (Northern Ireland) 1969 (c. 16) (N.I.),

(i) an offence under section 1 or 2 of the Theft Act 1978 (c. 31) (obtaining services, or evading liability, by deception),

(j) an offence under Article 3 or 4 of the Theft (Northern Ireland) Order 1978 (S.I. 1978/1407 (N.I. 23)),

(k) an offence under Article 8 or 9 of the Perjury (Northern Ireland) Order 1979 (S.I. 1979/1714 (N.I. 19)),

(l) an offence under Article 12 of that Order if it relates to an offence under Article 8 or 9 of that Order,

(m) an offence under any of the following provisions of the Forgery and Counterfeiting Act 1981 (c. 45)—

     (i)   section 1 (forgery),

     (ii) section 2 (copying false instrument),

     (iii) section 3 (using false instrument),

     (iv) section 4 (using copy of false instrument), and

     (v)   section 5(1) and (3) (false documents),

(n) an offence under any of sections 57 to 59 of the Sexual Offences Act 2003 (c. 42) (trafficking for sexual exploitation),

(o) an offence under section 22 of the Criminal Justice (Scotland) Act 2003 (asp 7) (trafficking in prostitution), and

(p) an offence under section 4 of this Act.

(3) The following provisions of the Immigration Act 1971 (c. 77) shall have effect for the purpose of making, or in connection with, an arrest under this section as they have effect for the purpose of making, or in connection with, arrests for offences under that Act—

(a) section 28C (entry and search before arrest),

(b) sections 28E and 28F (entry and search after arrest),

(c) sections 28G and 28H (search of arrested person), and

(d) section 28I (seized material).

(4) In section 19D(5)(a) of the Race Relations Act 1976 (c. 74) (permitted discrimination)—

    (a) for '(within the meaning of section 158 of the Nationality, Immigration and Asylum Act 2002)' substitute '(within the meaning of section 44 of the Asylum and Immigration (Treatment of Claimants, etc.) Act 2004)', and

    (b) at the end add 'and excluding section 14 of the Asylum and Immigration (Treatment of Claimants, etc.) Act 2004'.

15 Fingerprinting

(1) Section 141 of the Immigration and Asylum Act 1999 (c. 33) (fingerprinting) shall be amended as follows.

(2) In subsection (7) for paragraph (c) substitute—

    '(c) any person ("C") in respect of whom a relevant immigration decision has been made;'.

(3) In subsection (8) for paragraph (c) substitute—

    '(c) for C, on the service on him of notice of the relevant immigration decision by virtue of section 105 of the Nationality, Immigration and Asylum Act 2002 (c. 41);'.

(4) In subsection (9) for paragraph (c) substitute—

    '(c) for C—
       (i) the time when the relevant immigration decision ceases to have effect, whether as a result of an appeal or otherwise, or
      (ii) if a deportation order has been made against him, its revocation or its otherwise ceasing to have effect;'.

(5) After subsection (15) add—

    '(16) "Relevant immigration decision" means a decision of the kind mentioned in section 82(2)(g), (h), (i), (j) or (k) of the Nationality, Immigration and Asylum Act 2002 (c. 41).'

16 Information about passengers

In paragraph 27B of Schedule 2 to the Immigration Act 1971 (c. 77) (control on entry: provision of information about passengers) after sub-paragraph (4) insert—

    '(4A) The officer may ask the carrier to provide a copy of all or part of a document that relates to a passenger and contains passenger information.'

17 Retention of documents

Where a document comes into the possession of the Secretary of State or an immigration officer in the course of the exercise of an immigration function, the Secretary of State or an immigration officer may retain the document while he suspects that—

    (a) a person to whom the document relates may be liable to removal from the United Kingdom in accordance with a provision of the Immigration Acts, and

    (b) retention of the document may facilitate the removal.

18 Control of entry

After paragraph 2A(2) of Schedule 2 to the Immigration Act 1971 (control of entry: persons arriving with leave to enter) insert—

    '(2A) Where the person's leave to enter derives, by virtue of section 3A(3), from an entry clearance, he may also be examined by an immigration officer for the purpose of establishing whether the leave should be cancelled on the grounds that the person's purpose in arriving in the United Kingdom is different from the purpose specified in the entry clearance.'

Procedure for marriage

19 England and Wales

(1) This section applies to a marriage—

    (a) which is to be solemnised on the authority of certificates issued by a superintendent registrar under Part III of the Marriage Act 1949 (c. 76), and

    (b) a party to which is subject to immigration control.

(2) In relation to a marriage to which this section applies, the notices under section 27 of the Marriage Act 1949—

    (a) shall be given to the superintendent registrar of a registration district specified for the purpose of this paragraph by regulations made by the Secretary of State,

    (b) shall be delivered to the superintendent registrar in person by the two parties to the marriage,

    (c) may be given only if each party to the marriage has been resident in a registration district for the period of seven days immediately before the giving of his or her notice (but the district need not be that in which the notice is given and the parties need not have resided in the same district), and

    (d) shall state, in relation to each party, the registration district by reference to which paragraph (c) is satisfied.

(3) The superintendent registrar shall not enter in the marriage notice book notice of a marriage to which this section applies unless satisfied, by the provision of specified evidence, that the party subject to immigration control—

    (a) has an entry clearance granted expressly for the purpose of enabling him to marry in the United Kingdom,

    (b) has the written permission of the Secretary of State to marry in the United Kingdom, or

    (c) falls within a class specified for the purpose of this paragraph by regulations made by the Secretary of State.

(4) For the purposes of this section—

    (a) a person is subject to immigration control if—

        (i) he is not an EEA national, and

        (ii) under the Immigration Act 1971 (c. 77) he requires leave to enter or remain in the United Kingdom (whether or not leave has been given),

    (b) 'EEA national' means a national of a State which is a contracting party to the Agreement on the European Economic Area signed at Oporto on 2nd May 1992 (as it has effect from time to time),

    (c) 'entry clearance' has the meaning given by section 33(1) of the Immigration Act 1971, and

    (d) 'specified evidence' means such evidence as may be specified in guidance issued by the Registrar General.

20 England and Wales: supplemental

(1) The Marriage Act 1949 (c. 76) shall have effect in relation to a marriage to which section 19 applies—

    (a) subject to that section, and

    (b) with any necessary consequential modification.

(2) In particular—

    (a) section 28(1)(b) of that Act (declaration: residence) shall have effect as if it required a declaration that—

        (i) the notice of marriage is given in compliance with section 19(2) above, and

        (ii) the party subject to immigration control satisfies section 19(3)(a), (b) or (c), and

    (b) section 48 of that Act (proof of certain matters not essential to validity of marriage) shall have effect as if the list of matters in section 48(1)(a) to (e) included compliance with section 19 above.

(3) Regulations of the Secretary of State under section 19(2)(a) or (3)(c)—

    (a) may make transitional provision,

    (b) shall be made by statutory instrument, and

    (c) shall be subject to annulment in pursuance of a resolution of either House of Parliament.

(4) Before making regulations under section 19(2)(a) the Secretary of State shall consult the Registrar General.

(5) An expression used in section 19 or this section and in Part III of the Marriage Act 1949 (c. 76) has the same meaning in section 19 or this section as in that Part.

(6) An order under the Regulatory Reform Act 2001 (c. 6) may include provision—

    (a) amending section 19, this section or section 25 in consequence of other provision of the order, or

    (b) repealing section 19, this section and section 25 and re-enacting them with modifications consequential upon other provision of the order.

21 Scotland

(1) This section applies to a marriage—

    (a) which is intended to be solemnised in Scotland, and

    (b) a party to which is subject to immigration control.

(2) In relation to a marriage to which this section applies, notice under section 3 of the Marriage (Scotland) Act 1977 (c. 15)—

    (a) may be submitted to the district registrar of a registration district prescribed for the purposes of this section, and

    (b) may not be submitted to the district registrar of any other registration district.

(3) Where the district registrar to whom notice is submitted by virtue of subsection (2) is the district registrar for the registration district in which the marriage is to be solemnised, he shall not make an entry under section 4, or complete a Marriage Schedule under section 6, of the Marriage (Scotland) Act 1977 in respect of the marriage unless satisfied, by the provision of specified evidence, that the party subject to immigration control—

    (a) has an entry clearance granted expressly for the purpose of enabling him to marry in the United Kingdom,

    (b) has the written permission of the Secretary of State to marry in the United Kingdom, or

    (c) falls within a class specified for the purpose of this paragraph by regulations made by the Secretary of State.

(4) Where the district registrar to whom notice is submitted by virtue of subsection (2) (here the 'notified registrar') is not the district registrar for the registration district in which the marriage is to be solemnised (here the 'second registrar')—

    (a) the notified registrar shall, if satisfied as is mentioned in subsection (3), send the notices and any fee, certificate or declaration which accompanied them, to the second registrar, and

    (b) the second registrar shall be treated as having received the notices from the parties to the marriage on the dates on which the notified registrar received them.

(5) Subsection (4) of section 19 applies for the purposes of this section as it applies for the purposes of that section except that for the purposes of this section the reference in paragraph (d) of that subsection to guidance issued by the Registrar General shall be construed as a reference to guidance issued by the Secretary of State after consultation with the Registrar General for Scotland.

22 Scotland: supplemental

(1) The Marriage (Scotland) Act 1977 shall have effect in relation to a marriage to which section 21 applies—

    (a) subject to that section, and

    (b) with any necessary consequential modification.

(2) In subsection (2)(a) of that section 'prescribed' means prescribed by regulations made by the Secretary of State after consultation with the Registrar General for Scotland; and other expressions used in subsections (1) to (4) of that section and in the Marriage (Scotland) Act 1977 have the same meaning in those subsections as in that Act.

(3) Regulations made by of the Secretary of State under subsection (2)(a) or (3)(c) of that section—

    (a) may make transitional provision,

    (b) shall be made by statutory instrument, and

    (c) shall be subject to annulment in pursuance of a resolution of either House of Parliament.

23 Northern Ireland

(1) This section applies to a marriage—

    (a) which is intended to be solemnised in Northern Ireland, and

    (b) a party to which is subject to immigration control.

(2) In relation to a marriage to which this section applies, the marriage notices—

    (a) shall be given only to a prescribed registrar, and

    (b) shall, in prescribed cases, be given by both parties together in person at a prescribed register office.

(3) The prescribed registrar shall not act under Article 4 or 7 of the Marriage (Northern Ireland) Order 2003 (S.I. 2003/413 (N.I.3)) (marriage notice book, list of intended marriages and marriage schedule) unless he is satisfied, by the provision of specified evidence, that the party subject to immigration control—

    (a) has an entry clearance granted expressly for the purpose of enabling him to marry in the United Kingdom,

    (b) has the written permission of the Secretary of State to marry in the United Kingdom, or

    (c) falls within a class specified for the purpose of this paragraph by regulations made by the Secretary of State.

(4) Subject to subsection (5), if the prescribed registrar is not the registrar for the purposes of Article 4 of that Order, the prescribed registrar shall send him the marriage notices and he shall be treated as having received them from the parties to the marriage on the dates on which the prescribed registrar received them.

(5) The prescribed registrar shall not act under subsection (4) unless he is satisfied as mentioned in subsection (3).

(6) For the purposes of this section—

    (a) a person is subject to immigration control if—

        (i) he is not an EEA national, and

        (ii) under the Immigration Act 1971 (c. 77) he requires leave to enter or remain in the United Kingdom (whether or not leave has been given),

    (b) 'EEA national' means a national of a State which is a contracting party to the Agreement on the European Economic Area signed at Oporto on 2nd May 1992 (as it has effect from time to time),

    (c) 'entry clearance' has the meaning given by section 33(1) of the Immigration Act 1971, and

    (d) 'specified evidence' means such evidence as may be specified in guidance issued by the Secretary of State after consulting the Registrar General for Northern Ireland.

24 Northern Ireland: supplemental

(1) The Marriage (Northern Ireland) Order 2003 (S.I. 2003/413 (N.I.3)) shall have effect in relation to a marriage to which section 23 applies—

    (a) subject to section 23, and

    (b) with any necessary consequential modification.

(2) In section 23 'prescribed' means prescribed for the purposes of that section by regulations made by the Secretary of State after consulting the Registrar General for Northern Ireland and other expressions used in that section or this section and the Marriage (Northern Ireland) Order 2003 have the same meaning in section 23 or this section as in that Order.

(3) Section 18(3) of the Interpretation Act (Northern Ireland) 1954 (c.33 (N.I.)) (provisions as to holders of offices) shall apply to section 23 as if that section were an enactment within the meaning of that Act.

(4) Regulations of the Secretary of State under section 23—

    (a) may make transitional provision,

    (b) shall be made by statutory instrument, and

    (c) shall be subject to annulment in pursuance of a resolution of either House of Parliament.

25 Application for permission under section 19(3)(b), 21(3)(b) or 23(3)(b)

(1) The Secretary of State may make regulations requiring a person seeking permission under section 19(3)(b), 21(3)(b) or 23(3)(b)—

    (a) to make an application in writing, and

    (b) to pay a fee.

(2) The regulations shall, in particular, specify—

    (a) the information to be contained in or provided with the application,

    (b) the amount of the fee, and

    (c) how and to whom the fee is to be paid.

(3) The regulations may, in particular, make provision—
  (a) excepting a specified class of persons from the requirement to pay a fee;
  (b) permitting a specified class of persons to pay a reduced fee;
  (c) for the refund of all or part of a fee in specified circumstances.
(4) Regulations under this section—
  (a) shall be made by statutory instrument, and
  (b) shall be subject to annulment in pursuance of a resolution of either House of Parliament.

Appeals

26 Unification of appeal system

(1) For section 81 of the Nationality, Immigration and Asylum Act 2002 (c. 41) (appeals: adjudicators) substitute—

'Appeal to Tribunal
81 The Asylum and Immigration Tribunal
  (1) There shall be a tribunal to be known as the Asylum and Immigration Tribunal.
  (2) Schedule 4 (which makes provision about the Tribunal) shall have effect.
  (3) A reference in this Part to the Tribunal is a reference to the Asylum and Immigration Tribunal.'

(2) In section 82(1) of that Act (right of appeal: general) for 'to an adjudicator' substitute 'to the Tribunal'.
(3) In section 83(2) of that Act (appeal: asylum claim) for 'to an adjudicator' substitute 'to the Tribunal'.
(4) For Schedule 4 to that Act (adjudicators) substitute the Schedule set out in Schedule 1 to this Act (Asylum and Immigration Tribunal).
(5) The following provisions of that Act shall cease to have effect—
  (a) sections 100 to 103 (Immigration Appeal Tribunal), and
  (b) Schedule 5 (Immigration Appeal Tribunal).
(6) Before section 104 of that Act (pending appeal) insert—

'103A Review of Tribunal's decision

  (1) A party to an appeal under section 82 or 83 may apply to the appropriate court, on the grounds that the Tribunal made an error of law, for an order requiring the Tribunal to reconsider its decision on the appeal.
  (2) The appropriate court may make an order under subsection (1)—
    (a) only if it thinks that the Tribunal may have made an error of law, and
    (b) only once in relation to an appeal.
  (3) An application under subsection (1) must be made—
    (a) in the case of an application by the appellant made while he is in the United Kingdom, within the period of 5 days beginning with the date on which he is treated, in accordance with rules under section 106, as receiving notice of the Tribunal's decision,
    (b) in the case of an application by the appellant made while he is outside the United Kingdom, within the period of 28 days beginning with the date on which he is treated, in accordance with rules under section 106, as receiving notice of the Tribunal's decision, and
    (c) in the case of an application brought by a party to the appeal other than the appellant, within the period of 5 days beginning with the date on which he is treated, in accordance with rules under section 106, as receiving notice of the Tribunal's decision.

(4) But—

    (a) rules of court may specify days to be disregarded in applying subsection (3)(a), (b) or (c), and

    (b) the appropriate court may permit an application under subsection (1) to be made outside the period specified in subsection (3) where it thinks that the application could not reasonably practicably have been made within that period.

(5) An application under subsection (1) shall be determined by reference only to—

    (a) written submissions of the applicant, and

    (b) where rules of court permit, other written submissions.

(6) A decision of the appropriate court on an application under subsection (1) shall be final.

(7) In this section a reference to the Tribunal's decision on an appeal does not include a reference to—

    (a) a procedural, ancillary or preliminary decision, or

    (b) a decision following remittal under section 103B, 103C or 103E.

(8) This section does not apply to a decision of the Tribunal where its jurisdiction is exercised by three or more legally qualified members.

(9) In this section "the appropriate court" means—

    (a) in relation to an appeal decided in England or Wales, the High Court,

    (b) in relation to an appeal decided in Scotland, the Court of Session, and

    (c) in relation to an appeal decided in Northern Ireland, the High Court in Northern Ireland.

(10) An application under subsection (1) to the Court of Session shall be to the Outer House.

103B Appeal from Tribunal following reconsideration

(1) Where an appeal to the Tribunal has been reconsidered, a party to the appeal may bring a further appeal on a point of law to the appropriate appellate court.

(2) In subsection (1) the reference to reconsideration is to reconsideration pursuant to—

    (a) an order under section 103A(1), or

    (b) remittal to the Tribunal under this section or under section 103C or 103E.

(3) An appeal under subsection (1) may be brought only with the permission of—

    (a) the Tribunal, or

    (b) if the Tribunal refuses permission, the appropriate appellate court.

(4) On an appeal under subsection (1) the appropriate appellate court may—

    (a) affirm the Tribunal's decision;

    (b) make any decision which the Tribunal could have made;

    (c) remit the case to the Tribunal;

    (d) affirm a direction under section 87;

    (e) vary a direction under section 87;

    (f) give a direction which the Tribunal could have given under section 87.

(5) In this section "the appropriate appellate court" means—

    (a) in relation to an appeal decided in England or Wales, the Court of Appeal,

    (b) in relation to an appeal decided in Scotland, the Court of Session, and

    (c) in relation to an appeal decided in Northern Ireland, the Court of Appeal in Northern Ireland.

(6) An appeal under subsection (1) to the Court of Session shall be to the Inner House.

103C Appeal from Tribunal instead of reconsideration

(1) On an application under section 103A in respect of an appeal the appropriate court, if it thinks the appeal raises a question of law of such importance that it should be decided by the appropriate appellate court, may refer the appeal to that court.

(2) On a reference under subsection (1) the appropriate appellate court may—

    (a) affirm the Tribunal's decision;

    (b) make any decision which the Tribunal could have made;

    (c) remit the case to the Tribunal;

    (d) affirm a direction under section 87;

    (e) vary a direction under section 87;

    (f) give a direction which the Tribunal could have given under section 87;

    (g) restore the application under section 103A to the appropriate court.

(3) In this section—

    "the appropriate court" has the same meaning as in section 103A, and

    "the appropriate appellate court" has the same meaning as in section 103B.

(4) A reference under subsection (1) to the Court of Session shall be to the Inner House.

103D Reconsideration: legal aid

(1) On the application of an appellant under section 103A, the appropriate court may order that the appellant's costs in respect of the application under section 103A shall be paid out of the Community Legal Service Fund established under section 5 of the Access to Justice Act 1999 (c. 22).

(2) Subsection (3) applies where the Tribunal has decided an appeal following reconsideration pursuant to an order made—

    (a) under section 103A(1), and

    (b) on the application of the appellant.

(3) The Tribunal may order that the appellant's costs—

    (a) in respect of the application for reconsideration, and

    (b) in respect of the reconsideration,

    shall be paid out of that Fund.

(4) The Secretary of State may make regulations about the exercise of the powers in subsections (1) and (3).

(5) Regulations under subsection (4) may, in particular, make provision—

    (a) specifying or providing for the determination of the amount of payments;

    (b) about the persons to whom the payments are to be made;

    (c) restricting the exercise of the power (whether by reference to the prospects of success in respect of the appeal at the time when the application for reconsideration was made, the fact that a reference has been made under section 103C(1), the circumstances of the appellant, the nature of the appellant's legal representatives, or otherwise).

(6) Regulations under subsection (4) may make provision—

    (a) conferring a function on the Legal Services Commission;

    (b) modifying a duty or power of the Legal Services Commission in respect of compliance with orders under subsection (3);

    (c) applying (with or without modifications), modifying or disapplying a provision of, or of anything done under, an enactment relating to the funding of legal services.

(7) Before making regulations under subsection (4) the Secretary of State shall consult such persons as he thinks appropriate.

(8) This section has effect only in relation to an appeal decided in—

    (a) England,

    (b) Wales, or

    (c) Northern Ireland.

(9) In relation to an appeal decided in Northern Ireland this section shall have effect—

    (a) as if a reference to the Community Legal Service Fund were to the fund established under paragraph 4(2)(a) of Schedule 3 to the Access to Justice (Northern Ireland) Order 2003 (S.I. 2003/ 435 (N.I. 10)), and

    (b) with any other necessary modifications.

103E Appeal from Tribunal sitting as panel

(1) This section applies to a decision of the Tribunal on an appeal under section 82 or 83 where its jurisdiction is exercised by three or more legally qualified members.

(2) A party to the appeal may bring a further appeal on a point of law to the appropriate appellate court.

(3) An appeal under subsection (2) may be brought only with the permission of—
    (a) the Tribunal, or
    (b) if the Tribunal refuses permission, the appropriate appellate court.

(4) On an appeal under subsection (2) the appropriate appellate court may—
    (a) affirm the Tribunal's decision;
    (b) make any decision which the Tribunal could have made;
    (c) remit the case to the Tribunal;
    (d) affirm a direction under section 87;
    (e) vary a direction under section 87;
    (f) give a direction which the Tribunal could have given under section 87.

(5) In this section "the appropriate appellate court" means—
    (a) in relation to an appeal decided in England or Wales, the Court of Appeal,
    (b) in relation to an appeal decided in Scotland, the Court of Session, and
    (c) in relation to an appeal decided in Northern Ireland, the Court of Appeal in Northern Ireland.

(6) A further appeal under subsection (2) to the Court of Session shall be to the Inner House.

(7) In this section a reference to the Tribunal's decision on an appeal does not include a reference to—
    (a) a procedural, ancillary or preliminary decision, or
    (b) a decision following remittal under section 103B or 103C.'

(7) Schedule 2 (which makes amendments consequential on this section, and transitional provision) shall have effect.

(8) The Lord Chancellor may by order vary a period specified in—
    (a) section 103A(3)(a), (b) or (c) of the Nationality, Immigration and Asylum Act 2002 (c. 41) (review of Tribunal's decision) (as inserted by subsection (6) above), or
    (b) paragraph 29(5)(b) of Schedule 2 to this Act.

(9) An order under subsection (8)—
    (a) may make provision generally or only for specified cases or circumstances,
    (b) may make different provision for different cases or circumstances,
    (c) shall be made by statutory instrument, and
    (d) shall be subject to annulment in pursuance of a resolution of either House of Parliament.

(10) Before making an order under subsection (8) the Lord Chancellor shall consult—
    (a) the Lord Chief Justice, if the order affects proceedings in England and Wales,
    (b) the Lord President of the Court of Session, if the order affects proceedings in Scotland, and
    (c) the Lord Chief Justice of Northern Ireland, if the order affects proceedings in Northern Ireland.

27 Unfounded human rights or asylum claim

(1) Section 94 of the Nationality, Immigration and Asylum Act 2002 (c. 41) (no appeal from within United Kingdom for unfounded human rights or asylum claim) shall be amended as follows.

(2) After subsection (1) insert—

'(1A) A person may not bring an appeal against an immigration decision of a kind specified in section 82(2)(c), (d) or (e) in reliance on section 92(2) if the Secretary of State certifies that the claim or claims mentioned in subsection (1) above is or are clearly unfounded.'

(3) In subsection (2) for 'in reliance on section 92(4)' substitute 'in reliance on section 92(4)(a)'.

(4) In subsection (4) omit paragraphs (a) to (j).

(5) After subsection (5) insert—

'(5A) If the Secretary of State is satisfied that the statements in subsection (5) (a) and (b) are true of a State or part of a State in relation to a description of person, an order under subsection (5) may add the State or part to the list in subsection (4) in respect of that description of person.

(5B) Where a State or part of a State is added to the list in subsection (4) in respect of a description of person, subsection (3) shall have effect in relation to a claimant only if the Secretary of State is satisfied that he is within that description (as well as being satisfied that he is entitled to reside in the State or part).

(5C) A description for the purposes of subsection (5A) may refer to—
(a) gender,
(b) language,
(c) race,
(d) religion,
(e) nationality,
(f) membership of a social or other group,
(g) political opinion, or
(h) any other attribute or circumstance that the Secretary of State thinks appropriate.'

(6) For subsection (6) substitute—

'(6) The Secretary of State may by order amend the list in subsection (4) so as to omit a State or part added under subsection (5); and the omission may be—
(a) general, or
(b) effected so that the State or part remains listed in respect of a description of person.'

(7) After subsection (6) insert—

'(6A) Subsection (3) shall not apply in relation to an asylum claimant or human rights claimant who—
(a) is the subject of a certificate under section 2 or 70 of the Extradition Act 2003 (c. 41),
(b) is in custody pursuant to arrest under section 5 of that Act,
(c) is the subject of a provisional warrant under section 73 of that Act,
(d) is the subject of an authority to proceed under section 7 of the Extradition Act 1989 (c. 33) or an order under paragraph 4(2) of Schedule 1 to that Act, or
(e) is the subject of a provisional warrant under section 8 of that Act or of a warrant under paragraph 5(1)(b) of Schedule 1 to that Act.'

(8) After section 112(5) of that Act (orders, &c.) insert—

'(5A) If an instrument makes provision under section 94(5) and 94(6)—
(a) subsection (4)(b) above shall apply, and
(b) subsection (5)(b) above shall not apply.'

28 Appeal from within United Kingdom

For section 92(3) of the Nationality, Immigration and Asylum Act 2002 (c. 41) (appeal from within United Kingdom: person with entry clearance or work permit) substitute—

'(3) This section also applies to an appeal against refusal of leave to enter the United Kingdom if—
(a) at the time of the refusal the appellant is in the United Kingdom, and
(b) on his arrival in the United Kingdom the appellant had entry clearance.

(3A) But this section does not apply by virtue of subsection (3) if subsection (3B) or (3C) applies to the refusal of leave to enter.

(3B) This subsection applies to a refusal of leave to enter which is a deemed refusal under paragraph 2A(9) of Schedule 2 to the Immigration Act 1971 (c. 77) resulting from cancellation of leave to enter by an immigration officer—

    (a) under paragraph 2A(8) of that Schedule, and

    (b) on the grounds specified in paragraph 2A(2) of that Schedule.

(3C) This subsection applies to a refusal of leave to enter which specifies that the grounds for refusal are that the leave is sought for a purpose other than that specified in the entry clearance.

(3D) This section also applies to an appeal against refusal of leave to enter the United Kingdom if at the time of the refusal the appellant—

    (a) is in the United Kingdom,

    (b) has a work permit, and

    (c) is any of the following (within the meaning of the British Nationality Act 1981 (c. 61))—

        (i) a British overseas territories citizen,

        (ii) a British Overseas citizen,

        (iii) a British National (Overseas),

        (iv) a British protected person, or

        (v) a British subject.'

29 Entry clearance

(1) After section 88 of the Nationality, Immigration and Asylum Act 2002 (c. 41) (appeal: ineligibility) insert—

'88A Ineligibility: entry clearance

(1) A person may not appeal under section 82(1) against refusal of entry clearance if the decision to refuse is taken on grounds which—

    (a) relate to a provision of immigration rules, and

    (b) are specified for the purpose of this section by order of the Secretary of State.

(2) Subsection (1)—

    (a) does not prevent the bringing of an appeal on either or both of the grounds referred to in section 84(1)(b) and (c), and

    (b) is without prejudice to the effect of section 88 in relation to an appeal under section 82(1) against refusal of entry clearance.'

(2) In section 112 of that Act (regulations, &c.) after subsection (3) insert—

'(3A) An order under section 88A—

    (a) must be made by statutory instrument,

    (b) may not be made unless a draft has been laid before and approved by resolution of each House of Parliament, and

    (c) may include transitional provision.'

30 Earlier right of appeal

(1) Section 96 of the Nationality, Immigration and Asylum Act 2002 (earlier right of appeal) shall be amended as follows.

(2) For subsections (1) to (3) substitute—

'(1) An appeal under section 82(1) against an immigration decision ("the new decision") in respect of a person may not be brought if the Secretary of State or an immigration officer certifies—

    (a) that the person was notified of a right of appeal under that section against another immigration decision ("the old decision") (whether or not an appeal was brought and whether or not any appeal brought has been determined),

    (b) that the claim or application to which the new decision relates relies on a matter that could have been raised in an appeal against the old decision, and

    (c) that, in the opinion of the Secretary of State or the immigration officer, there is no satisfactory reason for that matter not having been raised in an appeal against the old decision.

  (2) An appeal under section 82(1) against an immigration decision ("the new decision") in respect of a person may not be brought if the Secretary of State or an immigration officer certifies—

    (a) that the person received a notice under section 120 by virtue of an application other than that to which the new decision relates or by virtue of a decision other than the new decision,

    (b) that the new decision relates to an application or claim which relies on a matter that should have been, but has not been, raised in a statement made in response to that notice, and

    (c) that, in the opinion of the Secretary of State or the immigration officer, there is no satisfactory reason for that matter not having been raised in a statement made in response to that notice.'

(3) In subsection (5) for 'Subsections (1) to (3) apply to prevent or restrict' substitute 'Subsections (1) and (2) apply to prevent'.

(4) At the end add—

'(7) A certificate under subsection (1) or (2) shall have no effect in relation to an appeal instituted before the certificate is issued.'

31 Seamen and aircrews: right of appeal

In section 82(2) of the Nationality, Immigration and Asylum Act 2002 (c. 41) after paragraph (i) insert—

'(ia) a decision that a person is to be removed from the United Kingdom by way of directions under paragraph 12(2) of Schedule 2 to the Immigration Act 1971 (c. 77) (seamen and aircrews),'.

32 Suspected international terrorist: bail

(1) At the end of section 24 of the Anti-terrorism, Crime and Security Act 2001 (c. 24) (suspected international terrorist: bail by Special Immigration Appeals Commission) add—

'(4) Where the Special Immigration Appeals Commission determines an application for bail, the applicant or a person who made representations to the Commission about the application may appeal on a question of law to the appropriate appeal court.

(5) Section 7(2) and (3) of the Special Immigration Appeals Commission Act 1997 (c. 68) (appeals from Commission) shall have effect for the purposes of an appeal under subsection (4) above.'

(2) In section 27(5) and (6) of the Anti-terrorism, Crime and Security Act 2001 (suspected international terrorist: Special Immigration Appeals Commission: procedure) for 'section 25 or 26 of this Act' substitute 'section 24, 25 or 26 of this Act'.

Removal and detention

33 Removing asylum seeker to safe country

(1) Schedule 3 (which concerns the removal of persons claiming asylum to countries known to protect refugees and to respect human rights) shall have effect.

(2) Sections 11 and 12 of the Immigration and Asylum Act 1999 (c. 33) (removal of asylum claimant to country under standing or other arrangements) shall cease to have effect.

(3) The following provisions of the Nationality, Immigration and Asylum Act 2002 (c. 41) shall cease to have effect—

    (a) section 80 (new section 11 of 1999 Act), and

    (b) section 93 (appeal from within United Kingdom: 'third country' removal).

34 Detention pending deportation

(1) In paragraph 2(1) of Schedule 3 to the Immigration Act 1971 (c. 77) (detention pending deportation on recommendation by court) for the words 'and that person is neither detained in pursuance of the sentence or order of any court nor for the time being released on bail by any court having power so to release him' substitute 'and that person is not detained in pursuance of the sentence or order of any court'.

(2) In paragraph 2(2) of that Schedule (detention following notice of deportation) for the words 'and he is neither detained in pursuance of the sentence or order of a court nor for the time being released on bail by a court having power so to release him' substitute 'and he is not detained in pursuance of the sentence or order of a court'.

35 Deportation or removal: cooperation

(1) The Secretary of State may require a person to take specified action if the Secretary of State thinks that—

    (a) the action will or may enable a travel document to be obtained by or for the person, and

    (b) possession of the travel document will facilitate the person's deportation or removal from the United Kingdom.

(2) In particular, the Secretary of State may require a person to—

    (a) provide information or documents to the Secretary of State or to any other person;

    (b) obtain information or documents;

    (c) provide fingerprints, submit to the taking of a photograph or provide information, or submit to a process for the recording of information, about external physical characteristics (including, in particular, features of the iris or any other part of the eye);

    (d) make, or consent to or cooperate with the making of, an application to a person acting for the government of a State other than the United Kingdom;

    (e) cooperate with a process designed to enable determination of an application;

    (f) complete a form accurately and completely;

    (g) attend an interview and answer questions accurately and completely;

    (h) make an appointment.

(3) A person commits an offence if he fails without reasonable excuse to comply with a requirement of the Secretary of State under subsection (1).

(4) A person guilty of an offence under subsection (3) shall be liable—

    (a) on conviction on indictment, to imprisonment for a term not exceeding two years, to a fine or to both, or

    (b) on summary conviction, to imprisonment for a term not exceeding twelve months, to a fine not exceeding the statutory maximum or to both.

(5) If a constable or immigration officer reasonably suspects that a person has committed an offence under subsection (3) he may arrest the person without warrant.

(6) An offence under subsection (3) shall be treated as—

    (a) a relevant offence for the purposes of sections 28B and 28D of the Immigration Act 1971 (c. 77) (search, entry and arrest), and

    (b) an offence under Part III of that Act (criminal proceedings) for the purposes of sections 28(4), 28E, 28G and 28H (search after arrest, &c.) of that Act.

(7) In subsection (1)—

'travel document' means a passport or other document which is issued by or for Her Majesty's Government or the government of another State and which enables or facilitates travel from the United Kingdom to another State, and

'removal from the United Kingdom' means removal under—

    (a) Schedule 2 to the Immigration Act 1971 (control on entry) (including a provision of that Schedule as applied by another provision of the Immigration Acts),

    (b) section 10 of the Immigration and Asylum Act 1999 (c. 33) (removal of person unlawfully in United Kingdom), or

    (c) Schedule 3 to this Act.

(8) While sections 11 and 12 of the Immigration and Asylum Act 1999 continue to have effect, the reference in subsection (7)(c) above to Schedule 3 to this Act shall be treated as including a reference to those sections.

(9) In so far as subsection (3) extends to England and Wales, subsection (4)(b) shall, until the commencement of section 154 of the Criminal Justice Act 2003 (c. 44) (increased limit on magistrates' power of imprisonment), have effect as if the reference to twelve months were a reference to six months.

(10) In so far as subsection (3) extends to Scotland, subsection (4)(b) shall have effect as if the reference to twelve months were a reference to six months.

(11) In so far as subsection (3) extends to Northern Ireland, subsection (4)(b) shall have effect as if the reference to twelve months were a reference to six months.

36 Electronic monitoring

(1) In this section—

    (a) 'residence restriction' means a restriction as to residence imposed under—

        (i) paragraph 21 of Schedule 2 to the Immigration Act 1971 (c. 77) (control on entry) (including that paragraph as applied by another provision of the Immigration Acts), or

        (ii) Schedule 3 to that Act (deportation),

    (b) 'reporting restriction' means a requirement to report to a specified person imposed under any of those provisions,

    (c) 'employment restriction' means a restriction as to employment or occupation imposed under any of those provisions, and

    (d) 'immigration bail' means—

        (i) release under a provision of the Immigration Acts on entry into a recognizance or bail bond,

        (ii) bail granted in accordance with a provision of the Immigration Acts by a court, a justice of the peace, the sheriff, the Asylum and Immigration Tribunal, the Secretary of State or an immigration officer (but not by a police officer), and

        (iii) bail granted by the Special Immigration Appeals Commission.

(2) Where a residence restriction is imposed on an adult—

    (a) he may be required to cooperate with electronic monitoring, and

    (b) failure to comply with a requirement under paragraph (a) shall be treated for all purposes of the Immigration Acts as failure to observe the residence restriction.

(3) Where a reporting restriction could be imposed on an adult—

    (a) he may instead be required to cooperate with electronic monitoring, and

    (b) the requirement shall be treated for all purposes of the Immigration Acts as a reporting restriction.

(4) Immigration bail may be granted to an adult subject to a requirement that he cooperate with electronic monitoring; and the requirement may (but need not) be imposed as a condition of a recognizance or bail bond.

(5) In this section a reference to requiring an adult to cooperate with electronic monitoring is a reference to requiring him to cooperate with such arrangements as the person imposing the requirement may specify for detecting and recording by electronic means the location of the adult, or his presence in or absence from a location—

    (a) at specified times,

    (b) during specified periods of time, or

    (c) throughout the currency of the arrangements.

(6) In particular, arrangements for the electronic monitoring of an adult—

    (a) may require him to wear a device;

    (b) may require him to make specified use of a device;

    (c) may prohibit him from causing or permitting damage of or interference with a device;

    (d) may prohibit him from taking or permitting action that would or might prevent the effective operation of a device;

    (e) may require him to communicate in a specified manner and at specified times or during specified periods of time;

    (f) may involve the performance of functions by persons other than the person imposing the requirement to cooperate with electronic monitoring (and those functions may relate to any aspect or condition of a residence restriction, of a reporting restriction, of an employment restriction, of a requirement under this section or of immigration bail).

(7) In this section 'adult' means an individual who is at least 18 years old.

(8) The Secretary of State—

    (a) may make rules about arrangements for electronic monitoring for the purposes of this section, and

    (b) when he thinks that satisfactory arrangements for electronic monitoring are available in respect of an area, shall notify persons likely to be in a position to exercise power under this section in respect of the area.

(9) Rules under subsection (8)(a) may, in particular, require that arrangements for electronic monitoring impose on a person of a specified description responsibility for specified aspects of the operation of the arrangements.

(10) A requirement to cooperate with electronic monitoring—

    (a) shall comply with rules under subsection (8)(a), and

    (b) may not be imposed in respect of an adult who is or is expected to be in an area unless the person imposing the requirement has received a notification from the Secretary of State under subsection (8)(b) in respect of that area.

(11) Rules under subsection (8)(a)—

    (a) may include incidental, consequential or transitional provision,

    (b) may make provision generally or only in relation to specified cases, circumstances or areas,

    (c) shall be made by statutory instrument, and

    (d) shall be subject to annulment in pursuance of a resolution of either House of Parliament.

(12) Before the commencement of section 26 a reference in this section to the Asylum and Immigration Tribunal shall be treated as a reference to—

    (a) a person appointed, or treated as if appointed, as an adjudicator under section 81 of the Nationality, Immigration and Asylum Act 2002 (c. 41) (appeals), and

    (b) the Immigration Appeal Tribunal.

Immigration services

37 Provision of immigration services

(1) For section 84(2) and (3) of the Immigration and Asylum Act 1999 (c. 33) (person qualified to provide immigration services) substitute—

    '(2) A person is a qualified person if he is—

        (a) a registered person,

        (b) authorised by a designated professional body to practise as a member of the profession whose members the body regulates,

        (c) the equivalent in an EEA State of—

            (i) a registered person, or

            (ii) a person within paragraph (b),

        (d) a person permitted, by virtue of exemption from a prohibition, to provide in an EEA State advice or services equivalent to immigration advice or services, or

        (e) acting on behalf of, and under the supervision of, a person within any of paragraphs (a) to (d) (whether or not under a contract of employment).

    (3) Subsection (2)(a) and (e) are subject to any limitation on the effect of a person's registration imposed under paragraph 2(2) of Schedule 6.'

(2) In section 85(1) of that Act (registration by the Commissioner) omit 'and (b)'.

(3) In section 89 of that Act (disciplinary charge upheld by Immigration Services Tribunal)—

    (a) for subsections (2) and (3) substitute—

    '(2) If the person charged is a registered person or acts on behalf of a registered person, the Tribunal may—

        (a) direct the Commissioner to record the charge and the Tribunal's decision for consideration in connection with the registered person's next application for continued registration;

        (b) direct the registered person to apply for continued registration as soon as is reasonably practicable.', and

    (b) in subsection (8) for 'employed by him or working' substitute 'acting on his behalf or'.

(4) In section 90(4) of that Act (orders by disciplinary bodies) for 'works under the supervision of' substitute 'is acting on behalf of'.

(5) In Schedule 5 to that Act (Immigration Services Commissioner)—

    (a) for paragraph 1(1)(b) substitute—

    '(b) those acting on behalf of registered persons,',

    (b) for paragraph 1(3)(b) substitute—

    '(b) any person acting on behalf of that person.',

    (c) for paragraph 3(3)(b) substitute—

       '(b) a person who is acting on behalf of a person who is within paragraph (a);',

    (d) for paragraph 4(1)(b) substitute—

       '(b) persons acting on behalf of persons who are within paragraph (a).',

    (e) in paragraph 5(3)(b) for 'employed by, or working under the supervision of,' substitute 'acting on behalf of',

    (f) for paragraph 5(3)(e) substitute—

       '(e) an alleged breach of a rule of a relevant regulatory body,',

    (g) for paragraph 6(3)(c) substitute—

       '(c) in any other case, refer the matter to any relevant regulatory body.',

    (h) in paragraphs 9(1)(a) and (b) for 'or a person employed by, or working under the supervision of,' substitute 'or is acting on behalf of',

    (i) for paragraph 9(1)(c) substitute—

       '(c) refer the complaint and his decision on it to a relevant regulatory body;',

    (j) for paragraphs 9(3)(a) and (b) substitute—

       '(a) imposing restrictions on the provision of immigration advice or immigration services by the relevant person or by a person acting on his behalf or under his supervision;
       (b) prohibiting the provision of immigration advice or immigration services by the relevant person or a person acting on his behalf or under his supervision.', and

    (k) for paragraphs 9(4)(b) to (d) substitute—

       '(b) a person acting on behalf of a registered person;'.

  (6) In Schedule 6 to that Act (registration)—

    (a) in paragraph 1(1) omit 'or (b)', and

    (b) in paragraph 3(7)(a) for 'section 89(3)(b)' substitute 'section 89(2)(b)'.

38 Immigration Services Commissioner: power of entry

  (1) After section 92 of the Immigration and Asylum Act 1999 (c. 33) (offences: enforcement) insert—

'92A Investigation of offence: power of entry

  (1) On an application made by the Commissioner a justice of the peace may issue a warrant authorising the Commissioner to enter and search premises.

  (2) A justice of the peace may issue a warrant in respect of premises only if satisfied that there are reasonable grounds for believing that—

    (a) an offence under section 91 has been committed,

    (b) there is material on the premises which is likely to be of substantial value (whether by itself or together with other material) to the investigation of the offence, and

    (c) any of the conditions specified in subsection (3) is satisfied.

  (3) Those conditions are—

    (a) that it is not practicable to communicate with a person entitled to grant entry to the premises,

    (b) that it is not practicable to communicate with a person entitled to grant access to the evidence,

    (c) that entry to the premises will be prevented unless a warrant is produced, and

    (d) that the purpose of a search may be frustrated or seriously prejudiced unless the Commissioner can secure immediate entry on arrival at the premises.

  (4) The Commissioner may seize and retain anything for which a search is authorised under this section.

  (5) A person commits an offence if without reasonable excuse he obstructs the Commissioner in the exercise of a power by virtue of this section.

  (6) A person guilty of an offence under subsection (5) shall be liable on summary conviction to—

    (a) imprisonment for a term not exceeding six months,

    (b) a fine not exceeding level 5 on the standard scale, or

    (c) both.

  (7) In this section—

    (a) a reference to the Commissioner includes a reference to a member of his staff authorised in writing by him,

    (b) a reference to premises includes a reference to premises used wholly or partly as a dwelling, and

    (c) a reference to material—

      (i) includes material subject to legal privilege within the meaning of the Police and Criminal Evidence Act 1984 (c. 60),

      (ii) does not include excluded material or special procedure material within the meaning of that Act, and

      (iii) includes material whether or not it would be admissible in evidence at a trial.

  (8) In the application of this section to Scotland—

    (a) a reference to a justice of the peace shall be taken as a reference to the sheriff,

    (b) for sub-paragraph (i) of subsection (7)(c) there is substituted—

    "(i) includes material comprising items subject to legal privilege (as defined by section 412 of the Proceeds of Crime Act 2002 (c. 29))," and

    (c) sub-paragraph (ii) of subsection (7)(c) shall be ignored.

  (9) In the application of this section to Northern Ireland the reference to the Police and Criminal Evidence Act 1984 shall be taken as a reference to the Police and Criminal Evidence (Northern Ireland) Order 1989 (S.I. 1989/1341 (N.I. 12)).'

(2) In paragraph 7 of Schedule 5 to the Immigration and Asylum Act 1999 (c. 33) (investigation of complaints, &c.: power of entry)—

  (a) in sub-paragraph (1)(b) after '(b)' insert ', (c)',

  (b) in sub-paragraph (1)(c) for 'registered person.' substitute 'registered or exempt person.',

  (c) in sub-paragraph (1A)(a) after '(b)' insert ', (c)',

  (d) in sub-paragraph (1A)(b) for 'registered person.' substitute 'registered or exempt person.', and

  (e) after sub-paragraph (8) insert—

    '(9) Sub-paragraphs (7) and (8) shall apply to an exempt person as they apply to a registered person, but with a reference to cancellation of registration being treated as a reference to withdrawal of exemption.

    (10) In this paragraph "exempt person" means a person certified by the Commissioner as exempt under section 84(4)(a).'

39 Offence of advertising services

After section 92A of the Immigration and Asylum Act 1999 (c. 33) (inserted by section 38 above) insert—

'92B Advertising

(1) A person commits an offence if—

    (a) he offers to provide immigration advice or immigration services, and

    (b) provision by him of the advice or services would constitute an offence under section 91.

(2) For the purpose of subsection (1) a person offers to provide advice or services if he—

    (a) makes an offer to a particular person or class of person,

    (b) makes arrangements for an advertisement in which he offers to provide advice or services, or

    (c) makes arrangements for an advertisement in which he is described or presented as competent to provide advice or services.

(3) A person guilty of an offence under this section shall be liable on summary conviction to a fine not exceeding level 4 on the standard scale.

(4) Subsections (3) to (7) of section 91 shall have effect for the purposes of this section as they have effect for the purposes of that section.

(5) An information relating to an offence under this section may in England and Wales be tried by a magistrates' court if—

    (a) it is laid within the period of six months beginning with the date (or first date) on which the offence is alleged to have been committed, or

    (b) it is laid—

        (i) within the period of two years beginning with that date, and

        (ii) within the period of six months beginning with a date certified by the Immigration Services Commissioner as the date on which the commission of the offence came to his notice.

(6) In Scotland, proceedings for an offence under this section may be commenced—

    (a) at any time within the period of six months beginning with the date (or first date) on which the offence is alleged to have been committed, or

    (b) at any time within both—

        (i) the period of two years beginning with that date, and

        (ii) the period of six months beginning with a date specified, in a certificate signed by or on behalf of the procurator fiscal, as the date on which evidence sufficient in his opinion to warrant such proceedings came to his knowledge,

    and any such certificate purporting to be so signed shall be deemed so signed unless the contrary is proved and be conclusive as to the facts stated in it.

(7) Subsection (3) of section 136 of the Criminal Procedure (Scotland) Act 1995 (c. 46) (date on which proceedings are deemed commenced) has effect to the purposes of subsection (6) as it has effect for the purposes of that section.

(8) A complaint charging the commission of an offence under this section may in Northern Ireland be heard and determined by a magistrates' court if—

    (a) it is made within the period of six months beginning with the date (or first date) on which the offence is alleged to have been committed, or

    (b) it is made—

        (i) within the period of two years beginning with that date, and

        (ii) within the period of six months beginning with a date certified by the Immigration Services Commissioner as the date on which the commission of the offence came to his notice.'

40 Appeal to Immigration Services Tribunal

Section 87(3)(f) of the Immigration and Asylum Act 1999 (c. 33) (appeal to Tribunal against deferral of decision) shall cease to have effect.

41 Professional bodies

(1) Section 86 of the Immigration and Asylum Act 1999 (designated professional bodies) shall be amended as follows.

(2) For subsection (2) substitute—

'(2) The Secretary of State may by order remove a body from the list in subsection (1) if he considers that the body—

(a) has failed to provide effective regulation of its members in their provision of immigration advice or immigration services, or

(b) has failed to comply with a request of the Commissioner for the provision of information (whether general or in relation to a particular case or matter).'

(3) For subsection (9)(b) substitute—

'(b) report to the Secretary of State if the Commissioner considers that a designated professional body—

(i) is failing to provide effective regulation of its members in their provision of immigration advice or immigration services, or

(ii) has failed to comply with a request of the Commissioner for the provision of information (whether general or in relation to a particular case or matter).'

(4) After subsection (9) insert—

'(9A) A designated professional body shall comply with a request of the Commissioner for the provision of information (whether general or in relation to a specified case or matter).'

(5) In section 166(2) of the Immigration and Asylum Act 1999 (c. 33) (regulations and orders) after 'in relation to' insert 'orders made under section 90(1),'.

(6) For paragraph 21(2) of Schedule 5 to the Immigration and Asylum Act 1999 (Commissioner: annual report) substitute—

'(2) The report must, in particular, set out the Commissioner's opinion as to the extent to which each designated professional body has—

(a) provided effective regulation of its members in their provision of immigration advice or immigration services, and

(b) complied with requests of the Commissioner for the provision of information.'

Fees

42 Amount of fees

(1) In prescribing a fee for an application or process under a provision specified in subsection (2) the Secretary of State may, with the consent of the Treasury, prescribe an amount which is intended to—

(a) exceed the administrative costs of determining the application or undertaking the process, and

(b) reflect benefits that the Secretary of State thinks are likely to accrue to the person who makes the application, to whom the application relates or by or for whom the process is undertaken, if the application is successful or the process is completed.

(2) Those provisions are—

(a) section 41(2) of the British Nationality Act 1981 (c. 61) (fees for applications, &c. under that Act),

(b) section 5(1)(a) and (b) of the Immigration and Asylum Act 1999 (fees for application for leave to remain, &c.), and

    (c) sections 10 and 122 of the Nationality, Immigration and Asylum Act 2002 (c. 41) (certificate of entitlement to right of abode; and fees for work permit, &c.).

(3) An Order in Council under section 1 of the Consular Fees Act 1980 (c. 23) (fees) which prescribes a fee in relation to an application for the issue of a certificate under section 10 of the Nationality, Immigration and Asylum Act 2002 (right of abode: certificate of entitlement) may prescribe an amount which is intended to—

    (a) exceed the administrative costs of determining the application, and

    (b) reflect benefits that in the opinion of Her Majesty in Council are likely to accrue to the applicant if the application is successful.

(4) Where an instrument prescribes a fee in reliance on this section it may include provision for the refund, where an application is unsuccessful or a process is not completed, of that part of the fee which is intended to reflect the matters specified in subsection (1)(b) or (3)(b).

(5) Provision included by virtue of subsection (4)—

    (a) may determine, or provide for the determination of, the amount to be refunded;

    (b) may confer a discretion on the Secretary of State or another person (whether in relation to determining the amount of a refund or in relation to determining whether a refund should be made).

(6) An instrument may not be made in reliance on this section unless the Secretary of State has consulted with such persons as appear to him to be appropriate.

(7) An instrument may not be made in reliance on this section unless a draft has been laid before and approved by resolution of each House of Parliament (and any provision making the instrument subject to annulment in pursuance of a resolution of either House of Parliament shall not apply).

(8) This section is without prejudice to the power to make an order under section 102 of the Finance (No. 2) Act 1987 (c. 51) (government fees and charges) in relation to a power under a provision specified in this section.

43 Transfer of leave stamps

(1) Section 5 of the Immigration and Asylum Act 1999 (c. 33) (charges) shall be amended as follows.

(2) For subsection (1)(c) (transfer of indefinite leave stamp to new document) substitute—

    '(c) the fixing of a limited leave stamp or indefinite leave stamp on a passport or other document issued to the applicant where the stamp was previously fixed on another passport or document issued to the applicant.'

(3) For subsection (5) substitute—

    '(5) In this section—

        (a) "limited leave stamp" means a stamp, sticker or other attachment which indicates that a person has been granted limited leave to enter or remain in the United Kingdom, and

        (b) "indefinite leave stamp" means a stamp, sticker or other attachment which indicates that a person has been granted indefinite leave to enter or remain in the United Kingdom.'

General

44 Interpretation: 'the Immigration Acts'

(1) A reference to 'the Immigration Acts' is to—

    (a) the Immigration Act 1971 (c. 77),

    (b) the Immigration Act 1988 (c. 14),

    (c) the Asylum and Immigration Appeals Act 1993 (c. 23),

    (d) the Asylum and Immigration Act 1996 (c. 49),

    (e) the Immigration and Asylum Act 1999,

    (f) the Nationality, Immigration and Asylum Act 2002 (c. 41), and

    (g) this Act.

(2) This section has effect in relation to a reference in this Act or any other enactment (including an enactment passed or made before this Act).

(3) For section 158(1) and (2) of the Nationality, Immigration and Asylum Act 2002 (c. 41) substitute—

> '(1) A reference to "the Immigration Acts" shall be construed in accordance with section 44 of the Asylum and Immigration (Treatment of Claimants, etc.) Act 2004.'

(4) In the following provisions for 'section 158 of the Nationality, Immigration and Asylum Act 2002' substitute 'section 44 of the Asylum and Immigration (Treatment of Claimants, etc.) Act 2004'—

    (a) section 32(5) of the Immigration Act 1971 (c. 77), and

    (b) section 167(1) of the Immigration and Asylum Act 1999 (c. 33).

45 Interpretation: immigration officer

In this Act 'immigration officer' means a person appointed by the Secretary of State as an immigration officer under paragraph 1 of Schedule 2 to the Immigration Act 1971.

46 Money

There shall be paid out of money provided by Parliament—

    (a) any expenditure incurred by a Minister of the Crown in connection with this Act, and

    (b) any increase attributable to this Act in the sums payable under any other enactment out of money provided by Parliament.

47 Repeals

The enactments listed in Schedule 4 are hereby repealed to the extent specified.

48 Commencement

(1) Sections 2, 32(2) and 35 shall come into force at the end of the period of two months beginning with the date on which this Act is passed.

(2) Section 32(1) shall have effect in relation to determinations of the Special Immigration Appeals Commission made after the end of the period of two months beginning with the date on which this Act is passed.

(3) The other preceding provisions of this Act shall come into force in accordance with provision made—

    (a) in the case of section 26 or Schedule 1 or 2, by order of the Lord Chancellor,

    (b) in the case of sections 4 and 5 in so far as they extend to Scotland, by order of the Scottish Ministers, and

    (c) in any other case, by order of the Secretary of State.

(4) An order under subsection (3)—

    (a) may make transitional or incidental provision,

    (b) may make different provision for different purposes, and

    (c) shall be made by statutory instrument.

(5) Transitional provision under subsection (4)(a) in relation to the commencement of section 26 may, in particular, make provision in relation to proceedings which, immediately before commencement—

    (a) are awaiting determination by an adjudicator appointed, or treated as if appointed, under section 81 of the Nationality, Immigration and Asylum Act 2002 (c. 41),

    (b) are awaiting determination by the Immigration Appeal Tribunal,

    (c) having been determined by an adjudicator could be brought before the Immigration Appeal Tribunal,

    (d) are awaiting the determination of a further appeal brought in accordance with section 103 of that Act,

    (e) having been determined by the Immigration Appeal Tribunal could be brought before another court by way of further appeal under that section,

    (f) are or could be made the subject of an application under section 101 of that Act (review of decision on permission to appeal to Tribunal), or

    (g) are or could be made the subject of another kind of application to the High Court or the Court of Session.

(6) Provision made under subsection (5) may, in particular—

    (a) provide for the institution or continuance of an appeal of a kind not generally available after the commencement of section 26,

    (b) provide for the termination of proceedings, or

    (c) make any other provision that the Lord Chancellor thinks appropriate.

49 Extent

(1) This Act extends (subject to subsection (2)) to—

    (a) England and Wales,

    (b) Scotland, and

    (c) Northern Ireland.

(2) An amendment effected by this Act has the same extent as the enactment, or as the relevant part of the enactment, amended (ignoring extent by virtue of an Order in Council).

(3) Her Majesty may by Order in Council direct that a provision of this Act is to extend, with or without modification or adaptation, to—

    (a) any of the Channel Islands;

    (b) the Isle of Man.

50 Short title

This Act may be cited as the Asylum and Immigration (Treatment of Claimants, etc.) Act 2004.

SCHEDULES

SCHEDULE 1   Section 26

NEW SCHEDULE 4 TO THE NATIONALITY, IMMIGRATION AND
ASYLUM ACT 2002

Schedule 4

The Asylum and Immigration Tribunal

Membership

1 The Lord Chancellor shall appoint the members of the Asylum and Immigration Tribunal.

2 (1) A person is eligible for appointment as a member of the Tribunal only if he—

   (a) has a seven year general qualification within the meaning of section 71 of the Courts and Legal Services Act 1990 (c. 41),

   (b) is an advocate or solicitor in Scotland of at least seven years' standing,

   (c) is a member of the Bar of Northern Ireland, or a solicitor of the Supreme Court of Northern Ireland, of at least seven years' standing,

   (d) in the Lord Chancellor's opinion, has legal experience which makes him as suitable for appointment as if he satisfied paragraph (a), (b) or (c), or

   (e) in the Lord Chancellor's opinion, has non-legal experience which makes him suitable for appointment.

  (2) A person appointed under sub-paragraph (1)(a) to (d) shall be known as a legally qualified member of the Tribunal.

3 (1) A member—

   (a) may resign by notice in writing to the Lord Chancellor,

   (b) shall cease to be a member on reaching the age of 70, and

   (c) otherwise, shall hold and vacate office in accordance with the terms of his appointment (which may include provision—

     (i) about the training, appraisal and mentoring of members of the Tribunal by other members, and

     (ii) for removal).

  (2) Sub-paragraph (1)(b) is subject to section 26(4) to (6) of the Judicial Pensions and Retirement Act 1993 (c. 8) (extension to age 75).

4 The Lord Chancellor may by order make provision for the title of members of the Tribunal.

Presidency

5 (1) The Lord Chancellor shall appoint—

   (a) a member of the Tribunal, who holds or has held high judicial office within the meaning of the Appellate Jurisdiction Act 1876 (c. 59), as President of the Tribunal, and

   (b) one or more members of the Tribunal as Deputy President.

  (2) A Deputy President—

   (a) may act for the President if the President is unable to act or unavailable, and

   (b) shall perform such functions as the President may delegate or assign to him.

Proceedings

6 The Tribunal shall sit at times and places determined by the Lord Chancellor.

7 (1) The jurisdiction of the Tribunal shall be exercised by such number of its members as the President, having regard to the complexity and other circumstances of particular cases or classes of case, may direct.

   (2) A direction under this paragraph—

     (a) may relate to the whole or part of specified proceedings or to the whole or part of proceedings of a specified kind,

     (b) may enable jurisdiction to be exercised by a single member,

     (c) may require or permit the transfer of the whole or part of proceedings—

       (i) from one member to another,

       (ii) from one group of members to another,

       (iii) from one member to a group of members, or

       (iv) from a group of members to one member,

     (d) may be varied or revoked by a further direction, and

     (e) is subject to rules under section 106.

8 (1) The President may make arrangements for the allocation of proceedings to members of the Tribunal.

   (2) Arrangements under this paragraph—

     (a) may permit allocation by the President or another member of the Tribunal,

     (b) may permit the allocation of a case to a specified member or to a specified class of member,

     (c) may include provision for transfer, and

     (d) are subject to rules under section 106.

Staff

9 The Lord Chancellor may appoint staff for the Tribunal.

Money

10 The Lord Chancellor—

     (a) may pay remuneration and allowances to members of the Tribunal,

     (b) may pay remuneration and allowances to staff of the Tribunal, and

     (c) may defray expenses of the Tribunal.

11 The Lord Chancellor may pay compensation to a person who ceases to be a member of the Tribunal if the Lord Chancellor thinks it appropriate because of special circumstances.

SCHEDULE 2   Section 26

ASYLUM AND IMMIGRATION TRIBUNAL:
CONSEQUENTIAL AMENDMENTS AND TRANSITIONAL PROVISION

Part 1

Consequential Amendments

Immigration Act 1971 (c. 77)

1 (1) Schedule 2 to the Immigration Act 1971 (control on entry) shall be amended as follows.

(2) In the following provisions for 'adjudicator' (or 'an adjudicator' or 'the adjudicator') substitute 'the Asylum and Immigration Tribunal'—

   (a) paragraph 22(1A), (2) and (3),

   (b) paragraph 23(1) and (2),

   (c) paragraph 24(2), and

   (d) paragraph 25.

(3) In paragraph 24(3) for 'An adjudicator, justice of the peace or sheriff before whom a person is brought by virtue of sub-paragraph (2)(a) above' substitute 'Where a person is brought before the Asylum and Immigration Tribunal, a justice of the peace or the sheriff by virtue of sub-paragraph (2)(a), the Tribunal, justice of the peace or sheriff'.

(4) In paragraph 29—

   (a) in sub-paragraph (2) for 'an adjudicator or the Immigration Appeal Tribunal' substitute 'the Asylum and Immigration Tribunal',

   (b) in sub-paragraph (3)—

      (i) for 'An adjudicator' substitute 'The Asylum and Immigration Tribunal',

      (ii) for 'that or any other adjudicator' substitute 'the Tribunal',

      (iii) omit the words from 'and where an adjudicator dismisses' to the end,

   (c) omit sub-paragraph (4), and

   (d) in sub-paragraph (6)—

      (i) for 'an adjudicator or the Tribunal' substitute 'the Asylum and Immigration Tribunal',

      (ii) for 'the adjudicator or Tribunal' substitute 'the Tribunal', and

      (iii) for 'the adjudicator or the Tribunal' substitute 'the Tribunal'.

(5) In paragraphs 30, 31, 32 and 33—

   (a) for 'an adjudicator and the Tribunal' substitute 'the Tribunal',

   (b) for 'an adjudicator or the Tribunal' substitute 'the Tribunal',

   (c) for 'the adjudicator or the Tribunal, as the case may be' substitute 'the Tribunal',

   (d) for 'the adjudicator or Tribunal' substitute 'the Tribunal',

   (e) for 'the adjudicator or the Tribunal' substitute 'the Tribunal',

   (f) for 'an adjudicator or Tribunal' substitute 'the Tribunal', and

   (g) for 'before an adjudicator or before the Tribunal' substitute 'before the Tribunal'.

(6) In paragraph 33—

   (a) in sub-paragraph (2)(a) for 'before an adjudicator' substitute 'before the Tribunal',

   (b) in sub-paragraph (2)(b) for 'before that adjudicator or before the Tribunal, as the case may be' substitute 'before it', and

   (c) in sub-paragraph (3) for 'An adjudicator, justice of the peace or sheriff before whom a person is brought by virtue of sub-paragraph (2)(a) above' substitute 'Where a person is brought before the Asylum and Immigration Tribunal, a justice of the peace or the sheriff by virtue of sub-paragraph (2)(a), the Tribunal, justice of the peace or sheriff'.

House of Commons Disqualification Act 1975 (c. 24)

2 (1) Schedule 1 to the House of Commons Disqualification Act 1975 (disqualifying offices) shall be amended as follows.

   (2) In Part II for the entry relating to the Immigration Appeal Tribunal substitute—

     'The Asylum and Immigration Tribunal.'

   (3) In Part III omit the entry relating to immigration adjudicators.

Northern Ireland Assembly Disqualification Act 1975 (c. 25)

3 (1) Schedule 1 to the Northern Ireland Assembly Disqualification Act 1975 (disqualifying offices) shall be amended as follows.

(2) In Part II for the entry relating to the Immigration Appeal Tribunal substitute—

'The Asylum and Immigration Tribunal.'

(3) In Part III omit the entry relating to immigration adjudicators.

British Nationality Act 1981 (c. 61)

4 In section 40A of the British Nationality Act 1981 (deprivation of citizenship: appeal)—

(a) in subsection (1) for 'an adjudicator appointed under section 81 of the Nationality, Immigration and Asylum Act 2002 (immigration appeal)' substitute 'the Asylum and Immigration Tribunal',

(b) for subsections (3) to (5) substitute—

'(3) The following provisions of the Nationality, Immigration and Asylum Act 2002 (c. 41) shall apply in relation to an appeal under this section as they apply in relation to an appeal under section 82 or 83 of that Act—

(a) section 87 (successful appeal: direction) (for which purpose a direction may, in particular, provide for an order under section 40 above to be treated as having had no effect),

(b) sections 103A to 103E (review and appeal),

(c) section 106 (rules), and

(d) section 107 (practice directions).', and

(c) omit subsections (6) to (8).

Legal Aid, Advice and Assistance (Northern Ireland) Order 1981 (S.I. 1981/228 (N.I. 8))

5 (1) For paragraph 6A of Part 1 of Schedule 1 to the Legal Aid, Advice and Assistance (Northern Ireland) Order 1981 (proceedings for which legal aid may be given under Part II of that Order) substitute—

'6A. Proceedings before the Asylum and Immigration Tribunal or the Special Immigration Appeals Commission.'

(2) The amendment made by sub-paragraph (1) is without prejudice to any power to amend or revoke the provision inserted by that sub-paragraph.

Courts and Legal Services Act 1990 (c. 41)

6 In Schedule 11 to the Courts and Legal Services Act 1990 (judges barred from legal practice) for the entries relating to the Immigration Appeal Tribunal and immigration adjudicators substitute—

'President or other member of the Asylum and Immigration Tribunal'.

Tribunals and Inquiries Act 1992 (c. 53)

7 (1) The Tribunals and Inquiries Act 1992 shall be amended as follows.

(2) In section 7 (dismissal) omit subsection (3).

(3) In Schedule 1 (tribunals under supervision of Council) for the entry for immigration appeals substitute—

'Immigration and asylum

22. The Asylum and Immigration Tribunal constituted under section 81 of the Nationality, Immigration and Asylum Act 2002.'

Judicial Pensions and Retirement Act 1993 (c. 8)

8 (1) The Judicial Pensions and Retirement Act 1993 shall be amended as follows.

(2) In Schedule 1 (qualifying judicial offices) for the entries relating to the Immigration Appeal Tribunal and immigration adjudicators substitute (in the place occupied by the first of those entries)—

'President or other member of the Asylum and Immigration Tribunal'.

(3) In Schedule 5 (retirement: relevant offices) for the entries relating to the Immigration Appeal Tribunal and immigration adjudicators substitute—

'President or other member of the Asylum and Immigration Tribunal'.

Asylum and Immigration Appeals Act 1993 (c. 23)

9 Section 9A of the Asylum and Immigration Appeals Act 1993 (bail) shall cease to have effect.

Special Immigration Appeals Commission Act 1997 (c. 68)

10 The Special Immigration Appeals Commission Act 1997 shall be amended as follows.

11 At the end of section 2B (deprivation of citizenship) insert '(and section 40A(3)(a) shall have effect in relation to appeals under this section).'

12 (1) In Schedule 1 (constitution, &c.) for paragraph 5(b) substitute—

'(b) at least one is or has been a legally qualified member of the Asylum and Immigration Tribunal.'

(2) A person is qualified for the purposes of paragraph 5(b) of that Schedule as it has effect after the commencement of sub-paragraph (1) above if he is qualified for the purposes of paragraph 5(b) as it had effect at any time since its commencement.

13 (1) Schedule 3 (bail) shall be amended as follows.

(2) In paragraph 1(2) for ' "adjudicator" ' substitute ' "Tribunal" '.

(3) In paragraph 1(3)(a) for ' "adjudicator" ' substitute ' "the Asylum and Immigration Tribunal" '.

(4) In paragraph 1(3)(b) for ' "adjudicator" ' substitute ' "the Asylum and Immigration Tribunal" '.

(5) In paragraph 1(4)(a) and (b) for ' "adjudicator" ' substitute ' "the Asylum and Immigration Tribunal" '.

(6) In paragraph 2(2)(a) for ' "an adjudicator" ' substitute ' "the Asylum and Immigration Tribunal" '.

(7) In paragraph 2(2)(b) for ' "the adjudicator" ' substitute ' "the Asylum and Immigration Tribunal" '.

(8) In paragraph 2(3)(a) for ' "an adjudicator" ' substitute ' "the Asylum and Immigration Tribunal" '.

(9) In paragraph 2(3)(b) for ' "the adjudicator" ' substitute ' "the Asylum and Immigration Tribunal" '.

(10) In paragraph 6(2)(a) for ' "an adjudicator or the Tribunal" ' substitute ' "the Tribunal" '.

(11) In paragraph 6(2)(b) for ' "the adjudicator or the Tribunal, as the case may be," ' substitute ' "the Tribunal" '.

(12) In paragraph 6(2)(c) for ' "the adjudicator or Tribunal" ' substitute ' "the Tribunal" '.

(13) In paragraph 6(3)(a) for ' "an adjudicator or the Tribunal" ' substitute ' "the Tribunal" '.

(14) In paragraph 6(3)(b) for ' "the adjudicator or Tribunal" ' substitute ' "the Tribunal" '.

(15) In paragraph 7(a) for ' "an adjudicator or the Tribunal" ' substitute ' "the Tribunal"'''.

(16) In paragraph 7(b) for ' "the adjudicator or Tribunal" ' substitute ' "the Tribunal" '.

(17) In paragraph 7(c) for ' "the adjudicator or the Tribunal" ' substitute ' "the Tribunal" '.

Access to Justice Act 1999 (c. 22)

14 For paragraph 2(1)(h) of Schedule 2 to the Access to Justice Act 1999 (Community Legal Service: excluded services) substitute—

'(h) the Asylum and Immigration Tribunal,'.

Immigration and Asylum Act 1999 (c. 33)

15 In section 156(3) of the Immigration and Asylum Act 1999 (escorts and custody) for paragraphs (a) and (b) substitute—

'(a) the Asylum and Immigration Tribunal;'.

Nationality, Immigration and Asylum Act 2002 (c. 41)

16 The Nationality, Immigration and Asylum Act 2002 shall be amended as follows.

17 In section 72(10) (serious criminal) omit 'adjudicator,'.

18 (1) In the provisions listed in sub-paragraph (2)—

    (a) for 'an adjudicator' substitute 'the Tribunal',

    (b) for 'the adjudicator' substitute 'the Tribunal',

    (c) for 'he' in relation to an adjudicator substitute 'it',

    (d) for 'him' in relation to an adjudicator substitute 'it', and

    (e) for 'his' in relation to an adjudicator substitute 'its'.

  (2) The provisions are—

    (a) section 85 (matters to be considered),

    (b) section 86 (determination of appeal), and

    (c) section 87 (successful appeal: direction).

19 In section 87—

    (a) for subsection (3) substitute—

'(3) But a direction under this section shall not have effect while—

    (a) an application under section 103A(1) (other than an application out of time with permission) could be made or is awaiting determination,

    (b) reconsideration of an appeal has been ordered under section 103A(1) and has not been completed,

    (c) an appeal has been remitted to the Tribunal and is awaiting determination,

    (d) an application under section 103B or 103E for permission to appeal (other than an application out of time with permission) could be made or is awaiting determination,

    (e) an appeal under section 103B or 103E is awaiting determination, or

    (f) a reference under section 103C is awaiting determination.', and

    (b) in subsection (4) for 'as part of the determination of the appeal for the purposes of section 101' substitute 'as part of the Tribunal's decision on the appeal for the purposes of section 103A'.

20 In section 104 (pending appeal)—

(a) for subsection (2) substitute—

'(2) An appeal under section 82(1) is not finally determined for the purposes of subsection (1)(b) while—

(a) an application under section 103A(1) (other than an application out of time with permission) could be made or is awaiting determination,

(b) reconsideration of an appeal has been ordered under section 103A(1) and has not been completed,

(c) an appeal has been remitted to the Tribunal and is awaiting determination,

(d) an application under section 103B or 103E for permission to appeal (other than an application out of time with permission) could be made or is awaiting determination,

(e) an appeal under section 103B or 103E is awaiting determination, or

(f) a reference under section 103C is awaiting determination.', and

(b) omit subsection (3) (remittal to adjudicator).

21 In section 106 (rules)—

(a) in subsection (1)(a) for ', 83 or 101' substitute 'or 83 or by virtue of section 109',

(b) in subsection (1)(b) for ', 83, 101(1) or 103' substitute 'or 83 or by virtue of section 109',

(c) after subsection (1) insert—

'(1A) In making rules under subsection (1) the Lord Chancellor shall aim to ensure—

(a) that the rules are designed to ensure that proceedings before the Tribunal are handled as fairly, quickly and efficiently as possible, and

(b) that the rules where appropriate confer on members of the Tribunal responsibility for ensuring that proceedings before the Tribunal are handled as fairly, quickly and efficiently as possible.',

(d) in subsection (2)(d) for 'an adjudicator or the Immigration Appeal Tribunal' substitute 'the Tribunal',

(e) in subsection (2)(e) and (f) omit 'an adjudicator or',

(f) in subsection (2)(g) for 'an adjudicator' substitute, in each place, 'the Tribunal',

(g) in subsection (2)(h) for 'an adjudicator' substitute, in each place, 'the Tribunal',

(h) omit subsection (2)(j) and (k),

(i) in subsection (2)(m) omit the words from '(which may' to the end,

(j) in subsection (2)(o) omit 'an adjudicator or',

(k) in subsection (2)(p) omit 'an adjudicator or',

(l) in subsection (2)(q) omit 'an adjudicator or',

(m) in subsection (2)(r) omit 'an adjudicator or',

(n) in subsection (2)(s) omit 'an adjudicator or',

(o) after subsection (2)(s) insert—

'(t) may make provision about the number of members exercising the Tribunal's jurisdiction;

(u) may make provision about the allocation of proceedings among members of the Tribunal (which may include provision for transfer);

(v) may make provision about reconsideration of a decision pursuant to an order under section 103A(1) (which may, in particular, include provision about the action that may be taken on reconsideration and about the matters and evidence to which the Tribunal may have regard);

(w) shall provide that a party to an appeal is to be treated as having received notice of the Tribunal's decision, unless the contrary is shown, at such time as may be specified in, or determined in accordance with, the rules;

     (x) may make provision about proceedings under paragraph 30 of Schedule 2 to the Asylum and Immigration (Treatment of Claimants, etc.) Act 2004 (transitional filter of applications for reconsideration from High Court to Tribunal) (and may, in particular, make provision of a kind that may be made by rules of court under section 103A(5)(b));

     (y) may make provision about the form and content of decisions of the Tribunal.',

   (p) in subsection (3)(a) omit 'an adjudicator or',

   (q) in subsection (3)(d) omit 'an adjudicator or',

   (r) in subsection (3)(e) omit 'an adjudicator or',

   (s) for subsection (3)(f) substitute—

     '(f) may enable the Tribunal to certify that an appeal had no merit (and shall make provision for the consequences of the issue of a certificate).', and

   (t) in subsection (4) omit 'an adjudicator or'.

22 (1) In section 107 (practice directions)—

     (a) for 'the Immigration Appeal Tribunal' substitute 'the Tribunal',

     (b) omit subsection (2), and

     (c) at the end add—

     '(3) A practice direction may, in particular, require the Tribunal to treat a specified decision of the Tribunal as authoritative in respect of a particular matter.'

   (2) The reference to a decision of the Tribunal in section 107(3) (as added by sub-paragraph (1) above) shall be treated as including a reference to a decision of the Immigration Appeal Tribunal.

23   In section 108 (forged document: proceedings in private)—

     (a) in subsection (1)(a) for ', 83 or 101' substitute 'or 83', and

     (b) in subsection (2) for 'The adjudicator or the Immigration Appeal Tribunal' substitute 'The Tribunal'.

24 (1) Section 112 (regulations, &c.) shall be amended as follows.

   (2) In subsection (2) after 'Regulations and rules under this Part' insert ', other than regulations under section 103D(4),'.

   (3) For subsection (6) substitute—

     '(6) Regulations under section 103D(4)—

       (a) must be made by statutory instrument, and

       (b) shall not be made unless a draft has been laid before and approved by resolution of each House of Parliament.

     (7) An order under paragraph 4 of Schedule 4—

       (a) may include consequential or incidental provision (which may include provision amending, or providing for the construction of, a reference in an enactment, instrument or other document to a member of the Asylum and Immigration Tribunal),

       (b) must be made by statutory instrument, and

       (c) shall be subject to annulment in pursuance of a resolution of either House of Parliament.'

Access to Justice (Northern Ireland) Order 2003 (S.I. 2003/435 (N.I. 10))

25 (1) For paragraph 2(i) of Schedule 2 to the Access to Justice (Northern Ireland) Order 2003 (civil legal services: excluded services) substitute—

     '(i) proceedings before the Asylum and Immigration Tribunal or the Special Immigration Appeals Commission,'.

(2) The amendment made by sub-paragraph (1) is without prejudice to any power to amend or revoke the provision inserted by that sub-paragraph.

Part 2

Transitional Provision

26 In this Part 'commencement' means the coming into force of section 26.

27 A person who immediately before commencement is, or is to be treated as, an adjudicator appointed under section 81 of the Nationality, Immigration and Asylum Act 2002 (c. 41) (appeals) (as it has effect before commencement) shall be treated as having been appointed as a member of the Asylum and Immigration Tribunal under paragraph 1 of Schedule 4 to that Act (as it has effect after commencement) immediately after commencement.

28 Where immediately before commencement a person is a member of the Immigration Appeal Tribunal—

 (a) he shall be treated as having been appointed as a member of the Asylum and Immigration Tribunal under paragraph 1 of Schedule 4 to that Act immediately after commencement, and

 (b) if he was a legally qualified member of the Immigration Appeal Tribunal (within the meaning of Schedule 5 to that Act) he shall be treated as having been appointed as a legally qualified member of the Asylum and Immigration Tribunal.

29 A person who immediately before commencement is a member of staff of adjudicators appointed or treated as appointed under section 81 of the Nationality, Immigration and Asylum Act 2002 (c. 41) or of the Immigration Appeal Tribunal shall be treated as having been appointed as a member of the staff of the Asylum and Immigration Tribunal under paragraph 9 of Schedule 4 to the Nationality, Immigration and Asylum Act 2002 immediately after commencement.

30 (1) This paragraph shall have effect in relation to applications under section 103A(1) or for permission under section 103A(4)(b) made—

 (a) during the period beginning with commencement and ending with such date as may be appointed by order of the Lord Chancellor, and

 (b) during any such later period as may be appointed by order of the Lord Chancellor.

 (2) An application in relation to which this paragraph has effect shall be considered by a member of the Asylum and Immigration Tribunal (in accordance with arrangements under paragraph 8(1) of Schedule 4 to the Nationality, Immigration and Asylum Act 2002 (inserted by Schedule 1 above)).

 (3) For the purposes of sub-paragraph (2)—

 (a) references in section 103A to the appropriate court shall be taken as references to the member of the Tribunal who is considering the application or who is to consider the application,

 (b) rules of court made for the purpose of section 103A(4)(a) in relation to the court to which an application is made shall have effect in relation to the application despite the fact that it is considered outside the appropriate court, and

 (c) section 103A(6) shall be subject to sub-paragraph (5) below.

 (4) Where a member of the Tribunal considers an application under section 103A(1) or 103A(4)(b) by virtue of this paragraph—

(a) he may make an order under section 103A(1) or grant permission under section 103A(4)(b), and

(b) if he does not propose to make an order or grant permission, he shall notify the appropriate court and the applicant.

(5) Where notice is given under sub-paragraph (4)(b)—

  (a) the applicant may notify the appropriate court that he wishes the court to consider his application under section 103A(1) or 103A(4)(b),

  (b) the notification must be given within the period of 5 days beginning with the date on which the applicant is treated, in accordance with rules under section 106 of the Nationality, Immigration and Asylum Act 2002, as receiving the notice under sub-paragraph (4)(b) above, and

  (c) the appropriate court shall consider the application under section 103A(1) or 103A(4)(b) if—

    (i) the applicant has given notice in accordance with paragraphs (a) and (b) above, or

    (ii) the applicant has given notice under paragraph (a) above outside the period specified in paragraph (b) above, but the appropriate court concludes that the application should be considered on the grounds that the notice could not reasonably practicably have been given within that period.

(6) Rules of court may specify days to be disregarded in applying sub-paragraph (5)(b).

(7) A member of the Tribunal considering an application under section 103A(1) by virtue of this paragraph may not make a reference under section 103C.

(8) An order under sub-paragraph (1)(a) or (b)—

  (a) shall be made by statutory instrument,

  (b) shall not be made unless the Lord Chancellor has consulted such persons as he thinks appropriate, and

  (c) shall not be made unless a draft has been laid before and approved by resolution of each House of Parliament.

SCHEDULE 3   Section 33

REMOVAL OF ASYLUM SEEKER TO SAFE COUNTRY

Part 1

Introductory

1 (1) In this Schedule—

'asylum claim' means a claim by a person that to remove him from or require him to leave the United Kingdom would breach the United Kingdom's obligations under the Refugee Convention,

'Convention rights' means the rights identified as Convention rights by section 1 of the Human Rights Act 1998 (c. 42) (whether or not in relation to a State that is a party to the Convention),

'human rights claim' means a claim by a person that to remove him from or require him to leave the United Kingdom would be unlawful under section 6 of the Human Rights Act 1998 (public authority not to act contrary to Convention) as being incompatible with his Convention rights, 'immigration appeal' means an appeal under section 82(1) of the Nationality, Immigration and Asylum Act 2002 (c. 41) (appeal against immigration decision), and 'the Refugee Convention' means the Convention relating to the Status of Refugees done at Geneva on 28th July 1951 and its Protocol.

(2) In this Schedule a reference to anything being done in accordance with the Refugee Convention is a reference to the thing being done in accordance with the principles of the Convention, whether or not by a signatory to it.

Part 2

First List of Safe Countries (Refugee Convention and Human Rights (1))

2   This Part applies to—

    (a) Austria,

    (b) Belgium,

    (c) Republic of Cyprus,

    (d) Czech Republic,

    (e) Denmark,

    (f) Estonia,

    (g) Finland,

    (h) France,

    (i) Germany,

    (j) Greece,

    (k) Hungary,

    (l) Iceland,

    (m) Ireland,

    (n) Italy,

    (o) Latvia,

    (p) Lithuania,

    (q) Luxembourg,

    (r) Malta,

    (s) Netherlands,

    (t) Norway,

    (u) Poland,

    (v) Portugal,

    (w) Slovak Republic,

    (x) Slovenia,

    (y) Spain, and

    (z) Sweden.

3 (1) This paragraph applies for the purposes of the determination by any person, tribunal or court whether a person who has made an asylum claim or a human rights claim may be removed—

    (a) from the United Kingdom, and

    (b) to a State of which he is not a national or citizen.

  (2) A State to which this Part applies shall be treated, in so far as relevant to the question mentioned in sub-paragraph (1), as a place—

    (a) where a person's life and liberty are not threatened by reason of his race, religion, nationality, membership of a particular social group or political opinion,

       (b) from which a person will not be sent to another State in contravention of his Convention rights, and

       (c) from which a person will not be sent to another State otherwise than in accordance with the Refugee Convention.

4   Section 77 of the Nationality, Immigration and Asylum Act 2002 (c. 41) (no removal while claim for asylum pending) shall not prevent a person who has made a claim for asylum from being removed—

       (a) from the United Kingdom, and

       (b) to a State to which this Part applies;

      provided that the Secretary of State certifies that in his opinion the person is not a national or citizen of the State.

5 (1) This paragraph applies where the Secretary of State certifies that—

       (a) it is proposed to remove a person to a State to which this Part applies, and

       (b) in the Secretary of State's opinion the person is not a national or citizen of the State.

    (2) The person may not bring an immigration appeal by virtue of section 92(2) or (3) of that Act (appeal from within United Kingdom: general).

    (3) The person may not bring an immigration appeal by virtue of section 92(4)(a) of that Act (appeal from within United Kingdom: asylum or human rights) in reliance on—

       (a) an asylum claim which asserts that to remove the person to a specified State to which this Part applies would breach the United Kingdom's obligations under the Refugee Convention, or

       (b) a human rights claim in so far as it asserts that to remove the person to a specified State to which this Part applies would be unlawful under section 6 of the Human Rights Act 1998 because of the possibility of removal from that State to another State.

    (4) The person may not bring an immigration appeal by virtue of section 92(4)(a) of that Act in reliance on a human rights claim to which this sub-paragraph applies if the Secretary of State certifies that the claim is clearly unfounded; and the Secretary of State shall certify a human rights claim to which this sub-paragraph applies unless satisfied that the claim is not clearly unfounded.

    (5) Sub-paragraph (4) applies to a human rights claim if, or in so far as, it asserts a matter other than that specified in sub-paragraph (3)(b).

6 A person who is outside the United Kingdom may not bring an immigration appeal on any ground that is inconsistent with treating a State to which this Part applies as a place—

       (a) where a person's life and liberty are not threatened by reason of his race, religion, nationality, membership of a particular social group or political opinion,

       (b) from which a person will not be sent to another State in contravention of his Convention rights, and

       (c) from which a person will not be sent to another State otherwise than in accordance with the Refugee Convention.

Part 3

Second List of Safe Countries (Refugee Convention and Human Rights (2))

7 (1) This Part applies to such States as the Secretary of State may by order specify.

    (2) An order under this paragraph—

(a) shall be made by statutory instrument, and

(b) shall not be made unless a draft has been laid before and approved by resolution of each House of Parliament.

8 (1) This paragraph applies for the purposes of the determination by any person, tribunal or court whether a person who has made an asylum claim may be removed—

(a) from the United Kingdom, and

(b) to a State of which he is not a national or citizen.

(2) A State to which this Part applies shall be treated, in so far as relevant to the question mentioned in sub-paragraph (1), as a place—

(a) where a person's life and liberty are not threatened by reason of his race, religion, nationality, membership of a particular social group or political opinion, and

(b) from which a person will not be sent to another State otherwise than in accordance with the Refugee Convention.

9 Section 77 of the Nationality, Immigration and Asylum Act 2002 (c. 41) (no removal while claim for asylum pending) shall not prevent a person who has made a claim for asylum from being removed—

(a) from the United Kingdom, and

(b) to a State to which this Part applies;

provided that the Secretary of State certifies that in his opinion the person is not a national or citizen of the State.

10 (1) This paragraph applies where the Secretary of State certifies that—

(a) it is proposed to remove a person to a State to which this Part applies, and

(b) in the Secretary of State's opinion the person is not a national or citizen of the State.

(2) The person may not bring an immigration appeal by virtue of section 92(2) or (3) of that Act (appeal from within United Kingdom: general).

(3) The person may not bring an immigration appeal by virtue of section 92(4)(a) of that Act (appeal from within United Kingdom: asylum or human rights) in reliance on an asylum claim which asserts that to remove the person to a specified State to which this Part applies would breach the United Kingdom's obligations under the Refugee Convention.

(4) The person may not bring an immigration appeal by virtue of section 92(4)(a) of that Act in reliance on a human rights claim if the Secretary of State certifies that the claim is clearly unfounded; and the Secretary of State shall certify a human rights claim where this paragraph applies unless satisfied that the claim is not clearly unfounded.

11 A person who is outside the United Kingdom may not bring an immigration appeal on any ground that is inconsistent with treating a State to which this Part applies as a place—

(a) where a person's life and liberty are not threatened by reason of his race, religion, nationality, membership of a particular social group or political opinion, and

(b) from which a person will not be sent to another State otherwise than in accordance with the Refugee Convention.

Part 4

Third List of Safe Countries (Refugee Convention Only)

12 (1) This Part applies to such States as the Secretary of State may by order specify.

(2) An order under this paragraph—

    (a) shall be made by statutory instrument, and

    (b) shall not be made unless a draft has been laid before and approved by resolution of each House of Parliament.

13 (1) This paragraph applies for the purposes of the determination by any person, tribunal or court whether a person who has made an asylum claim may be removed—

    (a) from the United Kingdom, and

    (b) to a State of which he is not a national or citizen.

(2) A State to which this Part applies shall be treated, in so far as relevant to the question mentioned in sub-paragraph (1), as a place—

    (a) where a person's life and liberty are not threatened by reason of his race, religion, nationality, membership of a particular social group or political opinion, and

    (b) from which a person will not be sent to another State otherwise than in accordance with the Refugee Convention.

14   Section 77 of the Nationality, Immigration and Asylum Act 2002 (c. 41) (no removal while claim for asylum pending) shall not prevent a person who has made a claim for asylum from being removed—

    (a) from the United Kingdom, and

    (b) to a State to which this Part applies;

provided that the Secretary of State certifies that in his opinion the person is not a national or citizen of the State.

15 (1) This paragraph applies where the Secretary of State certifies that—

    (a) it is proposed to remove a person to a State to which this Part applies, and

    (b) in the Secretary of State's opinion the person is not a national or citizen of the State.

(2) The person may not bring an immigration appeal by virtue of section 92(2) or (3) of that Act (appeal from within United Kingdom: general).

(3) The person may not bring an immigration appeal by virtue of section 92(4)(a) of that Act (appeal from within United Kingdom: asylum or human rights) in reliance on an asylum claim which asserts that to remove the person to a specified State to which this Part applies would breach the United Kingdom's obligations under the Refugee Convention.

(4) The person may not bring an immigration appeal by virtue of section 92(4)(a) of that Act in reliance on a human rights claim if the Secretary of State certifies that the claim is clearly unfounded.

16   A person who is outside the United Kingdom may not bring an immigration appeal on any ground that is inconsistent with treating a State to which this Part applies as a place—

    (a) where a person's life and liberty are not threatened by reason of his race, religion, nationality, membership of a particular social group or political opinion, and

    (b) from which a person will not be sent to another State otherwise than in accordance with the Refugee Convention.

Part 5

Countries Certified as Safe for Individuals

17   This Part applies to a person who has made an asylum claim if the Secretary of State certifies that—

    (a) it is proposed to remove the person to a specified State,

    (b) in the Secretary of State's opinion the person is not a national or citizen of the specified State, and

    (c) in the Secretary of State's opinion the specified State is a place—

        (i) where the person's life and liberty will not be threatened by reason of his race, religion, nationality, membership of a particular social group or political opinion, and

        (ii) from which the person will not be sent to another State otherwise than in accordance with the Refugee Convention.

18   Where this Part applies to a person section 77 of the Nationality, Immigration and Asylum Act 2002 (c. 41) (no removal while claim for asylum pending) shall not prevent his removal to the State specified under paragraph 17.

19   Where this Part applies to a person—

    (a) he may not bring an immigration appeal by virtue of section 92(2) or (3) of that Act (appeal from within United Kingdom: general),

    (b) he may not bring an immigration appeal by virtue of section 92(4)(a) of that Act (appeal from within United Kingdom: asylum or human rights) in reliance on an asylum claim which asserts that to remove the person to the State specified under paragraph 17 would breach the United Kingdom's obligations under the Refugee Convention,

    (c) he may not bring an immigration appeal by virtue of section 92(4)(a) of that Act in reliance on a human rights claim if the Secretary of State certifies that the claim is clearly unfounded, and

    (d) he may not while outside the United Kingdom bring an immigration appeal on any ground that is inconsistent with the opinion certified under paragraph 17(c).

Part 6

Amendment of Lists

20 (1) The Secretary of State may by order add a State to the list specified in paragraph 2.

    (2) The Secretary of State may by order—

      (a) add a State to a list specified under paragraph 7 or 12, or

      (b) remove a State from a list specified under paragraph 7 or 12.

21 (1) An order under paragraph 20(1) or (2)(a)—

      (a) shall be made by statutory instrument,

      (b) shall not be made unless a draft has been laid before and approved by resolution of each House of Parliament, and

      (c) may include transitional provision.

    (2) An order under paragraph 20(2)(b)—

      (a) shall be made by statutory instrument,

      (b) shall be subject to annulment in pursuance of a resolution of either House of Parliament, and

      (c) may include transitional provision.

SCHEDULE 4   Section 47

REPEALS

Short title and chapter	Extent of repeal
Immigration Act 1971 (c. 77)	In Schedule 2— (a) in paragraph 29(3), the words from 'and where an adjudicator dismisses' to the end, and (b) paragraph 29(4).
House of Commons Disqualification Act 1975 (c. 24)	In Part III of Schedule 1, the entry relating to immigration adjudicators.
Northern Ireland Assembly Disqualification Act 1975 (c. 25)	In Part III of Schedule 1, the entry relating to immigration adjudicators.
British Nationality Act 1981 (c. 61)	Section 40A(6) to (8).
Tribunals and Inquiries Act 1992 (c. 53)	Section 7(3).
Asylum and Immigration Appeals Act 1993 (c. 23)	Section 9A.
Asylum and Immigration Act 1996 (c. 49)	Section 8(9).
Immigration and Asylum Act 1999 (c. 33)	Sections 11 and 12. In section 72(10), 'adjudicator'. In section 85(1), 'and (b)'. Section 87(3)(f). Section 123. In Schedule 6, in paragraph 1(1), 'or (b)'.
State Pension Credit Act 2002 (c. 16)	In Schedule 2, paragraph 42.
Tax Credits Act 2002 (c. 21)	In Schedule 4, paragraph 22.
Nationality, Immigration and Asylum Act 2002 (c. 41)	Section 52. Section 80. Section 87(4). Section 93. Section 94(4)(a) to (j). Sections 100 to 103. Section 104(3). In section 106— (a) in subsection (2)(e) and (f), 'an adjudicator or', (b) subsection (2)(j) and (k), (c) in subsection (2)(m), the words from '(which may' to the end, and (d) in subsections (2)(o), (p), (q), (r) and (s), (3)(a), (d), (e) and (4), 'an adjudicator or'. Section 107(2). Schedule 5.
State Pension Credit Act (Northern Ireland) 2002 (c. 14 (N.I.))	In Schedule 2, paragraph 31.

APPENDIX 2

Useful Resources on the Internet

GENERAL

UK government websites

Immigration & Nationality Directorate (IND)

www.ind.homeoffice.gov.uk

Asylum in the UK: full text of current CIPU country assessments and country bulletins. Law & Policy: full text versions of current legislation and the Immigration Rules. Internal instructions: IND manuals for caseworkers, providing IND's guidance on its current policy and interpretation of the immigration rules: see manuals dealing with asylum policy, immigration & nationality instructions; nationality instructions; operational enforcement. The website also contains information on other matters, including guidance on obtaining a work permit and carriers' liability.

UK Visas

www.ukvisas.gov.uk

General guidance and application forms for applicants and sponsors.

Work Permits (UK)

www.workingintheuk.gov.uk

Full details of work permits and schemes dealing with employment related entry to the UK; application forms; guidance notes; links to IND policy documents.

Immigration Appellate Authority (IAA)

www.iaa.gov.uk

Daily court listings for adjudicator and Tribunal hearings; addresses of the hearing centres. Practice directions issued by the President of the IAT and Chief Adjudicator. Full text of 'starred' IAT determinations and reported country guidance decisions (see Practice Direction CA3 of 2003, in relation to the provisions governing citation of IAT determinations). Full text of IAA Gender guidelines.

Court Service

www.courtservice.gov.uk

Daily Court listings in the High Court and Court of Appeal; portal for access to Tribunal websites. Forms and guidance notes for judicial and statutory review and other applications in the higher courts.

Her Majesty's Stationery Office

www.hmso.gov.uk

Fully searchable database of legislation and statutory instruments.

Legal Services Commission

www.legalservices.gov.uk

Guidance and statutory material relating to funding by the Legal Services Commission.

ASYLUM AND HUMAN RIGHTS

*UK organizations working with immigrants and asylum seekers;
information on asylum and immigration in the UK*

Asylum Aid

www.asylumaid.org.uk

Useful resources and links relating to HIV/AIDS and women's issues; the organization also hosts the Refugee Women's Resource Project.

AIRE Centre

www.airecentre.org

Specialist law centre providing advice on European law.

Asylum support

www.asylumsupport.info

Extensive links relating to asylum support issues in the UK.

Bail for Immigration Detainees (BID)

www.biduk.org

Health for asylum seekers and refugees portal (HARP)

www.harpweb.org.uk

Immigration Law Practitioners' Association (ILPA)

www.ilpa.org.uk

Immigration Advisory Service (IAS)

www.iasuk.org

Joint Council for Welfare of Immigrants (JCWI)

www.jcwi.org.uk

Medical Foundation for the Care of Victims of Torture

www.torturecare.org.uk

Refugee Council

www.refugeecouncil.org.uk

Refugee Legal Centre

www.refugee-legal-centre.org.uk

Electronic Immigration Network

www.ein.org.uk

Subscription based online database (some parts of the site are also available to non-subscribers). Portal providing comprehensive access to case law (including asylum support decisions, the IAT, the Administrative Court, Court of Appeal, House of Lords, European Court of Human Rights and European Court of Justice), legislation, statutory instruments and practice directions; country of origin information (including main non-governmental country of origin reports, news service reports, and current and earlier versions of the CIPU assessments).

UK case law

Daily law notes

www.lawreports.co.uk

Free summaries of key cases from the House of Lords, Court of Appeal and High Court.

House of Lords judicial decisions

www.parliament.uk/judicial_work/judicial_work5.cfm

Full texts of House of Lords judgments and practice directions.

Casetrack

www.casetrack.com

Subscription based service; full access to judgments of the High Court and Court of Appeal.

Lawtel

www.lawtel.co.uk

Subscription based database providing full access to case summaries and judgments from the High Court and Court of Appeal.

British and Irish Legal Information Institute

www.bailii.org

Powerful search engine providing access to British and Commonwealth case law.

Institute of Advanced Legal Studies: Eagle-I service

www.ials.sas.ac.uk/links/eihuman.htm

Portal providing internet links to human rights organizations; also searchable by country and by a particular area of law.

Useful resources on the Internet

International case law: asylum and human rights; EU law

European Court of Human Rights

www.echr.coe.int

Access to basic texts and to decisions of the Court through the HUDOC search engine.

European Court of Justice

www.curia.eu.int/en

Access to basic texts and decisions of the European Court of Justice.

EUR-Lex

www.europa.eu.int/eur-lex/en/index.html

Portal website providing access to texts of treaties, legislation, case law, the Official Journal of the European Union and other public documents.

UN High Commissioner for Refugees Refworld

www.unhcr.ch/cgi-bin/texis/vtx/research

Search engine providing access to country of origin information and legal resources.

UN Committee Against Torture

www1.umn.edu/humanrts/cat/decisions/cat-decisions.html

Collection of the committee's decisions held by the University of Minnesota.

University of Minnesota Human Rights Library

www1.umn.edu/humanrts

Texts of international instruments; comprehensive library of links to websites containing information on asylum and human rights issues.

Refugee Caselaw

www.refugeecaselaw.org

University of Michigan Law School refugee case law website. Powerful search engine to search library of international refugee law by theme and country. Useful links to key texts of key international instruments and national case law; text of the Michigan guidelines on the Internal Protection alternative.

Asylumlaw.org

www.asylumlaw.org

Comprehensive links to international sources of information and case law.

European Council on Refugees and Exiles (ECRE)

www.ecre.org

Comprehensive information and fact-sheets on individual EU member states; general information on asylum within the EU; links to national case law collections; contact details for national ECRE partners.

Forced migration online

www.forcedmigration.org/guides

Useful thematic and country of origin research guides.

Centre for Gender & Refugee Studies, University of California

w3.uchastings/cgrs/summaries/summaries.html

Database of international case law relating to asylum applications based on gender.

National case law databases

Australasian Legal Information Institute

www.austlii.edu.au

Search engine providing access to decisions of the Australian courts, including the Refugee Review Tribunal.

Immigration and Refugee Board of Canada (RefLex database)

www.cisr-irb.gc.ca/en/decisions/reflex

Summaries and full texts of decisions from the Canadian Immigration and Refugee Board.

New Zealand Refugee Status Appeals Authority (RSAA)

www.refugee.org.nz

Full texts of decisions by the Refugee Status Appeals Authority.

US Department of Justice: Board of Immigration Appeals Precedent Decisions

www.usdoj.gov/eoir/efoia/bia/biaindx.htm

Country of origin research

Amnesty International

www.amnesty.org

Immigration and Refugee Board Of Canada (REFINFO)

www.cisr-irb.gc.ca/cgi-bin/foliocgi.exe/refinfo_e?

Very useful and fully searchable database of responses to specific information requests, received by the Research Division during the course of status determination of individual claims in Canada. The main country of information databases (Research Database; REFEXTEN and REFQUEST) are accessed through the homepage or directly at www.cisr-irb.gc.ca/en/researchpub/research/origin_e.htm

Danish Immigration Service fact-finding reports on countries of origin

www.udlst.dk/english/publications/Default.htm?CATEGORIES=23

Useful resources on the Internet

European Committee for the Prevention of Torture

www.cpt.coe.int/en

Database containing copies of the Committee's reports.

European Country of Origin Network

www.ecoi.net

Comprehensive database of country of origin information.

European Roma Rights Centre

www.errc.org

Human Rights Watch

www.hrw.org

International Federation for Human Rights (FIDH)

www.fidh.org

International Coalition for Religious Freedom

www.religiousfreedom.com

International Crisis Group

www.crisisweb.org

International Helsinki Federation for Human Rights

www.ihf-hr.org

Kurdish Human Rights Project

www.khrp.org

Global Internally Displaced Persons Project of Norwegian Refugee Council

www.idpproject.org

US Committee for Refugees

www.refugees.org

US State Department country reports on human rights

www.state.gov/g/drl/hr/c1470.htm

War Resisters International

www.wri-irg.org/from-of.htm

Survey of international military service obligations and recognition of conscientious objection.

Asylum support

NASS (National Asylum Support Service)

www.ind.homeoffice.gov.uk/ind/en/home/applying/national_asylum_support.html

NASS webpage, including policy bulletins and directory of contact details.

Asylum Support Adjudicators

www.asylum-support-adjudicators.org.uk

The site contains a database, searchable by theme and keyword, of asylum support adjudicators' decisions.

Rightsnet

www.rightsnet.org.uk

Welfare rights website for advisers.

Index

Advisory Panel on Country Information (APCI) 8.41–5
appeals 1.11, 7.01–3
see also **Special Immigration Appeals Commission**
AIT *see* **Asylum and Immigration Tribunal (AIT)**
background to provisions 7.04–14
bail 10.17
certification of repeat appeals 7.94–6
Court of Appeal 7.54–60
crew-members of ships and aircraft 7.91–3
entry clearance *see* **entry clearance**
EU scheme, right to effective remedy 12.34–9
failed asylum-seeker families, accommodation 4.100–101
failed asylum-seeker families, welfare 4.64–82
removal of right to appeal 4.80–82
High Court *see* **High Court review**
judicial review *see* **judicial review**
passport invalidity 3.46–8
public funding for review 7.71–6
removal of right of appeal before removal 7.77–8
entry clearance holder 7.82, 7.83–90
leave to enter granted before arrival 7.80–81
work permit holders 7.79
right to effective remedy (EU scheme) 12.34–9
third country removals, curtailment 9.08–10
arrest powers 5.01–3
arrest under immigration provision 3.67–70
assisting unlawful immigration 2.01–2
Asylum and Immigration Tribunal (AIT) 7.15
membership 7.16–19
powers 7.23
public funding for review 7.71–6
reconsideration 7.47–8
review *see* **High Court Review**
structure 7.20–21
three-member panels 7.22

back-dated benefits 4.116
abolition provision 4.124–7
background 4.117–23
entitlement 4.118, 4.121
refugee status requirement 4.127
bail
age dispute 10.56
appeal pending 10.17
deportation pending *see under* detention

bail—*continued*
examination/removal pending 10.16
persons believed to be threat to national security 10.20–21
power of arrest 10.19
recognizances, conditions and sureties 10.18–19
SIAC bail *see* **Special Immigration Appeals Commission**
under existing legislation 10.15–19
behaviour *see under* **credibility of claimant**

children failed asylum-seeker families, support to child 4.27–33, 4.42, 4.49
citizens of other European Economic Area states eligibility for welfare 4.07
claims
credibility *see* **credibility of claimant**
unfounded *see* **'clearly unfounded' certificate**
'clearly unfounded' certificate 8.01
designated states 8.04–5
extension of power to designate 8.21–38
removal of accession states 8.20
detention 10.13
duty to certify 9.52–6
extension of power to designate 8.21–38
Home Office assessments of countries of origin 8.39–45
present law 8.02–19
test case law and third country removals 8.08–19, 9.11
control of entry 5.07
credibility of claimant 3.01–6
behaviour
importance 3.02–6
obstructing/delaying handling 3.76–9
relating to passports *see under* **passport**
to conceal information/mislead 3.23–5
concealing information 3.23–5
deciding authorities 3.21–2
delaying handling of claim 3.76–9
failure to answer question 3.52–6
explanation for 3.57–62
failure to make claim in safe third-world country 3.71–5
importance of behaviour 3.02–6
misleading information 3.23–5
obstructing/delaying handling 3.76–9
overriding obligations 3.07–14

credibility of claimant—*continued*
passport *see under* **passport**
statements affected 3.15–20
ticket/travel documents
destroyed/altered/disposed of 3.49–51
timing of claim 3.63
after arrest under immigration provision
3.67–70
after notification of immigration decision
3.64–6

data protection 10.39
deportation pending 10.32–8
detention 10.01–3
see also **electronic monitoring**
bail *see* **bail**
'clearly unfounded' countries 10.13
common law limits 10.08
deportation pending
new provisions 10.34–5
bail implications 10.36–8
presumption of liberty 10.08
previous legislation 10.32–3
immigration v. criminal detention 10.02
limits on powers
common law 10.08
ECHR Art 5 10.09, 10.14
Home Office policy 10.10–14
previous powers 10.04–6
suspected international terrorist 10.24,
10.31
documents retention 5.06

electronic monitoring
age limits 10.56
categories of persons 10.54
criteria for imposition 10.58
requirements 10.53–7
time-limits 10.59
employer's liability for illegal working
extension of time for prosecution 2.10
penalty on conviction 2.09
enforcement powers
control of entry 5.07
fingerprinting 5.04
information about passengers 5.05
power of arrest 5.01–3, 10.45–50
retention of documents 5.06
entering the UK without a passport 2.03–6
entry clearance holder
removal of right of appeal 7.83–90
before removal 7.82
EU law rights, failed asylum-seeker families
4.45–53
EU scheme *see* **safe countries of origin (EU
scheme)**
European Asylum Procedures Directive *see*
appeals, EU scheme; **safe countries of
origin**; **third country removals**, EU
scheme

European Economic Area citizens eligibility for
welfare 4.07
European Union (EU)
law rights, failed asylum-seeker families
4.45–53
scheme *see* **safe countries of origin (EU
scheme)**

failed asylum-seeker families, accommodation
4.83
background 4.84–8
criteria, new regulatory scheme 4.89–93
human rights compliance 4.94–9
NASS role 4.85, 4.87–8
right of appeal 4.100–101
unpaid community work condition 4.83,
4.94–9
failed asylum-seeker families, welfare 4.02
appeals 4.64
para 7A decisions 4.75–9
procedure 4.68–74
removal of right to appeal 4.80–82
background 4.03–9
classes of ineligible persons 4.07–9, 4.10–13
compliance after issue of certificate 4.43–4
dependent persons 4.11–12
dual citizenship 4.51
ECHR rights
compliance after issue of certificate 4.43–4
'inhuman or degrading treatment' 4.35–6
respect for family life 4.37–44
EU law rights 4.45–53
exclusions 4.06
failure to take reasonable steps to leave UK
circumstances 4.16–19
persons affected 4.14–15
reasonable steps/excuses 4.20–26
Home Office decision-making 4.54–8
human rights 4.03, 4.08
Local Authority decision-making 4.59–63
support to child/British citizen 4.27–33, 4.42,
4.49
failed asylum-seeker ineligibility for welfare
4.07
fingerprinting 5.04
forgery of immigration documents 2.07
former asylum seekers, homelessness 4.102
accommodation in Scotland 4.113–15
background 4.103–7
local connection 4.103–7
accommodation in Scotland 4.113–15
NASS accommodation 4.108–112
NASS accommodation 4.108–112

Harmondsworth detention 10.13
High Court review 7.24–9
application 7.36–42
decisions 7.43
filter by AIT 7.49–53

High Court review—*continued*
   late applications 7.30–35
   reference to appellate court 7.44–6
   time-limit for application 7.30–35
Home Office assessments of countries of origin
   8.39–45
human rights
   credibility of claimant 3.07–14
   ECHR rights *see* **failed asylum-seeker**
      families, welfare; marriage; third
      country removals
   failed asylum-seeker families
      accommodation 4.94–9
      welfare 4.03, 4.08, 4.45–53
   legally privileged material, search and seizure
      11.27–34
   marriage 6.23–33
   third country removals 9.29–39, 12.32

immigration decision definition 3.64–6
immigration detention *see* **detention**
immigration documents 2.07
immigration officers, powers *see* **enforcement**
   powers
immigration services, regulation
   Commissioner's role 11.01–7
   evidence search and seizure
      application for search warrant 11.11–14
      excluded material 11.17–18, 11.33–4
      legally privileged material *see* **legally**
         privileged material
      limits on material that can be seized
         11.15–26
      original powers 11.08–10
      personal records 11.17–18
      power to enter premises 11.35
      special procedures material 11.19, 11.23–6,
         11.33–4
   legal professional bodies, powers to require
      information 11.36–7
   offering prohibited immigration services, new
      offence 11.38–9
   other changes 11.40–44
   premises, powers to enter 11.35
integration loan for refugees 4.128–32

judicial review 7.61
   power to quash 7.68
   preliminary, procedural, and ancillary decisions
      7.62–7
   where review has been refused 7.69–70

leave to enter granted before arrival 7.80–81
legal professional bodies, powers to require
   information from 11.36–7
legally privileged material
   definition 11.20–22
   search and seizure 11.15–16, 11.20–22
      human rights compliance 11.27–34

legally privileged material—*continued*
   onward transmission 11.29–30
   warrant procedures 11.31–2

marriage 6.01–2
   application districts 6.05
   compatibility issues 6.34–45
   different treatment for religion/nationality
      6.46–9
   ECHR
      case law 6.26–33
      right to marry 6.24–5
   existing immigration control 6.43–5
   existing rules 6.14–22
   human rights 6.23–33
   justification for provisions 6.34–40
   non-EEA nationals 6.41–2
   outline of provisions 6.03–13
   'subject to immigration control' 6.04, 6.06–7,
      6.09, 6.43–5
   target groups 6.41–2

National Asylum Support Service (NASS) 4.85,
   4.87–8, 4.108–112

Oakington detention 10.13
offences
   assisting unlawful immigration 2.01–2
   employment 2.09–10
   entering the UK without a passport 2.03–6
   failure to cooperate with obtaining travel
      documents 10.41–4
   forgery of immigration documents 2.07
   new immigration service offences 11.38–9
   offering prohibited immigration services
      11.38–9
   trafficking people for exploitation 2.08
offering prohibited immigration services new
   offence 11.38–9

passengers, information about 5.05
passport
   behaviour relating to 3.26–9
   definition 2.03, 3.27–9
   destruction/alteration/disposal 2.04–6,
      3.35–8
   invalidity
      alteration 3.44
      deception 3.45
      definition 3.41–3
      disputes on appeal 3.46–8
      production by claimant 3.39–40
      public interest factors 3.47–8
   not produced 3.30–34
person unlawfully in UK, ineligibility for welfare
   4.07
personal data transfer safeguards 10.39
power of arrest 5.01–3

refoulement 9.26, 9.50
refugees
back-dated benefits, refugee status requirement
4.127
integration loan for 4.128–32

safe countries of origin (EU scheme)
see also **third country removals**
application of concept 12.09–13
designation 12.13
minimum common list 12.04–5, 12.14
competence concerns 12.05
derogation 12.06–7
procedural concerns 12.05
quality of country information concerns
12.08
removal of countries from list 12.05
as third country 12.03
safe third country
see also **third country removals**
failure to make claim in 3.71–5
Scotland
accommodation in 4.113–15
Court of Sessions *see* **appeals**, Court of Appeal;
High Court review
Special Immigration Appeals Commission
(SIAC)
bail 10.20–21
new provisions 10.25–8
commentary 10.29–31
previous legislation/case law 10.23–4
support
failed asylum-seeker families 4.27–33, 4.42,
4.49
for immigrants 4.01
suspected international terrorist 10.24,
10.29–31

terrorist, suspected international 10.24,
10.29–31
third country removals 9.01
see also **safe countries of origin (EU scheme)**;
safe third country
appeals curtailment 9.08–10
categories of countries 9.12–13
amendment of lists 9.40–51, 12.32

third country removals—*continued*
'clearly unfounded' test case law 9.11
deeming provisions 9.14–23
human rights 9.29–39
ECHR challenges 9.26–7, 9.29–36
EU scheme 12.15
human rights 12.29–30, 12.32
'ordinary' safe third country 12.28–30
removal to member states 12.16–18
supersafe third country concept 12.19–27
first list countries 9.12
amendment 9.40–51, 12.32
human rights deeming provision 9.29–39,
12.32
levels of certification 9.07
new provisions 9.12–13
present law 9.02–11
refoulement 9.26, 9.51
supersafe third country concept 12.19–27
test case law 8.08–19, 9.11
ticket/travel documents
destroyed/altered/disposed of 3.49–51
trafficking people for exploitation 2.08
travel documents
destroyed/altered/disposed of 3.49–51
failure to cooperate with obtaining
commentary 10.51–2
degree of discretion 10.51
new offence 10.41–4
powers of arrest, search and entry 10.45–50
previous legislation 10.39–40
required actions 10.43–4

unfounded claims *see* **'clearly unfounded'**
certificate

welfare support
failed asylum-seeker families 4.27–33, 4.42,
4.49
for immigrants 4.01
welfare support for immigrants, *see also*
integration loans for refugees; back-
dated benefits; failed asylum-seeker
families; former asylum-seekers
work permit holders, removal of right of appeal
7.79